THE WRITING AND RATIFICATION OF THE U.S. CONSTITUTION

THE WRITING AND RATIFICATION OF THE U.S. CONSTITUTION

Practical Virtue in Action

JOHN R. VILE

ROWMAN & LITTLEFIELD PUBLISHERS, INC.

Lanham • Boulder • New York • Toronto • Plymouth, UK

Published by Rowman & Littlefield Publishers, Inc.
A wholly owned subsidiary of The Rowman & Littlefield Publishing Group, Inc.
4501 Forbes Boulevard, Suite 200, Lanham, Maryland 20706
www.rowman.com

10 Thornbury Road, Plymouth PL6 7PP, United Kingdom

British Library Cataloguing in Publication Information Available

Library of Congress Cataloging-in-Publication Data

Vile, John R.
  The writing and ratification of the U.S. Constitution : practical virtue in
action / John R. Vile.
     p. cm.
  Includes bibliographical references and index.
  ISBN 978-1-4422-1768-3 (cloth : alk. paper)—ISBN 978-1-4422-1770-6
(electronic)
  1. Constitutional law—United States—History. I. Title. II. Title: The writing
and ratification of the United States Constitution.
  KF4541.V555 2012
  342.7302'9—dc23

                                                                        2012013614

∞™ The paper used in this publication meets the minimum requirements of
American National Standard for Information Sciences—Permanence of Paper
for Printed Library Materials, ANSI/NISO Z39.48-1992.

Printed in the United States of America

Dedicated to my students and colleagues in the University Honors College and the Department of Political Science at Middle Tennessee State University

CONTENTS

PREFACE

I have examined and taught U.S. constitutional law, which largely involves teaching decisions by the Supreme Court, for more than three decades. As much as I enjoy reading court decisions, I am even more fascinated by the Constitution that the court seeks to interpret. I have presented my views of the Constitution and the major judicial decisions that have explained it in my *Companion to the United States and Its Amendments*, which is now in its fifth edition. Another work in which I take great pride is a two-volume work that ABC-CLIO published in 2005 entitled *The Constitutional Convention of 1787: A Comprehensive Encyclopedia of America's Founding*.

As the subtitle of these volumes suggest, that massive work is organized in an A-to-Z format and has hundreds of entries that relate in part or in whole to the Constitutional Convention of 1787. Although I think it can rightly claim to be one of the most comprehensive works on the subject, its A-to-Z format is designed primarily as a reference work that does not encourage lay persons, high school students, or college and university students to read straight through.

I am therefore most grateful to Rowman and Littlefield for giving me the opportunity to author this book, which should especially meet the needs of these audiences. As I worked on developing the narrative, I came to see great similarities between the way that members of the U.S. Supreme Court and other courts operate and the way that delegates to the Constitutional Convention worked. Individuals at the Convention, like members of the court, sought not simply to take votes but also to convince their colleagues, and the more general lay audience, through arguments that their reasoning was sound.

As I reread the notes that Madison and others took of the proceedings of the Constitutional Convention, which have been painstakingly collected in Max Farrand's *The Records of the Federal Convention of 1787* (1966), I came more than ever to appreciate both the style and substance of the debates. Facing what they believed to be a major crisis under the existing government, delegates directed their efforts by drafting rules, selecting a wise and respected leader to preside, and then proceeding deliberately and, for the most part, courteously, to draft a plan of government. Despite the summer heat and their absence from family and friends, the delegates participated in intense debates, often over subjects that they had already examined many times before.

At a time when presidential debates are largely reduced to one-minute statements from which commentators can take sound bites, and radio and television talk show hosts seek to highlight conflict rather than consensus, the framers of the U.S. Constitution engaged in a long-term reasoned discussion, not unlike that which one finds in court decisions where justices outline majority, concurring, and dissenting opinions. The analogy is not perfect. Since we have records of the debates at the convention, it is almost as though we were listening in on the arguments that the delegates made before they proposed and adopted their resolutions and then began defending them (perhaps reading *The Federalist*, which retrospectively seeks to defend the Constitution, is more like reading Supreme Court decisions).

Ironically, the authenticity of the arguments that delegates advanced at the Constitutional Convention was probably enhanced by the fact that the delegates conducted their debates in secret (where they did not have to tailor arguments to an outside audience) and correctly anticipated that the proceedings would not be published during their lifetimes. They were therefore able to speak with a candor that may not be nearly as likely in other public bodies. Like Supreme Court justices meeting in conference, the delegates were immediately intent with persuading one another, rather than with persuading the public.

Students who are familiar with my *Essential Supreme Court Decisions: Summaries of Leading Cases in U.S. Constitutional Law*, which is now in its fifteenth edition, or who are otherwise acquainted with the process of briefing cases, will see that this book is in some respect a "brief" of the convention's deliberations. Like such a brief, this book explains the key facts leading up to and surrounding the convention, identifies the issues that the delegates faced, records the decisions that they reached, and sometimes reconsidered, and presents the arguments that proponents and opponents of each decision offered. Taken together, these "briefs" of delegates' arguments also highlight the similarities and differences in viewpoints among both the delegates and the states that they represented. More importantly, many of the arguments and counterarguments that delegates raised in 1787 remain relevant to understanding not only the provisions within the original Constitution but also possible alternatives.

Although contemporary politicians sometimes substitute assertion for argument and speak of compromise as though it were a sign of either weakness or inconsistency, the delegates who met in Philadelphia in 1787 attempted to meet argument with argument and were not ashamed to engage in compromise. They recognized that they had assembled not as a group of political philosophers who were concerned about the fate of an abstract nation, but as representatives of individual states seeking to advance the common good. It is doubtful that any delegate emerged from the Pennsylvania State House on September 17, 1787 thinking that he had signed a perfect document, but 39 of 42 remaining delegates left the convention confident that the Constitution they had hammered out through arguments and compromises was far better than the existing government, which they and their fellow countrymen had weighed in the balance of experience and found wanting. The delegates were wise enough to recognize that unattainable perfection was the enemy of an attainable good, and they drafted and proposed a Constitution that they thought would be accountable to the people and that would avoid either anarchy or despotism. Although they debated in secret, the document the delegates produced was available for every citizen to review. Delegates were further willing to take these arguments on the hustings as they sought ratification of state conventions for their handiwork.

Congress now mandates publicly funded schools throughout America to celebrate the Constitution in order to be eligible for certain federal funds. I doubt that many of the framers would have approved of such a meddlesome federal mandate (indeed Antifederalist opponents of the document might view this as a confirmation of their worst fears), but I am confident that they would be pleased if they knew that students and other citizens were not only examining what the Constitution says, but seeking to understand why it does so. It is my profound hope that this volume will further these goals.

A NOTE ABOUT THE SUBTITLE

Although the title of this work is fairly straightforward, the subtitle requires some explanation. Given my particular admiration for James Madison, I initially sought a subtitle that would highlight his role at the convention, but taking a cue from Madison's own reluctance to accept sole paternity of the Constitution, I worked instead from a phrase that I found within the notes of a speech by William Paterson, who introduced the New Jersey Plan as an alternative to Madison's Virginia Plan. Although I would not advise elected officials to heed Paterson's observation that "we must follow the People; the People will not follow us," I agree with his observation that legislation and constitution-making must be accommodated to what he describes as "the Genius, the Temper, the Habits, [and, indeed, sometimes] the Prejudices of the People." He followed this by saying that "A little practicable Virtue is to be preferred to Theory" (Farrand 1966, 1:186). This is very similar to what I believe John Dickinson meant when he proclaimed that "Experience must be our only guide. Reason may mislead us" (2:278). Both Paterson and Dickinson appear to have been summarizing the ideas of Aristotelian philosophy. This Greek philosopher had thus written both about *phronesis,* or practical wisdom, and of *arête,* or virtue, which he believe to be the means between excess and deficiency.

I think the most remarkable aspect of the Constitutional Convention of 1787 is that while not kowtowing to public opinion, delegates looked to experience to guide their actions between extremes and to create the best document that they thought was attainable at the time. I think the pursuit of such "practicable virtue" is far to be preferred to the utopian quests that have too often dominated modern politics, and I believe that it has opened plenty of space for the nation to continue to keep its feet on the ground as it pursued noble ideals. Because I have modernized the term "practicable" to "practical," I have not put the two words in quotation marks, but I nonetheless want to credit Paterson as the inspiration for them.

A FURTHER NOTE ABOUT SOURCES

I have listed numerous sources about the Constitutional Convention and related events in a bibliography at the back of this volume. I have tried to minimize references within the text largely to enhance readability, but I decided to maintain references to the volume and page number of Max Farrand's four-volume *The Records of the Federal Convention of 1787* so that readers who chose to do so could readily look them up and examine their wider context. I have identified speakers within the texts. My references to quotations within these indispensable volumes typically consist only of a volume number and page number within parentheses.

SOURCES CITED IN THIS PREFACE

Farrand, Max, ed. 1966. *The Records of the Federal Convention.* 4 vols. New Haven, CT: Yale University Press. First published in 1911; revised edition published in 1937 and reissued in 1966.

Vile, John R. 2005. *The Constitutional Convention of 1787: A Comprehensive Encyclopedia of America's Founding.* 2 vols. Santa Barbara, CA: ABC–CLIO.

———. 2010. *Essential Supreme Court Decisions: Summaries of Leading Cases in U.S. Constitutional Law,* 15th ed. Lanham, MD: Rowman & Littlefield.

———. 2011. *A Companion to the United States Constitution and Its Amendments,* 5th ed. Lanham, MD: Rowman & Littlefield.

TIMELINE OF EVENTS

1215   The Signing of the Magna Carta

1619   Creation of the Virginia House of Burgesses

1620   The Signing of the Mayflower Compact

1754   Beginning of the French and Indian War

1763   End of the French and Indian War

1765   Imposition of the Stamp Act and meeting of the Stamp Act Congress

1773   Boston Tea Party signals continuing colonial opposition to British taxes

1774   First Continental Congress meets in Philadelphia

1775   Battles of Lexington and Concord

Meeting of the First Continental Congress

1776   States (led by New Hampshire and South Carolina) begin writing new constitutions

Meeting of the Second Continental Congress

Issuance of the Declaration of Independence

1777   Second Continental Congress Drafts Articles of Confederation

1781   The last state adopts the Articles of Confederation

The Colonists and their French allies defeat the British at Yorktown

1783   The Treaty of Paris marks an end to the Revolutionary War

1785   Virginia and Maryland delegates meet at Mt. Vernon to discuss common problems

1786   Annapolis Convention Issues a Call for a Convention

1786-87   Shays's Rebellion breaks out in Massachusetts

1787	The Meeting of the Constitutional Convention
1788	Ratification of the U.S. Constitution
1789	Inauguration of Washington
1789	Congressional proposal of the Bill of Rights
1790	Rhode Island is last state to ratify new Constitution
1791	State ratification of the Bill of Rights is completed
1836	James Madison, last attendee at the Constitutional Convention, dies
1840	Madison's notes of the Constitutional Convention are first published

DAY-BY-DAY TIMELINE OF THE CONSTITUTIONAL CONVENTION, 1787

Wednesday, May 3	James Madison arrives in Philadelphia.
Monday, May 14	This is the day the Convention had been slated to begin.
Friday May 25	A quorum of states is present, and the Constitutional Convention begins.
	The Convention selects George Washington as president.
	The Convention appoints a committee to draw up rules.
Monday, May 28	Convention modifies and adopts the report of the Rules Committee.
Tuesday, May 29	Randolph introduces the Virginia Plan, which proposes three branches of government.
Wednesday, May 30	The Convention meets as a Committee of the Whole with Nathaniel Gorham as Chairman.
	Committee of the Whole votes for a government of three branches.
	Committee of the Whole votes for a new method of apportioning congress to replace equal representation under the Articles of Confederation.
Thursday, May 31	Committee of the Whole agrees to a bicameral Congress.
	Committee of the Whole agrees that the people shall select members of the first house of Congress.

Committee agrees that Congress should legislate in cases in which individual states were incompetent.

Committee agrees that Congress shall have a negative of state laws that are contrary to the new constitution.

Friday, June 1   Committee of the Whole votes to create a national executive who would serve a seven-year term.

Saturday, June 2   Wilson proposes a mechanism for selecting the president that resembles today's electoral college.

Monday, June 4   Committee of the Whole proposes a single executive with a veto power, which two-thirds majorities of Congress could override.

Tuesday, June 5   Committee of the Whole proposes the establishment of federal courts.

Wednesday June 6   Committee of the Whole discusses possibility of allowing state legislatures to choose members of the first house of Congress. Madison gives his first major speech at the Convention.

Madison argues for allying the President and Judges in a Council of Revision but Convention disagrees.

Thursday, June 7   Committee of the Whole considers election and size of second house and decides to allow state legislatures to select its members.

Friday, June 8   Committee of the Whole discusses possible congressional veto of state laws but decides against it.

Saturday, June 9   Committee of the Whole votes against a plan introduced by Elbridge Gerry to vest election of the national executive in state governors.

Monday, June 11   Committee of the Whole agrees to "some equitable ratio of representation" for both houses of Congress.

Tuesday, June 12   Committee of the Whole votes for three-year term for members of the first house, for pay from the national treasury, and for making members ineligible for other national offices for one year after leaving office.

Wednesday, June 13   Committee of the Whole resolves remaining issues and presents its report to the Convention of the progress on the document to date in a series of 19 resolutions.

Thursday, June 14   William Paterson asks for time to contemplate the report of the Committee of the Whole and suggest an alternate plan.

Friday, June 15   William Paterson introduces the New Jersey Plan, which was closer in intent and structure to the Articles of Confederation than to the Virginia Plan.

Saturday, June 16   Delegates discuss merits and demerits of the New Jersey Plan.

Monday, June 18   Alexander Hamilton delivers one of the longest speeches at the Convention and proposes his own plan featuring an executive and a senate serving during good behavior.

Tuesday, June 19   James Madison gives a lengthy speech defending the Virginia Plan.

Committee of the Whole votes 7-3-1 to resume discussion of the Virginia Plan.

Wednesday, June 20   Convention replaces word "national" for the new government with "Government of the United States."

Sherman proposes proportional representation in one house of Congress and equal state representation in the other.

Thursday, June 21   In discussing bicameral Congress, the Convention renews discussion of federalism.

Convention decides on two-year term for members of the first house.

Friday, June 22   Convention sets minimum age of members of the first house at 25.

Saturday, June 23   Convention votes to prevent members of Congress from accepting other offices during their terms.

Monday, June 25   Charles Pinckney gives a long speech commenting on the lack of class distinctions among Americans.

	Convention votes that state legislatures would choose members of the second house of Congress.
Tuesday, June 26	Convention votes for 9-year terms for Senators and for the power of both houses to originate bills.
Wednesday, June 27	Luther Martin gives a long speech arguing for the need to preserve state governments.
Thursday, June 28	Benjamin Franklin proposes that the Convention should begin each session with prayer.
Friday, June 29	As discussions of representation continue, Ellsworth describes the government the Convention is seeking as "partly national; partly federal."
Saturday, June 30	Saying "*I do not, gentlemen, trust you,*" Delaware's Gunning Bedford suggests that if the large states dissolved the Confederation, smaller states might seek foreign allies.
Monday, July 2	Convention divides equally (5-5-1) as to whether to give states equal representation within the Senate.
	Convention votes for a Grand Committee of Eleven delegates to examine representation in Congress.
Tuesday, July 3	Grand Committee meets.
Wednesday, July 4	Convention takes day off for Independence Day Holiday.
Thursday, July 5	Grand Committee proposes proportional representation in first house, which alone could initiate money bills, and equality in the second.
Friday, July 6	Convention sets up another committee of five to review Grand Committee proposals relative to size of Congress.
Saturday, July 7	Convention votes to leave equal representation in the second house as part of the report of the Grand Committee.
Monday, July 9	Committee of Five recommends 56 members in first house of Congress.

	Convention decides to create a Committee of Eleven to consider this.
Tuesday, July 10	New Committee proposes increasing number of members of the first house to 65, and Convention rejects Madison's proposal to double that number.
Wednesday, July 11	Convention agrees to periodic census of free whites but rejects idea of counting each slave as three-fifths of a person.
Thursday, July 12	Convention agrees to link representation within Congress to direct taxation.
Friday, July 13	Convention splits evenly on giving each state an equal vote in the Senate.
Saturday, July 14	Convention rejects proposal that would limit the admission of new states to keep them from outnumbering the original.
Monday, July 16	Convention votes 5-4-1 to accept Committee report for proportional representation in one house and equal state representation in the other.
	After Randolph suggests an adjournment, Paterson suggests disbanding and seeking instructions from constituents.
Tuesday, July 17	Delegates from large states meet informally before convention and agreed that they would have to accept Great Compromise.
	Convention rejects congressional negative of state laws.
	Convention votes for a single executive to be selected by Congress for a single seven-year term.
Wednesday, July 18	Convention approves of a judicial branch headed by a Supreme Court whose members would serve during good behavior and for allowing the establishment of inferior tribunals.
	Guarantees states a republican form of government and protection against foreign or domestic violence.
Thursday, July 19	Convention votes to give each state from one to three electors to choose the president for a six-year term.

Friday, July 20	Convention votes to apportion electors for president based on state representation in the first house of Congress and to make president removable by impeachment.
Saturday, July 21	Convention gives executive a qualified veto but decides not to ally him with a Council of Revision.
Monday, July 23	Two delegates from New Hampshire finally arrive at the Convention.
	Convention votes to send Constitution to state conventions for ratification.
	Convention settles on two senators per state.
Tuesday, July 24	Convention chooses five delegates to the Committee of Detail.
Wednesday, July 25	Convention rejects motion to allow executive eligibility for only six of every twelve years.
Thursday, July 26	Convention votes to restore single seven-year executive term but rejects proposal that legislators should have a property qualification.
	Convention adjourns until August 6 to give Committee of Detail time to do its work.
Monday, August 6	Committee of Detail reports a document with 23 articles to the Convention, which delegates begin to debate article by article.
Tuesday, August 7	Convention debates congressional meeting times.
Wednesday, Aug. 8	Convention agrees to leave Committee's suggestion that state voting qualifications for members of first house of Congress align with those for most numerous branch of state legislatures but votes to require citizenship for House members for seven years rather than three.
	Convention votes to apportion house counting slaves as three-fifths of a person prompting discussions of slavery.
	Convention votes to delete origination of money bills in first house.
Thursday, August 9	Convention rejected 14-year citizenship requirement for Senators and retains proposal for congressional oversight of federal elections.

Friday, August 10	Convention voted against requiring property qualifications for members of Congress and requires two-thirds vote to expel members.
Saturday, August 11	Convention restores requirement that money bills originate in first house and requires keeping of a journal.
Monday, August 13	Convention votes to retain seven-year citizenship requirement for members of the House.
Tuesday, August 14	Delegates engage in renewed debate over congressional ineligibility for jobs and decide to pay members of Congress from the national treasury.
Wednesday, Aug. 15	In a decision it will later reverse, the Convention requires three-fourths of members of both houses of Congress to override presidential veto.
Thursday, August 16	Convention approves congressional powers over commerce but strikes out the provision for it to emit paper money.
Friday, August 17	Convention alters provision granting Congress power to "make" war so as to grant it power to "declare" it.
Saturday, August 18	Convention agrees to form a committee of eleven to make recommendations on governance of militia.
Monday, August 20	Proposals by Charles Pinckney submitted to the Committee of Detail.
	The Convention rejects George Mason's proposal for sumptuary laws and accepts the "necessary and proper clause."
	Convention discusses treason provision.
Tuesday, August 21	Committee of Eleven reports back to the Convention.
	Delegates vote to prohibit taxes on exports.
Wednesday, Aug. 22	Convention resumes discussion of slavery with George Mason delivering a powerful speech against it.
	Convention forms a committee of eleven to look into the matter. Convention adopts prohibitions against bills of attainder and ex post facto laws.

Thursday, August 23	Committee to deal with militia reports to Convention, which, after discussion, accepts most of it.
	Convention rejects congressional veto of state laws.
Friday, August 24	Committee of Eleven presents report allowing minimal taxes on slave imports through 1800.
	Convention strikes complicated mechanism for resolving disputes among the states and settles on a single executive.
Saturday, August 25	Convention agrees to allow slave importation until 1808 and made it clear that new government would accept treaties negotiated under the Articles.
Monday, August 27	Convention votes for oath requiring president to preserve, protect, and defend the Constitution.
Tuesday, August 28	Convention votes to mandate jury trials in criminal cases and to prohibit states from taxing imports or exports.
Wednesday, Aug. 29	Convention creates five-man committee to examine the full faith and credit clause and related matters.
	Convention discusses whether two-thirds vote of Congress should be required on commercial matters.
	Randolph indicates that he might not be able to sign off on the developing constitution.
Thursday, August 30	Convention grants Congress power over U.S. territories.
Friday, August 31	Convention agrees that new Constitution will go into effect among consenting states when approved by conventions in nine or more states.
	Convention creates 11-man Committee of Postponed Matters.
Saturday, Sept. 1	Convention receives partial report from Committee on Postponed Matters.
Monday, Sept. 3	Convention grants Congress power to establish uniform rule on bankruptcies.

	Convention votes to exclude members of Congress from offices created, or the emoluments of which were increased, during their tenure or from any other civil office during their sitting.
Tuesday, Sept. 4	Committee of Postponed Matters proposes nine measures, including a provision for an electoral college apportioned by state representation in Congress to select the president to four-year terms, which generated considerable discussion and debate.
Wednesday, Sept. 5	Committee of Postponed Matters offers five more proposals. Mason expresses concern over direction that the Convention is headed.
Thursday, Sept. 6	Convention votes to prevent congressmen from serving as electors and accepts presidential term of four years.
Friday, Sept. 7	Convention allows Congress to legislate on succession to the presidency and decides that the president must be a natural-born citizen 35 years or older with at least 14 years of residency. Convention provides that vice president will preside over the senate and that the president shall make treaties with the advice and consent of two-thirds of the Senate.
	Convention rejects the establishment of a Privy Council.
Saturday, Sept. 8	Convention limits introduction of money bills to the House but allows for Senate amendments.
	Delegates require two-thirds vote of Senate to convict on impeachment.
	Convention voted for a five-man Committee of Style.
Monday, Sept. 10	Convention accepts an amending mechanism allowing two-thirds of both houses of Congress to propose and three-fourths of the states to ratify future constitutional amendments.
Tuesday, Sept. 11	Convention adjourns as it awaits report from the Committee of Style.

Wednesday, Sept. 12	Committee of Style reports a letter to Congress and a new document of seven articles.
	Convention changes congressional majority needed to overturn presidential vetoes from three-fourths to two-thirds.
	Convention turns down a proposal by George Mason to add a bill of rights.
Thursday, Sept. 13	Convention creates a five-man committee to suggest sumptuary laws.
	Convention agrees to send proposed Constitution to Congress to forward on to the states.
Friday, Sept. 14	Convention rejects a proposal allowing Congress to appoint the National Treasurer by a joint ballot.
	Convention decides against giving Congress power to cut canals, to create corporations, or to establish a secular university.
Saturday, Sept. 15	Convention votes to add a provision entrenching state equality in the Senate against amendment without states' consent and rejects Randolph's proposal to allow state ratifying conventions to propose amendments that would be considered by yet another convention.
	Convention orders the Constitution to be engrossed.
Monday, Sept. 17	Franklin tries to persuade wavering delegates to sign. Proposes resolution indicating Constitution was unanimously approved by the states present.
	Convention decides to provide up to one representative for every 30,000 residents, instead of for every 40,000.
	Thirty-nine of 42 delegates present sign the Constitution.

1

REVOLUTION AND
ITS AFTERMATH

No morn ever dawned more favorable than ours did; and no
day was ever more clouded than the present! Wisdom, and
good example are necessary at this time to rescue the political
machine from the impending storm.

—Letter from George Washington to James Madison,
November, 1786 (Farrand 1966, 1:423)

Although they may not always be familiar with many of the particulars, the majority of Americans through most of its history have been justly proud of their constitution. Most citizens probably know that it is old, without necessarily knowing that 55 delegates from 12 states debated and formulated the document at a Constitutional Convention that met in Philadelphia in 1787 and that it went into effect two years later after being ratified by most of the states. Many Americans believe that the U.S. Constitution is the world's oldest continuing functioning written document of its type, although this honor actually goes to the Massachusetts Constitution (1780) that preceded it by almost a decade.

Each year the nation celebrates Constitution Week in mid-September, in the week that begins on September 17th, the day in 1787 that 39 (one by proxy) of 42 remaining delegates signed the document. This emphasis on the document's signing, however beneficial it might otherwise be, might incorrectly create the impression that, like the proverbial deus ex machina in some plays, the Constitution emerged from nowhere. Nothing could be further from the truth.

THE COLONIAL BACKGROUND

Indigenous peoples had occupied the Americas for millennia, but to European explorers, the Americas represented a "New World" for them to claim for their respective monarchs and to exploit for purposes as varied as the exercise of religious freedom and the pursuit of wealth. Although they explored both North and South America, Spanish and Portuguese eventually carved up most of Central and South America leaving the northern hemisphere largely to English, French, Dutch, and even Swedish claimants. The French and Indian War (1754–1763), which pitted French and Native American allies against England and her colonies, left the French in control in the eastern part of modern-day Canada and the English in control of the seaboard from there south to modern-day Florida, where Spain and France long retained their claims.

By the mid-1750s, there were 13 English-speaking colonies from New Hampshire in the north to Georgia in the south. Although largely sharing a common language, they varied significantly in terms of climate, size, and the temperaments of their peoples. Northern colonies tended to emphasize their Puritan roots (with Rhode Island having followed Roger Williams to develop its own nonconformist style), middle states like Pennsylvania and Delaware had a heritage of freedom that dated back to William Penn and his successors, and the South was not only tied more closely to the Anglican (Episcopal) Church but it also was more clearly shaped by the growing number of African American slaves—often shipped there by New England traders and merchants—who worked the large plantations.

Although their behavior did not always match their pretentions, northern colonists typically drew clear distinctions between their own civilized Christian heritage and that of the "savages" on the frontier. Similarly, white southerners not only distinguished themselves from Native Americans, some of whom had adopted their own style of living, but often seemed to value their own freedom more dearly as they contrasted such freedom to the bondage of the slaves living under them.

THE DEVELOPING SPLIT WITH ENGLAND

Despite vast regional differences, Americans were becoming a distinct people even before they recognized it. The free whites who wielded power had either taken the initiative to immigrate from Europe or reflected proudly on their forebearers who had done so, and they both developed, and highly valued, individual initiative and resilience, sometimes combined with a strong reliance on Divine Providence. Whatever aid they may have gotten from Europe, they largely attributed their success to their own perseverance in conquering and sustaining themselves in a strange land. Virginians traced their legislature, the House of Burgesses, back to 1619 while Pilgrims had signed a heralded compact of government, the Mayflower Compact, even before they disembarked from their ship the following year. Most colonies could trace their origins back to grants from the British kings, who had offered a fair degree of autonomy to adventurers and proprietors to settle the new land. The long distance between Europe and North America at a time of primitive communication and transportation often required colonies to exercise initiative that would not have been acceptable had the two continents been closer, or had the British been less preoccupied with other colonial possessions.

In time, the British began to question whether they had allowed this autonomy (often referred to as "salutary [beneficial] neglect") to go too far. When the British began to assert, or reclaim, their previously largely dormant powers, most notably in the area of taxation and trade, colonial spokesmen were already adept at utilizing legal claims familiar not only to English solicitors and barristers (as lawyers are there called) but also to the general British public, to press their own claims.

Although Great Britain was far from a democracy, the English people valued their liberties. Britain was sometimes described as a mixed, or balanced, government in which social classes were respectively represented in the monarchy, the House of Lords (the hereditary nobility in the upper house of Parliament), and the House of Commons (the lower house). Another prominent narrative of the history of British liberty focused on how the legislature, or Parliament, had protected popular liberties against the monarchs. Although it initially consisted of a group of noblemen, in time Parliament claimed to represent the English people as a whole. At least since King John had signed the Magna Carta in 1215, Englishmen (women's rights, such as they were, were usually subsumed under their fathers or husbands) had adhered to the principle of "no taxation without representation." Perhaps in part because of their own experience and in part because of convenience (the model certainly does not accord with denying voting rights to women!), colonists further thought that such representation had to be "actual" instead of "virtual." Since they were not represented within Parliament, and could not—given distances—easily have been so, it had no right to tax them.

Although colonists had sympathizers and supporters within the British Parliament, most British leaders were more concerned about paying debts incurred in protecting the colonies (as well as advancing their own interests) from the French and Indian War than in splitting legal hairs. Moreover, over the centuries of conflict with British monarchs, during which Parliament had stressed its role in representing all Englishmen (it was said that "the voice of the people is the voice of God"), the British Parliament considered itself to be legally all powerful or sovereign. William Blackstone, the great English legal commentator, once commented that Parliament could do anything except change a man into a woman or vice versa, that is, anything that was not physically impossible.

For a considerable time, colonists were able to rely on the argument that they could retain their rights as English citizens—much as later citizens of British Commonwealth nations—by adhering to the king, who had granted their charters, without accepting claims of parliamentary sovereignty. When colonial troops clashed with British troops who were attempting to remove military supplies from stockpiles in Lexington and Concord, Massachusetts, in April 1775 and King George III refused to support the colonial claim, however, the colonists had to choose to submit or to take up arms. The colonists chose the latter course.

Many revolutions begin and end in mob violence, and there was certainly some of that within the colonies, especially in some of the larger cities, where, however, there were sometimes unwritten rules—perhaps like those that often govern peaceful demonstrations of today—that they should not take place on Saturday and Sunday evenings, which were considered to be holy (Maier 1970, 17). Scholars still argue about whether there can be a *legal* "right" to revolution, but whatever the answer, it is certainly possible to distinguish those who seek revolution largely on an individual basis or in faceless mobs (in societies with few mediating institutions between the people and the government, they may have little choice) and those who seek to use existing structures to mount opposition to what they consider to be injustices. The American model of revolution comes much closer to the latter model, which may largely account both for its initial success in defeating the British and in its later success in establishing a stable government with which to replace British rule.

Initially, each colonial government became a potential rallying point for discontentment that had boiled up in individual districts and cities. Bostonians, furious at British use of general warrants and their confiscation of private homes to billet troops, could express outrage in their state assembly in the same city. Pennsylvanians who objected to British taxes could gather in Philadelphia. Representatives of far-flung Virginia who feared that their liberties were in jeopardy could gather to discuss their grievances in the colonial capital in Williamsburg.

Despite some earlier pleas for colonial unity, particularly when facing Indian attacks, colonies had distinct histories and had dealt individually with the British Crown and with Parliament. Now with similar grievances against the world's most powerful empire, it made sense for diverse colonies sharing the same continent to seek strength in numbers. In 1765, the colonies had thus sent representatives to a Stamp Act Congress to oppose British taxation. In 1775, and again in 1776, the colonists called two Continental Congresses to respond to perceived abuses, to boycott British goods, and to petition the king for redress of grievances.

In January 1776 Thomas Paine, a newly arrived English immigrant, published a pamphlet entitled *Common Sense*, that helped convince the colonies that they should cut the connection with the king, that he did not rule by "divine right," and that further American association with the king was likely to result in further loss of liberty and involve the continent in needless wars. The Second Continental Congress eventually decided that the time for negotiation was finished and that it was time to make what the English philosopher John Locke had called "an appeal to heaven," through a resort to force.

THE DECLARATION OF INDEPENDENCE

Once it made this decision, Congress had three main tasks—explaining and justifying its decision to resort to arms (important for both domestic and foreign audiences), securing foreign allies, and drawing up a new form of government so that the states did not slip into chaos. Congress, which did most of its work through committees, appointed five delegates to a committee to justify independence. They were Thomas Jefferson of Virginia, John Adams of Massachusetts, Benjamin Franklin of Pennsylvania, Roger Sherman of Connecticut, and Robert Livingston of New Jersey. Franklin had long represented colonial interests in London, Adams was perhaps the most notable congressional advocate of independence, Sherman and Livingston were respected colonial leaders, and Thomas Jefferson had arrived in Philadelphia from the most populous colony where he had recently taken the initiative in drafting a similar bill of particulars against the British in that colony. The committee asked Jefferson to take the lead in drafting the document, and he did so, with some kibitzing from Adams and Franklin and considerable more rewriting by the Continental Congress itself. Congress voted for independence on July 2 and adopted the Declaration of Independence as an explanation for its decision two days later on

July 4, which the nation now celebrates as Independence Day. Contrary to popular depictions of the event, the document was signed over a period of months rather than on a single day.

The longest part of the Declaration of Independence, while reads much like a legal brief (Jefferson was, after all, a lawyer), detailed a series of charges, or indictments, against the British king and Parliament, including war atrocities. The former colonists deemed these incidents as sufficient justification for separating from the mother country. The document, however, is better known for its introductory paragraph, which ably expressed the essence of colonial thinking about the existence of natural rights. Despite the fact that he was a slave owner with no immediate plans either to free his own slaves or to abolish this nefarious institution, Jefferson asserted on the Congress's behalf that all "men," including those in the colonies—which he believed had established their credentials as a separate people—were "created equal" and were thereby entitled to the God-given equal rights of "life, liberty, and the pursuit of happiness." Viewing government as a human creation rather than as a divine mandate, Jefferson argued that the colonies had the right to replace oppressive and nonresponsive governments with governments that were not oppressive and that were responsive to popular wishes. Although he did not outline such a government, it was clear that a legitimate government would have to rest more clearly on, and be more accountable to, what the Declaration described as "the consent of the governed." After declaring their independence from Great Britain, the 56 signatories of the Declaration pledged their "lives, fortunes and sacred honor" to the task that lay ahead.

The British authorities regarded this declaration as an act of treason. Pointing to the need for unity, Benjamin Franklin reportedly said that he and fellow signers would either hang together or hang separately from the ends of British nooses! Significantly, the colonists signed not simply as individuals but as representatives of individual states. They were seeking to bring about a fairly orderly revolution in government—what they believed was a restoration of earlier liberties—not unleash anarchy.

DEVELOPMENTS IN THE STATES

When directing his wrath at the English king in *Common Sense*, Thomas Paine had proposed that in America, the law should be king. There are few clearer indications of the colonists' desire to proceed in an orderly fashion than the decision of the Second Continental Congress in May, 1776 (see

Adams 2001, 61) to ask the states to "adopt such Government as shall, in the Opinion of the Representatives of the People, best conduce to the Happiness and Safety of their Constituents in particular and American in General" (59). New Hampshire and South Carolina had already drawn up new constitutions, and other states began so doing. In fashioning such documents, states relied as much on their colonial heritage as on English legal history.

Curiously, although it was common to refer to the British constitution, which included understandings that grew from many written documents like the Magna Carta and the British Bill of Rights (1689), the British had never outlined the essentials of their government in a single written document. They relied instead on what they called, not completely accurately, an "unwritten" constitution. It consisted of practices and understandings like parliamentary sovereignty, hereditary succession, and judicial decisions at common (case) law, which had developed around the operation of individual organs of government. In part because of their negative experiences under this arrangement and in part because of their earlier reliance upon their charters from the king, Americans sought greater security for their liberties, which they believed written documents might secure.

Many residents of the 13 colonies were Protestant nonconformists who had often cited Biblical passages to dismiss centuries of traditional practices and understandings, which had developed in the Catholic Church and which had, to a lesser degree, been accepted by the Church of England. Written constitutions, like written scripture, seemed more authoritative, and less subject to manipulation, than mere tradition. Puritans had put special emphasis on Old Testament passages that had described covenants between God and humans—Abraham, Moses, David, and other representatives of the Jews, for example. Indeed, Americans were accustomed to dividing their Bibles into the Old and New Testaments, or covenants. This idea blended with John Locke's description of a people leaving the precarious state of nature by agreeing to a social contract that bound them to one another to secure their lives, liberties, and property.

Constitutions were generally understood to be foundational. Although Congress rejected suggestions to propose a model state constitution (Adams 2001, 53–54), states—especially those in the same region—often borrowed from one another. It was typical for such documents to contain at least five elements. These included an explanation of why the document was being written; the recognition of a "people" within each jurisdiction; the creation of a government; a self-definition of common values, rights, and interests, and an outline of institutions and fundamental principles (Lutz 1988, 103).

Virginia's constitution of June 1776 was the first to include a Bill of Rights. At least 10 of the delegates who attended the U.S. Constitutional Convention, including Mason, had helped to write state constitutions.

As would be expected, institutions were in flux at the time of the Revolutionary War, so the idea of constitutions evolved with time. Initially, it was common for a sitting legislature, often faced with the need to prepare for war, to propose and/or ratify a constitution. The difficulty with such an approach was that voters had selected members of such bodies to write ordinary legislation rather than to write a constitution, and a body that could propose a constitution by an ordinary vote would be little different from its successor, which would presumably have the power to undo the same document. In his only published book, his *Notes on the State of Virginia* (1964), which he wrote to show that North America was equal to, if not better than, Europe, Thomas Jefferson nonetheless critiqued his state constitution for this perceived defect.

Over time, it became common to ground a constitution in a referendum of the people delivered either directly or through state ratifying conventions, the deliberations of which contemporaries equated with the popular will. The paramount example is the constitution of Massachusetts, which was largely written by John Adams in a constitutional convention of 1779, and then ratified in town meetings throughout the commonwealth. Most constitutions provided for methods of formal amendment that, like their own ratifications, were more difficult than the process of ordinary legislation, thus making them paramount to such laws.

As states adopted constitutions, they began gaining experience with what worked and what did not. This state experience with governments came to complement that on the national level. In time, the problems in the new structures began to outweigh their perceived benefits. Consistent with an analogy that Justice Louis Brandeis would later introduce, however, both states, and state constitutions, served as "laboratories," and when delegates assembled in Philadelphia to write the Constitution in 1787, most were quite familiar with the results of the "experiments" that had been conducted there.

THE ARTICLES OF CONFEDERATION

Delegates to the Second Continental Congress had begun to explore a form of government to replace British rule simultaneously with their decision to declare independence. The Continental Congresses were already operating under a largely unwritten template where each state legislature appointed delegates to a national meeting where each state was represented equally, but consistent with their belief in the importance of written constitutions, they recognized the value of spelling out such structures. To this end, they appointed John Dickinson of Pennsylvania and Delaware, the reluctant revolutionary and "penman of the Revolution," to draft a plan. Congress accepted a revision of this plan in 1777, and although the interim government essentially operated under the system proposed there, this system was not formally adopted until 1781, when Maryland became the 13th state to ratify.

At the time of the American Revolution, most individuals were probably as likely to think of their colony as a nation than as a state, or part of a nation. When delegates from the states met together in the Continental Congresses, they had assembled—much like modern diplomats—as equals, with each delegation representing a different colony with equal rights and privileges to the others. This pattern was repeated in the Articles of Confederation.

Under the Articles each state could send from two to seven delegates to Congress, but each state had an equal vote. Thus, the introduction to the Articles (the equivalent to "We the People" within the current U.S. Constitution) listed each state separately by name. The most important provision of the Articles was Article II, which had been added at the insistence of North Carolina Governor Thomas Burke and provided that "Each state retains its sovereignty, freedom, and independence, and every Power, Jurisdiction and right, which is not by this confederation expressly delegated to the United States, in Congress assembled." Congress was the only permanent part of the new government, and with a single chamber or house (such a legislature is described as unicameral), it was fairly simple in design.

State legislators chose, paid, and often "instructed" their delegates, who divided into committees to do most of the work of the current president. The Articles provided for a semi-judicial body to resolve boundary disputes among the states, but commissioners were selected in an ad hoc basis. During congressional recesses, provision was made for a "Committee of States," consisting of one delegate from each and presided over by a "president" (one of the congressional delegates) who served for a single-year term. Congress had a set of limited powers, but these did not include the power to regulate interstate and foreign commerce, the power to tax the people directly, or the power to create a national currency. Consistent with the doctrine of state sovereignty that the system embodied, Congress would requisition states for needed tax revenues, and in theory, the states would collect such taxes and submit them to Congress. The process for raising troops was also based on requisitioning states to do their duty.

In an effort further to protect state sovereignty, the exercises of most congressional powers required the consent of nine (roughly two-thirds) of the thirteen states. Congress could propose amendments to the states, but, like initial ratification of the Articles themselves, they required unanimous consent.

The British had a unitary form of government that did not have states with their own constitutions. By contrast, the Articles (like the later Confederate States of America) constituted a confederal form of government. Like the current federal government within the United States, such a government is based on a written constitution that divides power between a government at the center and those at the periphery. In contrast to today's federal government, the confederal government under the Articles vested primary power, or sovereignty, in the states, and allowed only the state governments to act directly on the people.

It retrospect, it may seem remarkable that the Articles registered as many successes as it did. The Articles certainly provided a transition from British rule to the current Constitution, with the Articles serving as a kind of laboratory for the former colonists to test out a new form of government. While many observers believe that the victory came largely in spite of, rather than because of, the weak system that it established, armies directed by the Articles achieved victory over the British in the Revolutionary War. Similarly, the Confederal Congress adopted the remarkable system of governing the nation's vast Northwest Territory during the sitting of, and, some believe, in conjunction with compromises adopted at, the Constitutional Convention of 1787.

THE CONFLUENCE OF STATE AND NATIONAL INFLUENCES

Historically, revolutionaries are often almost giddy after overthrowing rulers, colonial or domestic. Revolutions tend to breed high, often unrealistic, hopes for the future. People imagine being freer, richer, or more secure than they ever were before. Not infrequently, these hopeful dreams end in nightmares, with the new government being even more tyrannical than the old, and prosperity proving to be as elusive as ever.

The government under the Articles was hardly tyrannical. Largely in reaction to perceived abuses on the part of English monarchs, the Articles provided no independent executive power, and judicial power was largely ad hoc in nature. There were occasions early in the war when people might have echoed the sentiment of "one for all, and all for one," but the Confederal Congress was almost perpetually short of money, the defeat of the British removed a common foe, and state jealousies led many cash-strapped states to withhold their requisition until they thought other states paid their fair share. It was difficult to get southerners to rally against Indian attacks in the North or to get northerners to rally against such attacks in the South. Although the nation had successfully negotiated an end to the Revolutionary War, it did not have sufficient military might to enforce the treaty and had to borrow from foreign governments to keep the ship of state afloat.

As near sovereigns, states had a greater interest in their own advancement and preservation than in that of the Union as a whole. Individual state currencies, and lack of national regulation, led states to maximize their own trade advantages against others. Contemporaries thus likened New Jersey to a barrel with a cork in both ends because it was taxed in the north by New York and in the south by Pennsylvania. North Carolina was likened to a patient bleeding from both its Virginia and South Carolina "arms." Foreign diplomats found European governments skeptical that the new nation, conceived in freedom, would end in anything less than anarchy.

The weaknesses of the Articles were magnified by provisions within many state constitutions. Imitating the Articles, most had painfully weak executives, who often served terms of a single year. Facing debts, many from the grim years of the Revolution, states often yielded to the temptation to inflate their currencies simply by printing more. In a desire to keep legislators on a short lease, many state constitutions provided for annual elections; indeed, some proclaimed that "where annual elections end, tyranny begins." Although the Declaration of Independence had faulted the king for undermining judicial independence, some states removed judges who opposed arbitrary legislative policies.

In an age prior to monthly unemployment, inflation, and foreclosure reports, it is difficult to know with certainty how this time period compared to others, but there was widespread perception that victory had not brought about the expected economic prosperity. Individuals representing their states and nations could perceive that neither level of government was proving especially responsive to existing problems. Initially, many thought that national problems might be remedied by amendments, most notably granting Congress authority to level a uniform impost, or tariff, on imports. At one point, congressional leaders were able to get every state but Rhode Island to agree to such a plan, but it refused and then states that had given approval began to fall away. The unanimity requirement to amend the Articles appeared insuperable.

THE ANNAPOLIS CONVENTION

Virginia and Maryland called a meeting in March, 1785 at George Washington's house at Mt. Vernon to work out issues of navigation on common waterways. Although Governor Patrick Henry of Virginia had not notified all the participants of the event, it still resulted in a compact between Virginia and Maryland and was successful enough to suggest that other states might benefit from similar arrangements. In January of 1786, James Madison and other state leaders succeeded in getting the Virginia General Assembly to adopt a resolution to call a convention for May in Annapolis, Maryland, for all the states to discuss trade issues.

In a promising sign, nine states appointed delegates, but a week after the meeting was supposed to begin, only twelve delegates from five states (New York, New Jersey, Pennsylvania, Delaware, and Virginia) had actually arrived in time to meet in the old senate chamber at the State House. Notably, the host state did not even appoint a delegation, and Pennsylvania and New York delegations did not have quorums. The delegates did include such prominent individuals as Alexander Hamilton of New York, and Edmund Randolph, James Madison, and St. George Tucker of Virginia. The group elected John Dickinson, the primary author of the Articles of Confederation, as chair and appointed a committee to draft a report, which New York's Alexander Hamilton appears to have chiefly authored. Attempting to snatch victory from defeat, the convention suggested that the nation should address trade within a larger set of issues, "which may require a correspondent adjustment of other parts of the Foederal [this alternate spelling of federal, which was then used to describe what are today designated as confederal governments, is common in this period] System" (Jensen 1976, 184).

Perhaps in an attempt to disguise the revolutionary implications of revising the Articles as a whole, the convention report called for

> the appointment of Commissioners, to meet at Philadelphia on the second Monday in May next, to take into consideration the situation of the United States, to devise such further provisions as shall appear to them necessary to render the constitution of the Federal Government adequate to the exigencies of the Union; and to report such an Act

for that purpose to the United States in Congress Assembled, as when agreed to, by them, and afterwards confirmed by the Legislatures of every State will effectually provide for the same." (Jensen 1976, 184–85)

Initially tepid in its support, an eight-to-one majority in Congress ultimately offered a similar resolution of support in February of 1787 when faced with events that culminated in Shays's Rebellion in Massachusetts. It called for a cônvention of delegates to meet in Philadelphia "for the sole and express purpose of revising the Articles of Confederation" and to report to the states "such alterations and provisions therein as shall, when agreed to in Congress and confirmed by the states render the federal constitution adequate to the exigencies [pressing needs] of Government and the preservation of the Union" (Solberg 1958, 64).

SHAYS'S REBELLION

There are often gaps between members of the lower and middle classes and elites, or those who wield disproportionate power in relation to their numbers. These differences involve education, wealth, social class, manners, and more and may result in substantially different attitudes. Members of an elite can be relatively unaware of the sufferings and discontents of the lower classes. Contrariwise, elites—especially those who interact with foreign nations and diplomats—are often aware of problems that are of little concern to the lower classes.

There is general, albeit not universal, agreement that the period from the end of the American Revolution in 1783 to 1787 was a time of increased discontent among members of all classes. Internal tariffs and lack of federal control over interstate commerce made full utilization of a continental common market impossible. Governmental bonds, which had often been issued to Revolutionary War soldiers, were nearly valueless. The nation owed considerable interest on debts that it had used to win the war, and Congress was unable to carry out its own treaties, which meant that the British remained a major presence in the American Northwest Territories.

Enough members of the elite class had experience under the Congress of the Articles and in their own state assemblies to recognize that changes were needed. The experience in Massachusetts suggests that non-elites were also beginning to feel the pinch. As farmers in that state found it increasingly difficult to find money to pay their taxes, in August 1786, they rallied behind a Revolutionary War veteran named Daniel Shays to close down a courthouse, threaten the state's supreme court, and attempt to seize the federal arsenal at Springfield in January, 1787. Fearing the contagion of such violence, Congress attempted to raise military forces under the guise of preparing for possible Indian attacks.

Massachusetts eventually got the situation under control without direct national aid, but the rebellion confirmed to many colonial elites their view that the system under the Articles was incapable of protecting the nation. From his vantage point as an ambassador to France, Thomas Jefferson rather blithely observed that "The tree of liberty must be refreshed from time to time with the blood of patriots & tyrants," which he described as "its natural manure" (Jefferson 1905, 5:456), but those who observed from a closer vantage point were more likely to worry that the next bloodshed might be that of themselves or their neighbors. White southerners may well have been especially worried about the possibility of slave revolts.

THE STAGE IS SET

With the resolution from the Annapolis Convention calling for a new convention, Shays's Rebellion served as the catalyst to convince most states that the time of action had come. In time, all the states except Rhode Island would heed the call to send delegates to Philadelphia to consider revisions to the Articles of Confederation, but there was no guarantee that such a convention would succeed, that Congress would concur in its diagnoses or its proposed remedies, or that any solution it proposed could get through the amending gauntlet posed by the requirement for unanimity under the Articles of Confederation.

George Washington, who had led the nation to victory in the Revolutionary War, symbolically offered his sword to Congress, and returned to private life, likely reflected common sentiments when in a letter that he wrote to James Madison on November 5, 1786, he observed that "No morn ever dawned more favorable than ours did; and no day was ever more clouded than the present! Wisdom, and good example are necessary at this time to rescue the political machine from the impending storm." As states began appointing delegates to a convention, one of the great unanswered questions was whether the distinguished general, who had already retired from public life, and who had already cited his health as a reason to avoid addressing the Order of Cincinnati (a group of veterans that was being criticized for creating a hereditary aristocracy) that was to meet in Philadelphia in the summer of 1787, would be willing to lend his own immeasurable prestige to the proceedings. Even with his presence, could such a body formulate concrete solutions to existing problems, or would state jealousies continue to impede the hopes for freedom and prosperity that the Revolution had raised?

SOURCES CITED IN THIS CHAPTER

Adams, Willi Paul. 2001. *The First American Constitutions: Republican Ideology and the Making of State Constitutions in the Revolutionary Era.* Lanham, MD: Rowman & Littlefield.

Farrand, Max, ed. 1966. *The Records of the Federal Convention.* 4 vols. New Haven, CT: Yale University Press.

Jefferson, Thomas. 1905. *The Works of Thomas Jefferson.* 12 vols. Edited by Paul Leicester Ford. New York: G. G. Putnam's Sons, Knickerbocker Press.

———. 1964. *Notes on the State of Virginia.* New York: Harper and Row Publishers.

Jensen, Merrill. 1976. *Constitutional Documents and Records, 1776–1787.* Vol. 1 of *The Documentary History of the Ratification of the Constitution.* Madison: State Historical Society of Wisconsin.

Lutz, Donald S. 1988. *The Origins of American Constitutionalism.* Baton Rouge: Louisiana State University Press.

Maier, Pauline. 1970. "Popular Uprisings and Civil Authority in Eighteenth-Century America." *William and Mary Quarterly*, 3rd ser., 27 (January): 3–35.

Solberg, Winton, ed. 1958. *The Federal Convention and the Formation of the Union of the American States.* Indianapolis, IN: Bobbs-Merrill.

2

THE CONVENTION BEGINS AND RANDOLPH INTRODUCES THE VIRGINIA PLAN

A national government ought to be established consisting of a
supreme legislative, judiciary, and executive.

—Farrand 1966, 1:31

The Annapolis Convention, which had assembled in September, 1786
to discuss issues of navigation and trade among the states, had called
for another convention to meet on the "second Monday of May next" in
Philadelphia to propose changes to make the government "adequate to the
exigencies of the Union." However, there was initially no more guarantee
that a second convention, called to address even wider problems, would be
any more successful in attracting state delegations than was the first. Even
after Shays's Rebellion generated fears that induced Congress to give its
assent to a second meeting and more state legislatures began to appoint delegates, the success of the Convention was far from guaranteed. Moreover,
it was not altogether clear that the Articles of Confederation could be fixed
by the alterations that such a convention was likely to propose.

Although Virginia's James Madison, Jr. is often called the "father"
of the U.S. Constitution, a more discriminating author, who knows that
Madison was more influential in the days leading up to the convention and
in its opening weeks than in some subsequent proceedings, has recently
dubbed him its "midwife" (Brookhiser 2011, 84). Madison certainly played
among the most active roles in calling the convention and setting it on a
course consistent with our modern Constitution.

The son of a Virginia planter, Madison had served with distinction in
both the Articles of Confederation Congress and in the Virginia state assembly. A graduate of the College of New Jersey, today's Princeton, where he

had engaged in graduate study under its president, John Witherspoon (who had brought with him the wisdom of the Scottish Enlightenment), Madison was among the most cerebral of the framers. Although he was a master of political infighting and an eventual cofounder with Thomas Jefferson of one of the nation's first two political parties, he had the capacity to look beyond immediate circumstances to larger causes. Significantly, in the years leading up to 1787, Madison, who had served both in the Confederal Congress and in Virginia's state legislature, had been seeking information from books that his friend Jefferson was sending him from Europe. In preparation for the convention, Madison had composed two essays. One examined the history of ancient and modern confederacies, the governments most like those under the Articles of Confederation. A second identified what Madison believed to be the "vices," or ills, of the government under the Articles.

Madison was absolutely convinced that the ills were so great, and the flaws in the type of government under the Articles were so pronounced, that the nation needed not simply to *repair* but to *replace* the existing government. He also knew that the forces of inertia were so strong that he needed to do everything he could to assure the success of the new meeting. Madison spent months writing letters in an effort to lobby George Washington, and to lobby others (including Alexander Hamilton and Edmund Randolph) to lobby Washington, to attend this meeting and lend his wisdom and prestige to its deliberations. Madison had attended the Annapolis Convention and probably helped author its resolutions. He had helped write the resolution in Virginia calling for a convention, and he and his friends ultimately persuaded Washington to attend the Constitutional Convention. Had he done nothing more, Madison's contribution would have been major, but the records reveal that he did much more.

DELEGATES ASSEMBLE

Characteristically, Madison was the first delegate outside of Pennsylvania to appear in Philadelphia for the convention when he arrived on May 3 to stay at Mary House's Boarding House. There, as a member of Congress, he had once been engaged to Miss Kitty Floyd, the 16-year-old daughter of a member of Congress, who later ditched Madison for a Presbyterian minister and sealed her Dear John (Or Jemmy, as he was called) letter with sourdough! Other delegates would stay there or would board at the nearby Indian Queen, at Mrs. Daily's Boarding House, at Mrs. Marshall's Boarding House, or in private homes.

Philadelphia, a name meaning "city of brotherly love," was the nation's largest city, and the second-largest (behind London) in the English-speaking world. Founded by William Penn, it featured a busy port, eight newspapers, numerous churches, a museum, a medical school, a public library, a jail, and numerous shops and taverns. It was also home to the American Philosophic Society and would serve again from 1790 to 1800 as the nation's capital.

The delegates had to cool their heels from May 14, 1787 until May 25 to obtain a quorum with which to begin deliberations in the Pennsylvania State House—today's Independence Hall, near where the Liberty Bell, and Constitution Center, are now located. Designed in part by Andrew Hamilton, a one-time speaker of the Pennsylvania Assembly who had argued the famous *Peter Zenger* case involving freedom of the press, the building had two large rooms on the first floor, including the commodious East Room, the home of the Pennsylvania Assembly, where the delegates to the Constitutional Convention would meet. Both the Declaration of Independence and the Articles of Confederation had been proposed there.

Delegates from Virginia filtered in more quickly than those from many other states, and as they conferred together, Madison persuaded them not only to sign on to a plan to introduce at the beginning of the proceedings but to make it audacious. Effectively ignoring the congressional call for "revising the Articles of Confederation," this plan, which came to be known as the Virginia Plan, introduced a whole new scheme of government.

Thomas Jefferson would call the 55 delegates who convened in Philadelphia an "assembly of demigods," but, while the group was impressive, Jefferson's own assessment was an overstatement, in part because both he and John Adams were respectively serving in diplomatic capacities in France and England. The convention had men of great ability, but so had the Continental Congresses and so would the very first Congress that met under the new government. While some delegates were the very best the former colonies had to offer, others would prove to be relative nonentities. Fortunately, the best of the best dominated most of the proceedings and raised arguments that continue both to explain most provisions of the Constitution and to provide vantage points to defend and critique them.

A COLLECTIVE PORTRAIT OF THE DELEGATES

Consistent with the norms of the day and the makeup of the Confederal Congress and the state legislatures, all the delegates were white males.

Delegates ranged in age from 26 (New Jersey's Jonathan Dayton) to 81 (Franklin), but averaged 43. Although there were a few bachelors, most were married, or like James Madison, would someday be so. Almost all were politically experienced. Political scientist Martin Diamond thus noted that 6 of the delegates had signed the Declaration of Independence, 6 had signed the Articles of Confederation, 24 had served in the Continental Congress, 46 had served in state or colonial legislatures, 10 had helped draft state constitutions, and 39 had served or were serving in Congress (Diamond 1981, 17).

Eight of the fifty-five delegates had been born abroad, about two-thirds had served in the military, and at least thirty had attended college—nine had graduated from Princeton, four from Yale, three from Harvard, and three from William and Mary. An overwhelming majority of the delegates were Protestants, with Episcopalians being the most numerous, but a few were known for their religious enthusiasm, and there were two Roman Catholics and a few known Deists. Thirty-four of the delegates were lawyers, while others were planters, merchants, career politicians, and doctors (Vile 2005, 1:218). Seventeen of the delegates owned slaves. The number of delegates who attended each day averaged about 30 to 35.

When delegates signed the Constitution, they did so under the names of their respective states from north to south. Although it was not always clear precisely where one section began and other ended, at the time contemporaries often classified states into eastern (northern or New England), middle, and southern divisions. Differences among these three regions, as well as between the eastern states and the anticipated western states, often figured prominently in Convention debates.

In 1785, Spain had sent Don Diego De Gardoqui as a minister plenipotentiary to negotiate with John Jay, the U.S. secretary of foreign affairs whose home state was New York, over Spain's decision to cut off American rights to navigate the Mississippi River. Despite congressional instructions to the contrary, Jay had sought to exchange this right for that of marketing fish and grain to Spain, which would have favored New Englanders. Although southern states had managed to block this move, it had exacerbated relations between the two regions, and had a large impact on the majorities required to ratify treaties. Toward the end of the convention, Charles Pinckney of South Carolina gave a further peek into regional variations when he observed that New England states were especially interested in "the fisheries & W. India trade," New York in "free trade," New Jersey and Pennsylvania in "wheat & flour," Maryland, Virginia, and North

Carolina in tobacco, and South Carolina and Georgia in rice and indigo (Farrand 1966, 2:449).

DELEGATIONS FROM THE EASTERN
(NORTHERN OR NEW ENGLAND) STATES

The New Hampshire delegates, John Langdon and Nicholas Gilman, did not arrive until July 23, after the convention's most important compromise on state representation, so their impact was limited. Langdon, who had served as president of New Hampshire from 1784 to 1786, was a wealthy merchant and shipbuilder who fronted the money for Gilman and himself to attend the convention. The latter, a lifelong bachelor, is not recorded as speaking a single time during the convention deliberations, but later served terms in both the U.S. House of Representatives and Senate.

Massachusetts sent four delegates. They were Elbridge Gerry, Nathaniel Gorham, Rufus King, and Caleb Strong. Strong, who was a lawyer and judge, had to leave the convention early. Gerry, a merchant, was a consistent defender of the existing confederal system and one of three members remaining on the last day who refused to sign the Constitution. His name later became the base of the word "gerrymandering," which refers to configuring electoral districts for political advantage, and he would go on to serve as vice president under James Madison. Nathaniel Gorham was another merchant who had served in Congress and who served in the opening weeks of the convention as chair of the Committee of the Whole. Rufus King was a lawyer with lots of political experience who would serve on a record six committees during the convention's deliberations, suggesting that he was both popular and respected. In 1816, he would lose an election to the presidency to Virginia's James Monroe.

Connecticut was a small state with a powerful delegation that included Oliver Ellsworth, William Samuel Johnson, and Roger Sherman. In addition, Georgia's delegate, Abraham Baldwin, had emigrated from there. Whereas delegates from other states were chosen by legislatures, those from Connecticut were chosen directly by the people (Farrand 1996, 1:314). Ellsworth was a lawyer, and later chief justice of the U.S. Supreme Court, who is particularly associated with the Great, or Connecticut, Compromise regarding representation of the states in Congress. William Samuel Johnson, who had just been appointed as president of King's College, would serve on a number of committees, including one that dealt with the slave trade and navigation. Roger Sherman, a former cobbler and merchant who had gotten a law degree and signed both the Declaration of Independence and the Articles of Confederation, played a key role at the convention, helping to formulate the Connecticut Compromise and often besting Madison on major issues.

DELEGATIONS FROM THE MIDDLE STATES

New York's delegation was badly split. Alexander Hamilton was a strong nationalist, and John Lansing and Robert Yates were allied with Governor George Clinton, who was far more satisfied with maintaining the status quo under the Articles. Hamilton, a precocious immigrant from the British West Indies, had served under Washington during the revolution, married into a wealthy family, and established himself as a skilled lawyer. He was the only one of New York's three delegates who was present when the Constitution was signed, but he did not participate in critical debates from the end of June through August 12. Often engaged in political conflict, including the Federalist/Antifederalist debates in which he was the lead author of *The Federalist*, Hamilton's life would end in 1804 after a notorious duel with a political rival, Aaron Burr.

John Lansing, the mayor of Albany, was a wealthy landowner and lawyer who owned slaves and who questioned the convention's right to do any more than revise the Articles of Confederation; his life ended in mystery in 1829 when he disappeared after going to post a letter. Robert Yates, who served on the New York Supreme Court for more than 20 years, took unofficial notes that help provide a picture of convention debates until he and Lansing left, in apparent disgust, on July 10. Yates may have authored essays printed in New York newspapers under the name of Brutus that opposed adoption of the new Constitution.

David Brearly, Jonathan Dayton, William Churchill Houston, William Livingston, and William Paterson all represented New Jersey and were associated with the defense of the small states, but only the latter made a substantial contribution to the proceedings. Brearly had served as chief justice of the New Jersey and would serve on two committees at the Convention. Dayton (b. 1760), a Revolutionary War hero for whom a city in Ohio would later be named, was the youngest delegate at the convention and, perhaps because of his young age, did not speak frequently. William Churchill Houston had immigrated to New Jersey from South Carolina, had earned a law degree and had served in a number of state posts, but he did not speak at the convention, which he left by June 6, probably because of the tuberculosis that would end his life the following year. Livingston was a wealthy lawyer who rarely participated in convention debates, perhaps in part because he was simultaneously serving as state governor. The physically diminutive William Paterson, a lawyer, is best known for his able advocacy of the New Jersey Plan, which represented the interests of the small states. He left the convention on July 23 but returned in September to sign the document and went on to serve on the U.S. Supreme Court.

Pennsylvania's delegation included eight delegates, four of whom had signed the Declaration of Independence and all of whom would sign the Constitution. They were George Clymer, Thomas Fitzsimons, Jared Ingersoll, Thomas Mifflin, Robert Morris, Benjamin Franklin, James Wilson, and Gouverneur (this was a family name, not a title of a state executive) Morris, the last of whom also had strong New York connections. In addition, Delaware's John Dickinson had once served in the Pennsylvania Assembly.

Five of the Pennsylvania delegates said almost nothing during the convention proceedings. Clymer was a wealthy merchant who may have been more engaged at the time in simultaneously representing his state in its legislature. Fitzsimons, also a merchant, is perhaps best known for being one of two Roman Catholics at the convention. Mifflin was another merchant who had served as a quartermaster general during the Revolutionary War but was not recorded as giving a single speech or serving on a single committee at the convention. Although Robert Morris's land speculations would eventually land him in a debtor's prison, he had served as the financier of the revolution and was associated at the convention with those who supported representation based on population.

Franklin, Wilson, and Gouverneur Morris must all be ranked as among the convention's most influential members. Franklin, the self-educated journalist who was the oldest member (81) at the convention, was among the best-known men not only in America but throughout the world and had been a popular U.S. ambassador when he served in France. Wilson, who had been born in Scotland and had studied law under John Dickinson, was one of the convention's most ardent supporters of a strong single executive. Wilson was second only to Gouverneur Morris in the number of recorded speeches that he gave at the convention. Morris, who would become known for giving the final polish to the convention, was conversant in both law and business and was handsome despite a withered arm and a peg leg, both due to accidents.

Delaware's five representatives to the Philadelphia Convention were Richard Bassett, Gunning Bedford, Jr., Jacob Broom, John Dickinson, and George Read. Bassett, who was trained as a lawyer and founded a political dynasty in the state, may be best known for having attended almost every day of the convention without giving a single speech. Bedford, who had once roomed with James Madison, Jr. at Princeton, was a lawyer who had served as his state's attorney general and would become best known at the convention for his passionate, even intemperate, advocacy on behalf of the small states. Broom was a surveyor and public servant who mostly seconded motions by others and is depicted in Louis Glanzman's painting of the convention of 1787 with his back to viewers because he is the only delegate present at the signing of whom there is no known portrait. John Dickinson, the "penman of the American Revolution," was a London-trained lawyer who had been selected to both the Delaware and Pennsylvania state legislatures. He had authored the plan for the Articles of Confederation and presided over the Annapolis Convention. After he had to leave because of illness, he asked George Read to sign the Constitution on his behalf. Read, another lawyer, sometimes designated "Dionysius, Tyrant of Delaware" (Gillespie and Lienesch 1989, 32) for his role in his state during the Revolutionary War, was a strong defender of the rights of the small states and later served as a U.S. senator.

Maryland also sent five delegates to the convention. They were Daniel Carroll, Luther Martin, James McHenry, John Francis Mercer, and Daniel of St. Thomas Jenifer. Carroll, the convention's other Roman Catholic (his brother became the nation's first Roman Catholic bishop), had been educated in Flanders and inherited his father's extensive business and land. He was not seated at the convention until July 9 and would later be appointed as one of three commissioners responsible for helping to lay out Washington, D.C. Martin was a lawyer known for passionate but desultory speeches, who strongly defended the rights of the small states and left the convention early and printed a negative critique called *The Genuine Information*. McHenry, who had been born and educated in Ireland, had served as a surgeon at Valley Forge and missed most of the first two months of the convention, but left some notes of proceedings while he was there. Although he criticized a number of proposals and compromises, he eventually decided to sign in deference to the judgment of other delegates whose judgment he respected (Farrand 1966, 2:649) and went on to serve as a secretary of war to the first two presidents. Mercer had read law under Thomas Jefferson and had once served in the Virginia legislature, but he only attended the convention from August 6 through August 17, where he expressed concern over the creation of an aristocracy and supported a strong executive. He opposed ratification at his state's ratifying convention. Daniel of St. Thomas Jenifer, a lifelong bachelor, was a planter and merchant who often found himself at odds at the convention with Luther Martin. Jenifer freed his slaves at his death and willed all of his French books to James Madison.

DELEGATIONS FROM THE SOUTHERN STATES

Virginia shared characteristics of both the Middle Atlantic states and those farther south. Virginia's delegation included George Washington, James Madison, Edmund Randolph, George Mason, George Wythe, John Blair, and Dr. James McClung. Washington, a wealthy (although sometimes cash-strapped) planter, had a worldwide reputation based on successfully leading colonial forces against the British and then, like the Roman patriot Cincinnatus with whom he was frequently compared, returning to private life rather than seeking further power. Madison, a planter's son, came close to being a career politician and would be one of the convention's most important participants. Randolph, the state's winsome governor, was a planter/lawyer who had split with his own father in siding with the patriots during the revolution. He was one of three delegates who declined to sign the document at the convention but supported it during his state's ratifying convention. He later served under George Washington as secretary of state. Mason, who appears to have been commissioned as a leader of the local militia during the French and Indian War (and whom Madison consistently identified as "Col. Mason") was a Virginia planter who was the chief author of the Virginia Declaration of Rights—Madison had also served on the drafting committee—and a neighbor to George Washington. Mason played a major role in the convention. However, he ultimately refused to sign the Constitution largely because it lacked a bill of rights; as a result, he became estranged from Washington.

Wythe, who was often compared to Aristides "the Just" of ancient Greece, had mentored many lawyers including Thomas Jefferson and had in 1779 become the nation's first professor of law at William and Mary. Wythe headed the convention's Committee on Rules but left for home shortly thereafter because of his wife's illness and eventually resigned from the convention after her death. Blair, a lawyer, was the son of a merchant who owned Raleigh's tavern in Williamsburg. Although he was a long-time judge and later associate justice of the U.S. Supreme Court, Blair said almost nothing at the convention and was not selected to any committees. McClurg was a surgeon who had served in a number of governmental positions and who also said little at the convention, which he left near the end of July or the beginning of August. James Monroe, a Revolutionary War hero and future president, would pout about the fact that McClung had been sent to represent the state rather than him.

North Carolina sent five delegates to the convention. They were William Blount, William Richardson Davie, Alexander Martin, Richard Dobbs Spaight, and Hugh Williamson. Blount was an avaricious landowner who did not arrive until June 20 (he was delayed by an attack of hemorrhoids) and spoke only at the signing of the document. Later influential in the establishment of Tennessee, he is the first and only U.S. senator to have been impeached (but not convicted) on charges that he tried to stir up an Indian war against Spain. Davie was a lawyer who would later found the University of North Carolina. He appears to have favored adoption of the Great Compromise, and left the convention on August 13, but supported the Constitution at his state ratifying convention. Martin, a lifelong bachelor, who, however, acknowledged paternity of a son, had been born and raised in New Jersey. Although he stayed at the convention until late August, he did little more than second a few motions. Spaight, a planter who had been educated at the University of Glasgow, participated more actively than Martin without, however, being a major player; he died in 1802 after a duel with a political opponent. Williamson was the intellectual leader of the North Carolina delegation and had a variety of degrees including one in medicine from the University of Utrecht. He attended the entire convention and served on five different committees. He moved to New York in 1793.

South Carolina was ably represented at the convention by four delegates—Pierce Butler, Charles Pinckney, Charles Cotesworth Pinckney, and John Rutledge. Butler, who had been born in Ireland and sent to America as a British major, switched sides in the conflict and became a planter. He had state legislative experience and participated actively in convention proceedings but spent his later years in Philadelphia. Charles Pinckney, at 31, who did nothing to disabuse delegates of the notion that he was the youngest delegate (the distinction belonged to Dayton), was a lawyer/planter who proposed the Rules Committee at the convention and who appears to have introduced an early plan that was eclipsed by the proposal from Virginia. This did not deter him from addressing most major issues at the convention and from giving a major speech on the three classes that he believed predominated in America. His cousin, General Charles Cotesworth Pinckney, was another wealthy lawyer and planter who participated actively in proceedings and continued with a life of public service that included unsuccessful bids for the presidency against Jefferson and Madison in 1804 and 1808. Rutledge had studied law at the Inns of Court in England and had helped write the state's first constitution. He served on a number of committees during the course of the Convention and later served as a U.S. Supreme Court justice.

Georgia, the southernmost state, was represented at the convention by Abraham Baldwin, William Few, William Pierce, and William Houston. Baldwin was a chaplain for Connecticut troops during the Revolutionary War who subsequently got a law degree and whose ties to the Connecticut delegation may have been influential in the adoption of the Connecticut Compromise regarding representation in Congress. After the convention he served on the committee in the first Congress that helped draft the Bill of Rights and helped found the University of Georgia. Few, who had been born in Maryland and was admitted to the Georgia bar without formal legal training, attended the entire convention without making a single recorded speech, and he later moved to New York, where he served in the state legislature. Pierce had been born in Virginia and is best known for his engaging character sketches of fellow delegates. He left the convention early to attend to his duties in Congress. Houston had been born in Scotland and educated in law at the English Inns of Court. He participated in some debates but left the convention sometime in late July or early August because of ill health. He spent most of his later years in New York.

Delegates arrived in Philadelphia as representatives of loosely bound states. The question remained whether they could create a more unified nation. If this were to happen, it was important to establish an atmosphere that would be conducive to reason and compromise.

Delegates met 6 days a week—88 of 116 days—from May 25 to September 17. Most days they worked from 10:00 a.m. until 3:00 or 4:00 p.m. Other than Sundays, their only recesses were on the very first Saturday (used by the Rules Committee), the July 3 and 4 recess (used by a Committee of Five) and from Friday, July 27 until August 6, during which a Committee of Detail met. Delegates closed the windows to enhance privacy, which undoubtedly increased the heat during the summer months.

SELECTING OFFICERS AND RECORDING DEBATES

Of all the delegates, none were better known or more respected that Benjamin Franklin, the journalist and diplomat who had authored almanacs and described his ascent from poverty in his autobiography, and George Washington, who had successfully led colonial forces in the war with Great Britain. Despite rheumatism and painful false teeth, the 55-year-old Washington was much younger, and in much better health, than the gout-stricken Franklin, who generally had Wilson deliver his speeches for him. Conventioneers were probably relieved when Robert Morris, the wealthy delegate from Franklin's own state of Pennsylvania, nominated Washington (whom he was hosting in his house) when the Convention convened on Friday 25, and the delegates unanimously selected him.

Leadership can take many forms, not all of which involve lofty rhetoric. One can comb convention records in vain for long speeches by Washington. His only recorded words at the convention are those humbly accepting this nomination and decrying his own qualifications for such an honor and those suggesting a revision in the formula for congressional representation near the end of the convention. Still, his presence called out the best in men who, knowing both the risks that he had made of his own life and fortune and his refusal to claim kingly power, did not want to embarrass themselves in his august presence. At a time of deep state loyalties, Washington was the nation's most fitting human symbol of the importance of a commitment to the common good. As the "father" of the nation and a representative of the largest state, Washington's austere presence lent a quiet dignity to the proceedings that might be almost impossible to duplicate in another such gathering.

The convention followed its action in electing a president by selecting a doorman and messengers and by choosing as the convention secretary Major William Jackson, who had served for a time as an aide to Washington during the Revolutionary War and would serve again in this capacity when he became U.S. president. Benjamin Franklin, who graciously assented to Washington's selection as president, was embarrassed that the convention chose Jackson over Franklin's grandson, Temple Franklin, who had worked with him when he was a diplomat to France. At the convention, Jackson, who appears primarily to have been motivated by the hope of fame, did little more than keep a tally of votes, which John Quincy Adams later had to reorganize.

Fortunately, Jackson's sketchy records are supplemented by reports of actual debates. The most extensive of these were kept by none other than James Madison, who had discovered in his own research how little was known about the founding of some of the republics that he had studied. Madison explained his technique for recording the debates:

I chose a seat in front of the presiding member, with the other members, on my right and left hand. In this favorable position of hearing all that passed, I noted in terms legible and in abbreviations and marks intelligible to myself what was read from the Chair or spoken by the members; and losing not a moment unnecessarily between the adjournment and reassembling of the Convention, I was enabled to write out my daily notes during the session or within a few finishing days after its close. (Benton 1986, 1:3–4)

Claiming with a melodrama that was consistent with his own hypochondria—although he appears to have had a condition similar to epilepsy and as a young man anticipated a short life, he was the last surviving member of the convention—Madison observed that "the confinement to which his attendance in Convention subjected him, almost killed him; but that having undertaken the task, he was determined to accomplish it" (Farrand, 1907, 52).

Although Madison's records were not published until 1840, after his own death, they remain the backbone of most primary collections of writings, most notably a four-volume set first published by historian Max Farrand in 1911, and subsequently supplemented by a fifth volume of additional materials about the convention in 1987. Most of the quotations from convention deliberations in this and other books on the convention are the product of Madison's painstaking efforts, which did not, however, improve his spelling, especially of delegates' names. Some other delegates, most notably New York's Robert Yates, also took notes that, while generally sketchier, confirm and sometimes supplement convention records and Madison's notes.

RULES OF THE CONVENTION

A majority of the delegates to the Constitutional Convention had previous experience in state or national legislatures and/or at state constitutional conventions. One indication of this experience is their early and frequent use of committees to promote deliberation and expedite their work. On the opening day, the delegates appointed Virginia's George Wythe to chair a three-man committee to draft rules for the convention, which it reported back on Monday, May 28. Such rules were designed to promote "a blend of orderly procedures and good manners" (Farrand 1966, 2:683).

As under the Articles of Confederation, each state delegation had a single vote (with ties cancelling the votes of states with equal numbers of representatives), and seven states (a majority of 13) were required to be present for a quorum. Members stood when speaking, with the president deciding who had risen first. The president was supposed to allow new speakers to express their views before giving the floor back to those who had already spoken on a subject. Votes were recorded by states. The convention had rejected the idea of recording votes under the names of individual delegates. The convention had decided to allow for re-votes, and delegates wanted individuals to be free to change their minds, and feared that recorded votes might make this less likely.

The most controversial, but arguably most effective, rule at the convention would probably be impossible to enforce with today's mass media. It provided "That nothing spoken in the House be printed, or otherwise published, or communicated without leave" (Farrand 1966, 1:15). George Washington limited the substance of his daily dairy entries, and Madison kept his near-lifelong correspondence with Jefferson to a minimum. Delegates sometimes shadowed the aging and loquacious Franklin for fear that he might inadvertently spill the beans on the convention proceedings. North Carolina's William Blount wrote a letter on July 19 that probably violated the rule against secrecy (Hutson 1987, 175), but it does not appear to have been circulated. When the New York *Daily Advertiser* published an article on August 18 suggesting that the convention was considering appointing the son of George III as a king, the convention did uncharacteristically authorize a statement for publication in the *Pennsylvania Herald* noting that "'tho we cannot, affirmatively, tell you what we are doing; we can, negatively, tell you what we are not doing—we never once thought of a king" (Van Doren 1948, 145). William Pierce, a convention delegate from Georgia, noted that on one occasion during the convention, Washington was highly disturbed when a member dropped a copy of a resolution being debated. Pierce further reports that after Washington solemnly called this breach of the rules to the convention's attention and threw the resolution on the table for its owner to retrieve, no delegate had the courage to claim it (Farrand 1966, 3:86–87).

Maryland's Luther Martin, who left the convention early, later charged that the convention had engaged in a giant conspiracy to foist a new government on an unwilling and uninformed people. From the perspective of the majority of delegates, however, they were simply attempting to discuss issues without the fear that riots might develop in the streets or that delegates might be influenced by pressure groups rather than by reason.

Moreover, although deliberations at the convention would be kept secret for decades, the constitution that it produced was available to scrutiny by all and would be ratified in a relatively open process.

John Langdon, one of the two New Hampshire delegates who had arrived late, wrote a letter on August 2, 1787 describing his impression of how the convention operated under its rules and the ever watchful eyes of its president:

> Figure to yourself the Great Washington, with a Dignity peculiar to himself, taking the Chair. The Notables are seated, in a Moment and after a short Silence the Business of the day is open'd with great Solemnity and good Order. The Importance of the Business, the Dignified Character of Many, who Compose the Convention, the Eloquence of Some and the Regularity of the whole gives a Ton[e] to the proceedings which is extremely pleasing. (Hutson 1987, 201)

In the early weeks, the convention operated through a Committee of the Whole, which Nathaniel Gorham of Massachusetts chaired. This mechanism, which would have been familiar to students of both the English Parliament and the Congress under the Articles of Confederation, allowed a smaller majority of delegates to operate in an expedited fashion subject to eventual approval of the entire body. The convention abandoned this mechanism after June 13, after which Washington presided over the entire body.

RANDOLPH INTRODUCES THE VIRGINIA PLAN

Virginia's James Madison had been planning for months for the Constitutional Convention, and as an experienced legislator, he appreciated the value of agenda-setting. If he could get the convention to start with a new plan, rather than with a revision of the Articles, he could point it in a more positive direction. Being more concerned about getting things done than in getting the credit for it, he persuaded the more charismatic and more rhetorically gifted Governor Edmund Randolph to introduce it!

Randolph's opening speech, the bulk of which Madison almost surely authored, was divided into four sections. These dealt respectively with the properties that were necessary for good government, the defects in the existing Articles of Confederation, the danger that these defects posed, and the proposed remedy (Farrand 1966, 1:18). Randolph said that the government should be able to protect against foreign invasion and against internal dissentions and seditions (a not-so-subtle reminder of Shays's Rebellion); should be able to secure the blessings of unity and protect itself against state encroachments; and should be paramount to the states. The defects in the current government, which Madison had identified prior to the convention, were evident in its failure satisfactorily to achieve any of these objectives. The existing dangers posed "the prospect of anarchy from the laxity of government every where" (1:19).

As if to disguise the radical nature of the proposed remedies, the first of Randolph's resolutions proposed that "the articles of Confederation ought to be corrected & enlarged as to accomplish the objects proposed by their institution; namely, 'common defence, security of liberty, and general welfare'" (1:20). The substance of subsequent proposals called for far more.

The Virginia Plan can only be fully appreciated by contrast to the Articles of Confederation. Under that plan, a unicameral congress in which each state was represented equally by delegates chosen by state legislatures exercised very limited powers. The Articles required supermajorities for key actions and unanimous consent to ratify constitutional amendments. The Articles had no independent executive or judiciary.

By contrast, the Virginia Plan called for a bicameral legislature apportioned according to tax contributions or the number of free inhabitants. The Virginia Plan proposed that the people would directly elect members of the first branch (today's House of Representatives) and that members of this branch would in turn select members of the second (today's Senate) from among nominees made by individual states. The plan called for broadly vesting Congress not only with the authority it had exercised under the Articles but also in "all cases to which the separate States are incompetent, or in which the harmony of the United States may be interrupted by the exercise of individual Legislation" (1:21). The plan further proposed granting Congress the power "to negative all laws passed by the several States, contravening in the opinion of the National Legislature the articles of Union" and even the power "to call forth the force of the Union agst. any member of the Union failing to fulfill its duty under the articles thereof" (1:21).

Rather than relying, as under the Articles, chiefly on Congress, the Virginia Plan proposed a system of separated powers with three branches of government. The plan did not specify whether the national executive would be singular or plural, but it did specify that whoever served would be selected by Congress and would be limited to a single term. The plan also left some details about the national judiciary to be filled in later but provided that Congress would choose the members of one or more such tribunals who would serve "during good behavior" (1:21). In a hybrid proposal that did not ultimately survive the Convention—but is partly reflected in the current presidential veto—the Virginia Plan also called for a Council of Revision. It would combine the executive with a number of judges, who would examine all acts of the state and national legislatures before they went into effect and have the power to veto them, subject to override by congressional supermajorities.

Other provisions of the Virginia Plan wisely called for the admission of new states, for the general government to guarantee republican governments to the states, for a constitutional amending provision that did not require congressional consent, for continuity between the current government and the one that would replace it, for eventual ratification of the proposals by special conventions elected by the people, and for a provision that all individuals holding office under the new government must take an oath to support it. The Committee of the Whole debated these proposals during the first two weeks of the convention.

Although the Virginia Plan contained many provisions, the most notable were its proposals for a significantly stronger national government of three branches rather than one, and its call for a significantly different system of representation (by tax contributions or population) that favored the more populous states in a bicameral Congress. Although Virginia delegates clearly anticipated that they would play a much larger role in the proposed government than they were able to play within a system that put them on par with other states, they undoubtedly thought that such a proposed system was more representative and also fairer.

CLARIFYING WHAT THE VIRGINIA PLAN WAS PROPOSING TO DO

With everything now being on the table, some members of the convention wanted to clarify what was happening. Whereas Randolph had introduced the Virginia Plan on Tuesday, May 29, as a way to "correct and enlarge" the Articles, delegates proposed new resolutions on the following day. One would have indicated "that a union of the States, merely federal [the designation that was then used for a form of government like that under the Articles of Confederation rather than for the system that emerged from the Convention], will not accomplish the objects proposed by the articles of confederation" (Farrand 1966, 1:30). A second, ultimately adopted, suggested "that a national government ought to be established consisting of a supreme legislative, judiciary and executive" (1:31).

Delegates queried Randolph who assured them that the Virginia Plan did not intend to abolish existing state governments, but Gouverneur Morris advanced the need for compulsive power in the new government, and George Mason stressed the need for a government that could operate directly on individuals. Connecticut's Roger Sherman, a onetime shoemaker and experienced legislator, who had just arrived at the convention and whose state would register the only negative to creating a new national government, observed that while it was necessary to increase congressional powers, especially related to the raising of revenues, he did not want to push things beyond what states were likely to approve.

By modern terminology, which was not yet available to the delegates, the Virginia Plan was nudging delegates from a confederal plan (then identified as "federal") where states were sovereign, to a federal plan where the balance between the national government and the states was more equal and where both state and national authorities would have power, as in taxation, to operate directly on the people. Everyone present seemed to realize that the Virginia Plan went far beyond mere tinkering with existing governmental machinery, but their perception that they were living in a time of crisis gave them courage to try something new. George Washington may well have summarized convention sentiments when he said:

> It is too probable that no plan we propose will be adopted. Perhaps another dreadful conflict is to be sustained. If to please the people, we offer what we ourselves disapprove, how can we afterwards defend our work? Let us raise a standard to which the wise and honest can repair. The event is in the hand of God. (Peters 1987, 18)

One of the most striking departures of the Virginia Plan from the Articles of Confederation was its proposed change in state representation within Congress. This posed an immediate difficulty for delegates from Delaware whose commissions from their state had specified that they could not assent to any change in the state's equal representation. However, no one had yet called for a vote on this issue, they decided to stay, and the discussion continued.

DISCUSSIONS OF THE PROPOSED CONGRESS

Many of the delegates had fought for freedom in the Revolutionary War, and probably all would have affirmed, with the Declaration of Independence, that government should rest on the consent of the governed. This did not mean that the delegates necessarily embraced democracy, at least not as it is currently understood. On May 31 the convention concurred relatively quickly with the idea that the new Congress should be bicameral—with only the Pennsylvania delegation, which had a unicameral state legislature, dissenting. Still, delegates were not as unified in thinking that the people should select members of one or both houses of Congress by direct election. Connecticut's Roger Sherman observed that state legislators might be able to make a better choice since the people as a whole "want information and are constantly liable to be misled" (Farrand 1966, 1:48). Elbridge Gerry proffered that "The evils we experience flow from the excess of democracy." Like Sherman, he did not think the people were vicious; they "do not want virtue," but they "are the dupes of pretended patriots" (1:48). He feared "the levilling [sic.] spirit," which he thought that Shays's Rebellion had epitomized (1:48).

At least three delegates took up cudgels for the more democratic view. Virginia's George Mason favored direct election of the larger house of Congress, which he viewed as "the grand depository of the democratic principle of the Govt." and a body which he likened to the British House of Commons (1:48). Acknowledging that one could be "too democratic," he also thought it was possible to run incautiously "into the opposite extreme" (1:49). Noting that members of the upper classes would in time "distribute their posterity throughout the lowest classes of Society," he thought that "every selfish motive" recommended a system that protected such classes (1:49). Speaking with his Scottish brogue over thick glasses, Pennsylvania's James Wilson, who would later serve on the U.S. Supreme Court, further noted the need for governments, especially republican, or representative governments, to have "the confidence of the people," and he attributed most opposition to national policies not to the hoi polloi but to state elected officials. Madison further weighed in on the side of popular election. Although he was a strong proponent of representative over direct democracy, here he argued that the idea of "refining the popular appointments by successive filtrations" could "be pushed too far," and "the great fabric to be raised would be more stable and durable if it should rest on the solid foundation of the people themselves, than if it should stand merely on the pillars of the Legislatures" (1:50).

After consenting to election of the first branch of Congress, the committee still had to decide about the second. The Virginia Plan had proposed that members of the first branch should select the members of the second branch from among nominees that the state legislatures proposed. Early in the debate, Randolph suggested that the upper house should be small enough "to be exempt from the passionate proceedings to which numerous assemblies are liable." He further associated such a branch with a means of curing some of "the turbulence and follies of democracy" that had been evident under the Articles (1:51). Wilson favored election of *both* houses by the people but settled for a system (not so far from statewide electorates) in combining districts for such selection. Having decided to reject the proposal within the Virginia Plan without settling on a replacement, the committee moved on to other matters.

The Virginia Plan had proposed to give Congress power over matters in which states were incompetent. Randolph, perhaps doing Madison's heavy lifting, had to deny that he favored "any intention to give indefinite powers to the national Legislature" (1:53). Madison tried to render support by saying that he favored enumerating congressional powers in theory but wondered whether this would be practical. After the Committee recommended accepting the idea of enumerating congressional powers, however, Madison backed away from the idea, which was part of the Virginia Plan, that the national government might need to use force against states and suggested looking for other solutions, a decision in which the rest of the committee concurred.

DISCUSSION OF THE PROPOSED EXECUTIVE

On Friday, June 1 the convention began considering the proposed new executive. Wilson, who would consistently favor an energetic executive, proposed almost immediately that the executive should consist of a single individual. Few in the convention could doubt that, if the executive were unitary, the first individual to fill the post would be George Washington. Although he was not presiding over the Committee of the Whole, his presence in the room would have been about as obvious as the proverbial elephant in the room. This was probably why this proposal led to "a considerable pause" (Farrand 1966, 1:65) after which Franklin cajoled members to speak their mind on the subject.

In addition to deciding whether the office should be vested in a single individual, the convention would have to decide whether to vest him with the powers of war and peace. More generally, should he share the prerogatives of the English king, and, if so, which ones? Whereas Wilson had argued for the "energy[,] dispatch and responsibility" of a single executive (1:65), Gerry favored "annexing a Council" to the office, and Randolph, who feared that an executive might become "the foetus of monarchy," suggested that a team of three executives might be preferable to one.

Madison proposed that the committee should decide what powers to allocate to the executive before deciding whether it would be singular or plural, but the committee ended up by agreeing to little more than that it should establish some kind of executive. After failing to agree on whether the executive would be chosen (as Wilson favored) by the people, or (as Sherman favored, and as the Virginia Plan had proposed) by Congress, the committee debated terms of three years or seven before temporarily agreeing on the latter.

In debates that followed the following day, Saturday, June 2, delegates suggested the legislative intrigues that might occur if Congress had the responsibility of selecting the executive. Wilson outlined a proposal that resembles today's electoral college (1:77), and Franklin proposed a motion, with a long speech that he apparently deposited in Madison's safekeeping, that such an individual should serve—as Washington would initially do— without a salary (1:78). Deferring a vote, probably in deference to Franklin's feelings, the delegates probably realized that, however public-spirited Franklin's proposal was, it would have left the office open only to those wealthy enough to serve without a salary.

Having not yet determined whether the legislature should *select* the president, the convention began debating whether it should *remove* him, perhaps through impeachment. This raised issues involving separation of powers. John Dickinson observed that the three branches of the new government "ought to be made as independt. as possible" (1:86). Seeing the separate states, like the three branches of government and the bicameral legislature, as means of creating stability within the new government, Dickinson also anticipated the convention's most important eventual compromise by suggesting that states might be equally represented in one house and by population or property in the other (1:87).

When the committee reassembled on Monday, June 4, delegates were finally ready to vote for a single executive, in part because they feared that a plural executive might result in tumult. Discussions of the proposed Council of Revision led to questions as to whether it was appropriate to involve judges in such decisions or as to whether, as Wilson argued, the president alone should share in an absolute negative. After Franklin observed that the governor had misused the veto in Pennsylvania, Madison sagely suggested that the president's veto need not be absolute but could be subject to override by legislative majorities. Mason feared the potential of an elective monarch, but perhaps to soothe Washington's feelings, Franklin observed that "The first man, put at the helm will be a good one. No body knows what sort may come afterwards" (1:103). The Committee voted decisively to enable two-thirds majorities of both houses of Congress to override presidential vetoes and almost as decisively to allow the president to exercise the veto alone, without the concurrence of the Council of Revision (1:104).

DISCUSSIONS OF THE PROPOSED JUDICIARY AND RELATED MATTERS

The Articles of Confederation provided only for ad hoc national judicial bodies to deal with conflicts among the states. By contrast, the Virginia Plan had proposed one or more permanent national tribunals appointed by Congress, with judges serving during good behavior. Discussion shifted to this proposal on Tuesday, June 5.

Wilson was interested in vesting the appointment power in the executive branch rather than in Congress. John Rutledge wanted to rely on state courts subject to the supervision of a single Supreme Court. Franklin enlivened the mood by suggesting that the nation should consider following what he claimed was the practice in Scotland of allowing lawyers to make the appointments, reasoning that they would appoint their best colleagues in order to split the fees from their practices! After Madison suggested that the Senate might make selections, rather than the full Congress, the committee voted to strike the provision for legislative appointment and allow full determination of the issue at a later time.

This did not stop renewed discussion later in the day when Rutledge and Sherman renewed fears of inferior federal tribunals, but Madison and Wilson—who was especially concerned about the need for national jurisdiction over admiralty matters—argued for their necessity. Pointing to the possibility of "improper Verdicts in State tribunals obtained under the biased [sic.] directions of a dependent Judge, or the local prejudices of an undirected jury," Madison argued that "A Government without a proper Executive & Judiciary would be the mere trunk of a body without arms or legs to act or move" (Farrand 1966, 1:124). Although South Carolina's Pierce Butler proposed that "We must follow the example of Solon who gave the Athenians not the best Govt. he could devise; but the best they wd. receive" (1:125), in its second try, the motion for inferior federal courts carried.

The convention postponed a decision on the mechanism for amending the Constitution, but Sherman nonetheless objected to attempting to bypass the process of amending the Articles by providing for such ratifications by state conventions. Reflecting the growing consensus that constitutions were designed to be paramount to ordinary legislation, Madison observed that the ratification of the Articles themselves was arguably defective. Preparing the way for change, he further noted that the Articles were a treaty, which at least some parties had violated (presumably by failing to meet their requisitions), and which technically "absolved the other parties" from their obligations (1:122). Madison's notes indicated that Gerry, consistent with Gerry's earlier reservations about democracy, "seemed afraid of referring the new system to them [the people of the states]" (1:123). Wilson suggested that states that wanted to do so should be able to join together in a new union and allow others to enter later. Charles Pinckney suggested that an agreement among nine or more states should be sufficient to bring a new government into play.

FURTHER DISCUSSIONS OF THE PROPOSED
LEGISLATURE WAX PHILOSOPHICAL

Congress was the central branch under the Articles and would remain so under the proposed Virginia Plan, so it continued to garner the greatest discussion and provoke the most philosophical arguments. Charles Pinckney's reintroduction of a proposal on June 6, to allow state legislatures to choose members of the first house of Congress, generated considerable discussion. Elbridge Gerry, who was perpetually skittish about popular input, recognized that a government could err in either extreme. Reflecting a popular, albeit far from universal, sentiment, Wilson thought that "The Legislature ought to be the most exact transcript of the whole Society" (Farrand 1966, 1:132), but he recommended election from large districts where he thought there would be less chance of "intrigue" (1:133). Sherman argued that if state governments were to be retained, then they needed to select members of the national legislature. Recognizing that small states like Rhode Island (the only state not represented at the convention) might be so small as to be "too subject to faction" (1:133), others were too large to govern effectively, and the new government would rest on dividing duties between the two levels of authority so that many "civil & criminal" matters would remain with the states. George Mason concurred in Wilson's earlier argument that larger districts would be more likely to elect better representatives.

It is difficult to imagine a better stage for James Madison to launch into his first major speech (excluding the opening speech on the Virginia Plan by Randolph, which Madison probably wrote and which almost surely reflected Madison's own sentiments). Madison's heart must have skipped a beat when Sherman mentioned the proclivity of small states to faction, and other delegates began to discuss the ideal size of legislative districts. Madison was a man of ideas. With the possible exception of his passionate defense of religious liberty (which was related in that he believed such liberty was more secure the more denominations there were), Madison remains today most closely associated with an argument in his celebrated essay in Federalist No. 10 in defense of the new Constitution. In assessing problems that had arisen under the Articles of Confederation, Madison had concluded that they were similar to the main problem with earlier confederacies. The smaller districts and societies were, the more likely a single faction, or interest, could dominate and threaten individual rights. Madison set forth all these arguments in his speech of June 6. He so warmed to this theme that he seems to have been the first to breach the verboten subject of slavery: "We have seen the mere distinction of colour made in the most enlightened period of time, a ground of the most oppressive dominion ever exercised by man over man" (1:135). By enlarging the sphere of government, one could multiply factions and make it unlikely that any faction would dominate. Representatives chosen from the larger districts that would be needed to elect a national assembly would be less likely to represent factions than would state legislatures.

Did other delegates share Madison's views? Did they even understand them? Did they recognize how important Madison's view of factions played in his own philosophy of government? Was the Constitution based on adherence to Madison's view or is its philosophy independent of them? Scholars still debate these issues. Interestingly, Alexander Hamilton, who later recruited Madison to help write the *Federalist*, expressed doubts in notes that he took of that day's session that larger districts would necessarily be more likely to choose better leaders (1:147).

Although Delaware's George Read appeared to suggest that it might be time to sacrifice the states to a national entity, John Dickinson and William Pierce probably represented convention sentiments more closely when they proposed that the people should be represented by the first branch and the states by the second. This was consistent with General Pinckney's desire "to have a good national Govt. & at the same time to leave a considerable share of power in the States" (1:137). Although Wilson had favored a strong national government, he made it clear that he had done so not in an effort to eliminate the states but because he thought the states were posing a greater threat to the government of the whole than the existing government under the Articles was posing to the existence of the states.

DISCUSSION OF THE PROPOSED COUNCIL OF REVISION

As debates continued on June 6, James Wilson asked for a reconsideration of the decision to give a veto to the president alone rather than in conjunction with a Council of Revision. The soft-voiced Madison, who was beginning to hit his stride, chimed in to support one of his own pet ideas. Madison was concerned that an executive might need special support within a republican government that was unaccustomed to vesting a single individual with preeminence. Madison argued that allying the executive with members of the executive might actually defend both institutions against "Legislative encroachments" (Farrand 1966, 1:138). Recognizing that some delegates feared that such a prior consideration of legislation might bias judges about cases that they would later hear, he did not think this would happen very often, and he thought it would be balanced by the good that would proceed "from the perspicuity, the conciseness, and the systematic character whc. the Code of laws wd. receive" from such review (1:139). Madison did not think that an alliance of the executive and judiciary on a Council of Revision would improperly mix their powers in a way that violated the maxim of separation of powers. As on the earlier occasion, however, the committee decided to leave the veto power in the executive office alone.

DISCUSSIONS OF THE PROPOSED SECOND HOUSE

Up to this point, most discussions of the proposed new Congress had focused on the first house. On Thursday, June 7, however, the committee directed attention to the second house when Dickinson initiated discussion of a proposal to allow state legislatures to select members of this house directly rather than, as suggested in the original Virginia Plan, having the first house select members of the second from state nominees. This discussion became entwined with the issue of what the proper size of that body should be.

Sherman thought state selection of senators might lead to greater harmony between state and national authorities. He further argued that popular sentiments would be "better collected" (Farrand 1966, 1:150) through state governments than from "the people at large" and that state legislatures would be more likely to choose distinguished characters to this body, making it more equivalent to the British House of Lords. Dickinson expressed the further hope that the Senate could be large enough (80 or more members) to balance the powers of the other house.

The more democratically inclined Wilson wanted the people to select members of both houses. Madison indicated his desires to proportion the Senate according to population and to keep it from becoming too large. Seizing a favorite philosophical bone with zest, he repeated concerns that factions were more likely to arise in more numerous bodies.

After Gerry reviewed the existing options for selecting senators, John Dickinson introduced a metaphor, that would recur from time to time in the debates and that must have had special appeal in an age of Enlightenment, when educated men marveled at the orderly universe that Isaac Newton had explained and sought to reflect such harmony by establishing checks and balances within governments. Pointing to the necessity of preserving a degree of individual state autonomy, Dickinson suggested that the proposed new system was like the solar system "in which the States were the planets, and ought to be left to move freely in their proper orbits" (1:153). A larger Senate would be likely to give greater representation to "family weight & other causes" (1:153).

Reading into Wilson's earlier comments a desire to obliterate the states, Dickinson mixed metaphors in opposing reforms that "would only unite the 13 small streams into one great current pursuing the same course without any opposition whatever" (1:153). He further questioned how far Madison would be willing to go in reducing the size of the Senate. Responding to Dickinson, Wilson assured the delegates that he did not favor extinguishing the states as planets, although he did warn that they could not "warm or enlighten the Sun" (1:153), an apparent reference to the proposed national government.

Madison was uncertain as to how one system would be more likely to represent family weight than another. He further questioned how state legislatures that had "run into schemes of paper money &c" (1:154) could be expected to do a better job than the people of keeping reins on Congress. By contrast, Gerry, a merchant who continued his distrust of the people, believed that state legislatures would better be able to secure the "commercial and monied interest" (1:154), and he raised a number of objections to voting districts. Pinckney wanted the Senate to be "permanent and independent" and suggested that states might be divided into three classes, one with one senator, a second with two, and a third with three (1:155). After George Mason pointed to the need for state legislatures to defend themselves "agst. Encroachments of the Natl. Govt" (1:155), the Committee voted unanimously to allow them to select senators.

DISCUSSIONS OF THE PROPOSED CONGRESSIONAL NEGATIVE OF STATE LAWS

The Virginia Plan had called for giving Congress a negative, similar to modern exercises of judicial review, over laws that conflicted with national laws or treaties, but on Friday, June 8, Charles Pinckney proposed widening this power to include any laws that Congress considered to be improper. It seems unlikely that increased the chances of the proposal's success when he observed that such a veto would be similar to the one that the British Crown had previously exercised over the colonies, but, perhaps despite the analogy, he found that Madison was more than willing to second this alteration of his earlier handiwork. Madison appears to have concluded that such a veto might be an adequate substitute for the use of force against recalcitrant states, from which he had been backing away almost since the introduction of the Virginia Plan. Picking up on Dickinson's earlier planetary analogy, Madison argued that such a veto could work against "the centrifugal tendency of the States; which, without it, will continually fly out of their proper orbits and destroy the order & harmony of the political system" (Farrand 1966, 1:165).

North Carolina's Hugh Williamson feared any veto that might restrict states in the exercise of their internal state police powers, while Elbridge Gerry thought the proposed congressional veto power was too broad. Although he could see the value of a veto over state issues of paper money or the like, he feared congressional interference with state affairs, especially related to their militia. He even suggested that national authorities might use such a power to "enslave the States" (1:165). Sherman wanted the delegates to be specific about the cases where the veto could be used.

Like Madison, James Wilson often couched his arguments in terms of larger theories. Although he was unable to decide on the practicality or expediency of the proposed Council of Revision, he was convinced that the principle behind the proposal was "right" (1:166). He likened control of individuals to that of states. Just as individuals gave up their absolute freedom within the state of nature and agreed to obey the law, so too, individual states had to give up their freedom within the new national system. While delegates to the First Continental Congress had described themselves as "one nation of brethren," who needed to "bury all local interests & distinctions," they had subsequently given way to "jealousy & ambition," with each endeavoring "to cut a slice from the common loaf, to add to its own morsel, till at length the confederation became frittered down to the impotent condition in which it now stands" (1:166). In an analogy that Chief Justice John Marshall would later use in ruling that a state cannot tax a national bank, Wilson observed that the whole (the national government) would have no desire to sacrifice a part, but that individual parts were often willing to sacrifice the common good. Dickinson agreed that states posed a greater threat to national unity than did the national government to state autonomy.

Both Madison and Wilson were from populous states. In a scenario that would be increasingly repeated after the introduction of the New Jersey Plan on June 14, Delaware's Gunning Bedford spoke for smaller states. Surmising that Delaware would have about one-ninetieth a share in the legislature and that Virginia and Pennsylvania would collectively have about a third, he rhetorically asked, "Will not these large States crush the small ones whenever they stand in the way of their ambitions or interested views?" (1:167). Perhaps reflecting on Pinckney's analogy to the king's veto, he asked whether states should have to wait for authorities seven or eight hundred miles away before they could enforce their own laws. Madison suggested both that the national government might develop a mechanism to give at least temporary approval of state measures and that the power to veto state laws might be more properly lodged in the Senate than in Congress as a whole. As to the interests of the smaller states, what would be their fate if the Union were to dissolve?

Although delegates from more populous states had apparently dominated the debates, the vote showed that debates might not always reflect convention sentiments. Only Massachusetts, Pennsylvania, and Virginia voted to widen the veto power. Seven states voted against it, and the Delaware delegation was divided.

CHOOSING THE EXECUTIVE

As if to echo the discussion of who should choose members of the Senate, Elbridge Gerry of Massachusetts proposed that state governors should choose the national executive, with their votes apportioned according to their representation within the Senate. In addition to helping to protect state sovereignty, such a proposal promised to promote separation of powers by lessening the president's dependency on Congress. Perhaps because of their own executive experience, Gerry also suggested that governors would "be most likely to select the fittest men" (Farrand 1966, 1:176).

Virginia's Randolph was less confident. Moreover, he feared that such an appointment mechanism would produce undue presidential dependence on the states. In colorful language he suggested that "They will not cherish the great Oak which is to reduce them to paltry shrubs" (1:176). Although Delaware's delegates divided its vote, none of the other states favored Gerry's proposal.

APPORTIONING CONGRESS:
A PREVIEW OF THINGS TO COME

This vote did not mean that everyone was on board with other elements of the Virginia Plan. In a dress rehearsal for arguments that would in another week dominate the convention, William Paterson introduced a resolution, seconded by David Brearly, also of New Jersey, to revisit the Virginia Plan's formula for state representation. Brearly observed that Congress had already debated the issue of representation when it had created the Articles and that it had accorded equal representation to each state in order to protect the interests of the less populous states. Representing states by population "carried fairness on the face of it; but on a deeper examination was unfair and unjust" (Farrand 1966, 1:177). By his calculations, Virginia would end up with sixteen votes in Congress to Georgia's one. New Jersey's experience suggested that when larger and smaller counties were combined into similar districts, the interests of the former dominated, and he feared similar results at the national level. Admitting that it seemed unfair to give the largest and smallest states the same representation, Brearly suggested the ultimate redistricting plan, albeit one that would only work if people were equally spread throughout the entire nation. Delegates should spread out a map and divide it into "13 equal parts" (Farrand 1966, 1:177)!

Paterson continued as though he were a member of the small-state tag team. He reminded the delegates that the Confederal Congress had concurred in a convention to revise, rather than replace, the existing government. When states selected delegates to represent them at the Philadelphia Convention, "The idea of a national Govt. as contradistinguished from a federal one, never entered into the mind of any of them" (1:178). Like Brearly, he suggested that if the Articles were to be changed from a confederacy into a national government, "all State distinctions must be abolished, the whole must be thrown into hotchpot, and when an equal division is made, then there may be fairly an equality of representation" (1:178). His meaning must have seemed clear even to non-lawyer delegates who were not familiar with the meaning of hotchpot, a legal term for combining, and then equally dividing, all the properties of an estate among members of a family when the family head died without a will. Paterson further suggested that it was no fairer to give larger and richer states a greater vote than to give rich men a greater vote than the poor. He observed that one of the obstacles to American representation in the British parliament prior to the Revolutionary War was that, even with such representation, the states would have been entitled to no more than a third of the total representatives. Interpreting Wilson's speech of June 5 as an invitation for the larger states to join together and wait for others to follow, Paterson threw down his own gauntlet:

> Let them unite if they please, but let them remember that they have no authority to compel the others to unite. N. Jersey will never confederate on the plan before the Committee. She would be swallowed up. He had rather submit to a monarch, to a despot, than to such a fate. He would not only oppose the plan here but on his return home do everything in his power to defeat it there. (1:179)

Paterson's response brought out the political theorist in James Wilson. Starting with the proposition that "all authority was derived from the people," he thought that it was clear that an equal number of people should have an equal number of representatives (1:179). Individuals were as sovereign as states.

Philosophers have long speculated as to what happens when an irresistible force hits an immovable object. The convention seemed about to provide an answer. The initial vote, taken on June 11, seemed conclusive, with seven states favoring representation in the first house according to population, three states opposing, and another divided, but the impassioned rhetoric should have given delegates a clue that those opposed to state representation by population alone were so fervent in their opposition that they were unwilling to agree to any plan that included such a provision.

Perhaps delegates could accommodate utilizing differing methods of representation in the House and Senate. Consistent with an earlier suggestion that Dickinson had made, Connecticut's Sherman proposed representing states by population in the House and equally in the Senate. Just as the House of Lords served to balance the House of Commons in England, so the second house could serve as a state balance to the more popular branch in America. With a view to difficulties under the Articles, Dickinson suggested that states should be awarded representation commensurate with their actual tax contributions. Rufus King pointed out that this might unfairly disadvantage states without ports if the new government chiefly collected taxes from imposts.

As the convention came close to a boil, Franklin attempted to intervene with a measured speech that James Wilson read to the committee on his behalf. Franklin observed that to this point the debates had been carried out "with great coolness & temper"; this was appropriate since states had sent delegates "to *consult* not to *contend*, with each other" (1:197). Franklin favored representation based on population, and did not see what larger states would gain from swallowing the smaller ones. Scottish fears that they might be swallowed up in the British Parliament had proved to be unfounded. Larger states had just as much to fear from smaller states as the reverse. If practical, he would not oppose equalizing states, but he was not sure it was practical. This speech was followed by a vote whose outcome was identical to the previous one in favor of representation according to population.

As if the tension in the room were already insufficient, Wilson introduced a modification of this rule, seconded by Pinckney, that would include indentured servants among free citizens and would count three-fifths "of other persons" excluding Indians (1:201). Many years later, as he examined the provisions in the Constitution relative to slavery, Abraham Lincoln observed that the framers had used circumlocutions, or ambiguous language, to hide the institution slavery "just as an afflicted man hides away a wen [cyst] or a cancer which he dares not cut out at once, lest he bleed to death" (Kammen 1987, 102). The original Virginia Plan had called for representation on the basis of free inhabitants. Now Wilson had proposed to modify this by counting slaves, whose continuing existence so violated the maxim of equality that the Declaration of Independence had declared that they were too embarrassing to mention by name, in the formula.

Wilson's concern in this matter is not immediately apparent so he may have introduced this proposal on behalf of a southern delegate like Madison. Had the vote on representation emboldened southern delegates to push their luck still further? They certainly did not intend to allow slaves to vote! Gerry's words were unsettling, but no wonder he queried why individuals who were regarded as mere property had any more right being counted than the "cattle & horses of the North" (1:201). With almost no recorded debate, the convention adopted the new emendation by a vote of nine to two, with New Jersey and Delaware dissenting.

Sherman introduced a motion proposing to represent states equally in the Senate, and it failed (five to six) by a single vote. A similar vote affirmed that the Senate should be apportioned the same way as the House. Delegates further voted to guarantee republican government and the territory of each state by a vote of seven to three. Delegates continued to agree on the need for an amending process but were not certain that it should include a provision making the assent of Congress unnecessary. Gerry questioned whether state officials should have to take an oath of loyalty to the national government, but a narrow six-to-five majority agreed that they should.

THE END OF THE BEGINNING

June 12 and 13 would be the last days in which the Virginia Plan would be the sole object of focus. After taking a vote to submit any proposed plan to the people of each state for ratification, discussion centered on the terms of members of the first branch of Congress. Rutledge favored two years, Jenifer and Madison favored three years, and Gerry favored terms of one year. He equated shorter terms with the popular will and, with considerable hyperbole, three-year terms with "tyranny" (Farrand 1966, 1:215). Madison pointed out that public opinion could be fickle and argued that if the convention focused less on what the people wanted and more on what was right, the results would gain the support of "the most enlightened & respectable citizens" (1:215). The committee approved a three-year term by a vote of seven to four.

What about legislative pay? Madison wanted the national government rather than the states to provide such pay, and he wanted it fixed, perhaps—in what appears to have been a rather impractical suggestion—around the price of a commodity like wheat. Mason supported national financing for fear that states would pay differentially or that states would be unable to provide salaries adequate for those who could not pay their own way. After the committee approved of national financing, it also approved a resolution making members of Congress ineligible for other national offices for one year after they left that body.

Delegates agreed that members of the second house should serve longer terms than those of the first, but they proposed a broad range of terms. Spaight, Randolph, and Madison favored a seven-year term, Sherman preferred five, Pierce preferred three. Those favoring the longer term, which initially prevailed, argued that it would give the upper house additional firmness and stability. In favoring a five-year term, Sherman was aiming for a mean between the executive and the first house. Pierce presumably favored three in order to keep members on a shorter lease, although his central focus was on opposing terms of seven years. Delegates voted on a variety of lesser issues. It is unclear whether there was little debate, whether Madison simply had inadequate time to record it, or whether he simply considered the issues to be too inconsequential for such discourse.

June 13 also appeared to be a day for cleaning up. One cannot help but wonder whether some delegates might have begun packing their bags. The committee tinkered with the jurisdiction of the Supreme Court, and agreed that its members would be selected by the Senate rather than by Congress as a whole. Gerry favored limiting the origination of money bills to the first house. This generated considerable discussion, largely about whether the mechanism could be evaded by various parliamentary maneuvers, and the proposal was eventually defeated.

REPORT OF THE COMMITTEE OF THE WHOLE

The first two and a half weeks had witnessed intense discussions and had registered lots of votes, but because everything had been done through a Committee of the Whole, it was now necessary to write a report to present to the convention itself. Summaries of the proceedings to date, prepared on June 13, consisted of 19 resolutions.

The committee had agreed to establish a national government of three branches and a Congress of two houses. The people would select members of the first house according to population (including three-fifths of the slaves) for three-year terms. State legislatures would select members of the second house, who would also be apportioned according to population and would be chosen for seven-year terms. Members of both houses would be paid out of the national treasury and would be ineligible for other offices for one year after they finished serving. Both houses would be able to originate acts. Congress would have power to legislate in all cases in which states were incompetent and could negative state laws contrary to the Union or its treaties.

The national executive would have the power to veto laws subject to override by both houses of Congress. The national judiciary would consist of at least one tribunal whose members would be appointed by the second house and serve during good behavior, but Congress could establish additional tribunals. The Report of the Committee of the Whole also specified that the new Constitution would provide for the admission of new states, for the continuation of the Articles until the new government went into effect, and for amendments when needed. The Constitution would require state officials to be bound by oath to support the Union, and the results of the convention would be subject to ratification in state conventions called for this purpose.

Called to revise the Articles of Confederation, the delegates had considered and refined the Virginia Plan instead. Its bold outlines remained, with some changes consistent with more than two weeks of reasoned discussion. Madison and representatives of the most populous states had reason to be feeling good, but deliberations were about to take an unexpected turn that would call into question the convention's early work and prolong the meeting until summer's end.

SOURCES CITED IN THIS CHAPTER

Benton, Wilbourne E., ed. 1986. *1787: Drafting the U.S. Constitution.* 2 vols. College Station: Texas A & M University Press, 1986.

Brookhiser, Richard. 2011. *James Madison.* New York: Basic Books.

Diamond, Martin. 1981. *The Founding of the Democratic Republic.* Itasca, IL: F. F. Peacock Publishers.

Farrand, Max. 1907. "The Records of the Federal Convention." *American Historical Review* 13 (October): 44–65.

———. 1966. *The Records of the Federal Convention of 1787.* 4 vols. New Haven, CT: Yale University Press.

Gillespie, Michael Allen and Michael Lienesch, eds. 1989. *Ratifying the Constitution.* Lawrence: University Press of Kansas.

Hutson, James H., ed. 1987. *Supplement to Max Farrand's* The Records of the Federal Convention of 1787. New Haven, CT: Yale University Press.

Kammen, Michael. 1987. *A Machine That Would Go of Itself: The Constitution in American Culture.* New York: Alfred A. Knopf.

Peters, William. 1987. *A More Perfect Union.* New York: Crown Publishers.

Van Doren, Charles. 1948. *The Great Rehearsal: The Story of the Making and Ratifying of the Constitution of the United States.* New York: Viking Press.

Vile, John R. 2005. *The Constitutional Convention of 1787: A Comprehensive Encyclopedia of America's Founding.* 2 vols. Santa Barbara, CA: ABC-CLIO.

3

PATERSON AND HAMILTON OFFER ALTERNATIVE PLANS

If the sovereignty of the States is to be maintained, the Representatives must be drawn immediately from the States, not from the People; and we have no power to vary the idea of equal sovereignty.

—William Paterson, June 16, 1787 (Farrand 1966, 1:251)

The first two and a half weeks had gone smoothly for those who had introduced the Virginia Plan. Delegates had given it a nick here and a tuck there, but its overall outlines were not far from what Madison had envisioned and what Randolph had introduced on May 28. The Committee of the Whole summarized 19 propositions that called for a national government of three branches with expanded powers, a bicameral legislature representing the people of the states according to population, a single national executive wielding a veto subject to an override by two-thirds majorities of both houses of Congress, and an independent judiciary. The Council of Revision was, for the moment, gone, but Congress retained power to veto state laws that contravened the articles of union or national treaties, and while new state delegations had continued to arrive, none had as yet deserted the convention.

INTRODUCTION OF THE NEW JERSEY PLAN

On June 14, William Paterson of New Jersey asked for time to examine the report of the Committee of the Whole in anticipation of introducing a "purely federal" plan (Farrand 1966, 1:240). By this, he meant to refer to a plan more like the existing Articles of Confederation with its unicameral

Congress in which sovereign states were represented equally. On the following day, Paterson introduced the plan, which the convention agreed not to debate until the following day, presumably so that its members could first examine and think about it.

Although Paterson introduced the plan, his delegation was so influential in its making that it is generally known as the New Jersey Plan. Madison observed that the plan had been written by delegates from Connecticut, New York, New Jersey, and Delaware (all, with the exception of New York, classified as small states), possibly with the help of Maryland's Martin Luther. One indication of the verisimilitude of Madison's notes is the fact that he recorded that John Dickinson had told him that the introduction of the New Jersey Plan was "the consequence of pushing things too far" (1:242). Consistent with a speech that Paterson had made before the Committee of the Whole on June 9, Dickinson had further admonished Madison that while some members of the small states favored both a strengthened national government and a bicameral legislature, many "would sooner submit to a foreign power, than submit to be deprived of an equality of suffrage, in both branches of the legislature, and thereby be thrown under the domination of the large States" (1:242).

Despite Dickinson's private comments, it is difficult to know whether other delegates generally attributed the Virginia Plan to Madison, who appears largely to have authored it, or to Edmund Randolph who had introduced it. It is notable that immediately after Paterson introduced the New Jersey Plan, Madison left others to critique it. Perhaps his role as the faithful scrivener of the convention's proceedings gave him some cover. However much he might have favored the Virginia Plan, delegates could see that he was listening to and recording both sides of the debates.

Paterson introduced nine resolutions. The first almost mirrored the congressional call for a convention to correct and enlarge the Articles "so as to render the federal Constitution adequate to the exigencies of Government, & the preservation of the Union" (1:242). Whereas the Virginia Plan advanced a whole new plan of government, the New Jersey Plan proposed a series of emendations of the existing Articles. Thus, the Virginia Plan called for a bicameral Congress; the New Jersey Plan did not do so because it sought to leave the existing unicameral Congress in place. Similarly, the Virginia Plan called for allocating representatives within Congress according to population, but the New Jersey Plan simply intended to keep the existing system, which gave each state a single vote. The Virginia Plan called for a new amending process whereas the New Jersey Plan simply would have left the existing requirement for unanimous state approval in place.

Consistent with Dickinson's observation that smaller states were willing to grant greater powers to Congress, the second resolution called for vesting Congress with power to levy taxes on imports and regulate trade with foreign nations and with one another. However, in contrast to the Virginia Plan, the New Jersey Plan would have allowed the resolution of disputes over such matters to originate in state courts.

The third resolution provided that Congress could requisition states for money based on their total number of free citizens and three-fifths of the slaves. It also called for the adoption of laws to deal with states that did not comply with such requests. It further would have required an initially unspecified majority of the states to enforce them.

It is critical to realize that Paterson introduced the New Jersey Plan *after* more than two weeks of discussion on the Virginia Plan, which had thus set the initial agenda. The new plan accordingly featured a number of decisions to which the convention had already agreed, but which its authors might not have advanced had they chosen to introduce a plan at the beginning of the convention. The fourth resolution thus called for establishing an executive, albeit a plural one, and listed a number of functions that this office would perform. Whereas the Virginia Plan would have permitted Congress to begin impeachment proceedings, the New Jersey Plan called for state governors to initiate this process.

The fifth resolution favored the creation of an independent judiciary. Whereas the Virginia Plan had called for vesting the appointment of judges in one or both houses of Congress, however, the New Jersey Plan wanted to vest this power in the executive branch. The plan made no provision for inferior federal judicial tribunals, presumably because it intended to continue relying, like the existing Articles of Confederation, on those of the states.

However else it differed from the Virginia Plan, the New Jersey Plan clearly recognized the need for expanded national powers. The sixth resolution served as the foundation for the provision in Article VI of the U.S. Constitution that would become known as the supremacy clause. This resolution was designed to make federal laws and treaties superior to state laws. The resolution even authorized the executive to use force against states to compel obedience to such acts. Resolutions seven, eight, and nine respectively provided for the admission of new states, for uniform rules for naturalization, and for mutual state recognition of criminal convictions rendered in other states.

After weeks of discussions centering on the Virginia Plan, another was now on the table. The New Jersey Plan conceded the need for greater power, especially in regard to requisitioning revenue from the states. According to Yates's notes, Paterson even expressed willingness to allow the national government to have "a small standing force" (1:246). Although the New Jersey Plan was willing to accept a more independent executive and judiciary, Paterson did not think the delegates needed to start from scratch as the Virginia Plan had done.

The convention faced a choice. It could move forward with the Virginia Plan and seek approval in nine or more state conventions, or it could reconsider revising the existing Articles and seek congressional and unanimous state approval of proposed amendments. Both plans called for vesting greater powers in Congress, but the Virginia Plan was much more likely to appeal to delegates from more populous states who chafed under their equal representation in Congress, whereas the New Jersey Plan was the darling of small states, who wanted to keep their current status. Which plan, if either, would win? Would the people approve either plan? If not, might delegates be able to meld elements of the two plans into an acceptable compromise?

THE INITIAL DEFENSE OF THE NEW JERSEY PLAN

The first person recorded as speaking to the New Jersey Plan was not Paterson but New York's Robert Lansing, who would later oppose the Constitution during ratification debates. He contrasted the Virginia and New Jersey Plans and came down on the side of the latter. He favored the New Jersey Plan both because he thought that it was within the convention's authorization and, perhaps largely in consequence, because he thought states were more likely to adopt and ratify it.

Paterson followed with the same arguments, suggesting that if the convention were to continue to draft a whole new form of government, delegates should first go back to their constituents with a request to increase their authority. Contrasting what some delegates might consider to be the best government in and of itself (was he conceding that the Virginia Plan was better or simply seeking support among those who might think so?), Paterson suggested that delegates should pay more attention to what government was more likely to be adopted. Conceiving of the Articles as a treaty among all 13 states, he observed that "[w]hat is unanimously done, must be unanimously undone" (Farrand 1966, 1:250). Moreover, however much they were now complaining, the large states had actually shown more zest for the Articles than the small one, with New Jersey and Maryland being the last to ratify. "If the sovereignty of the States is to be maintained, the Representatives must be drawn immediately from the States, not from the people: and we have no power to vary the idea of equal sovereignty" (1:251). The only alternative was that "of throwing the States into Hotchpot" (1:251), which while it had been criticized as impractical, had remained untested.

Paterson questioned the need for a bicameral Congress. States already served as checks on one another. The people were not criticizing Congress for being unicameral but for lacking adequate powers. The smaller Confederal Congress could act with greater "energy & wisdom" (1:251) than the larger, more complex, and more expensive Congress that the Virginia Plan proposed.

FURTHER DISCUSSION OF THE NEW JERSEY PLAN

James Wilson offered the first negative critique of the New Jersey Plan. He began by comparing the two plans with respect to 13 particulars. Recognizing, like Paterson, that the Virginia Plan was a major departure from the existing Articles, Wilson drew a different conclusion than proponents of the New Jersey Plan as to the convention's authority: "With regard to the *power of the convention*, he conceived himself authorized to *conclude nothing*, but to be at liberty to *propose any thing*" (Farrand 1966, 1:253). As to popular opinion, who could know it? As to state attachments, no citizen of a state should consider himself degraded by being considered a citizen of the United States!

Although he had outlined scores of differences between the Virginia and New Jersey Plans, Wilson limited his critique of the New Jersey Plan to a few major points. He observed that he would be reluctant to increase the powers of the existing Congress both because it was not accountable to the people and because it consisted of a single house. Inequality of representation was "a poison contaminating every branch of Govt." (1:253). The smaller states that now professed to favor a national impost had previously opposed it when Congress had proposed it as a constitutional amendment. A bicameral legislature would provide better checks against despotism than a unicameral legislature, whereas a single executive would be better than a plural one: "In order to control the Legislative authority, you must divide it. In order to control the Executive you must unite it" (1:254).

To what degree did the New Jersey Plan represent a viable alternative to the Virginia Plan, and to what degree was it designed chiefly as a way of preserving the existing system of representation? General Charles

Cotesworth Pinckney, who thought the convention was authorized to recommend whatever it thought to be necessary, expressed the rather cynical, but not necessarily mistaken, view that if the convention gave New Jersey an equal vote, "she will dismiss her scruples, and concur in the Natil. system" (1:255).

Governor Randolph followed with a defense of the Virginia Plan. Fearing that the very "salvation of the Republic was at stake," Randolph suggested that it would be "treason to our trust" to propose less than was needed to meet the crisis (1:255). This might, indeed, be the last favorable opportunity to take such action.

In Randolph's view, there was clear choice between a federal plan and a national plan. The former had already displayed its weaknesses. The New Jersey Plan called for strengthening the existing plan with coercion over the states whereas the Virginia Plan relied on legislation directed to individuals. The former was "*impracticable, expensive, cruel to individuals,*" and would breed the use of further force (1:256). The current Congress was "a mere diplomatic body" whose members were subject to state recall and who were therefore "always obsequious [overly deferential] to the views of the States, who are always encroaching on the authority of the U. States" (1:256). Only a truly national government could provide adequate remedies.

ALEXANDER HAMILTON SPEAKS

Few if any delegates to the convention had keener minds or more ambitious hearts than did Alexander Hamilton of New York, a brilliant lawyer who would go on to help found one of the nation's first two political parties (the Federalists) and become the new nation's first secretary of the treasury. Representing a state with two other delegates who favored revising the Articles rather than establishing a new national government, Hamilton had little chance of having his own views reflected in his state's vote, but this did not mean that he could not try to influence the convention as a whole. To this point, he had said almost nothing, but on June 18, he delivered one of the longest and most memorable speeches of the entire convention. Gouverneur Morris, who was himself capable of giving a stem-winder, reported that the speech took between five and six hours and that it was among "the most able and impressive he had ever heard" (Farrand 1966, 1:293, citing J. C. Hamilton 1864, 3:283–84).

Hamilton was born and raised in the West Indies (rather than in one of the American colonies) and had come to New York as a teenager. He had identified with the patriot cause before he had a chance to form strong state loyalties or even to complete his education at King's College (today's Columbia). Although expressing greater disdain for the New Jersey Plan—he did not think any mere amendment of the existing system could be adequate—than for the Virginia Plan, Hamilton professed to be unfriendly to both.

Hamilton prided himself on being a hard-headed realist. He believed that the general government required five key supports, all of which the Articles lacked. The first consisted of "an active & constant interest in supporting it" (1:284). Under the Articles, states pursued their individual interests rather than those of the whole. The second support was connected to the love of power. Under the Articles, demagogues were more devoted to the power of their states than to that of the Union as a whole. The government's third support was "an habitual attachment of the people" (1:284), but under the current arrangement, citizens were more attached to their states than to the Articles. The government's fourth support was force, but the Articles lacked both coercive military and coercive legal power. The government's fifth support was influence, but states were dispensing current honors and rewards rather than the Union. Hamilton proceeded to review the history of evils that had plagued ancient republics in a survey that was almost as extensive as those that Randolph and Madison had invoked.

To avoid such evils, the general government needed to get the five key supports on its side. The New Jersey Plan continued to rely on requisitions from the states, which were almost impossible to apportion fairly. Equal representation for states, regardless of their population, "shocks too much the ideas of Justice, and every human feeling" (1:286). Hamilton was unsure whether the government under the Articles allowed Congress to maintain military forces, but even if it did, there is little hope that states would use it against one another. Experience suggests that "Two Sovereignties can not co-exist within the same limits" (1:287).

What was the solution? Madison—whom Hamilton did not reference in this speech—had argued for the merit of extending the sphere of republican government. By contrast, Hamilton found the size of America discouraging; indeed, he almost despaired over whether such a government "could be established over so great an extent" (1:288). He thought the Union could save money by abolishing the states, but he realized that such abolition would shock public opinion. Perhaps he knew that the sentiment would be equally shocking, but he believed that the government of Britain was the world's best. Hamilton thought that the aristocratic House of Lords was "a noble institution" (1:288), but he was not sure that the proposed Senate would be its equal, or that seven years would provide a long enough term. It would be difficult to establish an executive "on Republican principles" (1:289). He favored allowing members of both institutions to serve during good behavior, that is, for life. He feared that an executive limited to a seven-year term might engage in war as an excuse to perpetuate his power beyond the limits of his term.

HAMILTON'S PLAN

After engaging in this far-reaching excursus on the problems of both the Virginia and New Jersey Plans, Hamilton advanced a plan with 22 provisions, some undoubtedly shaped by the plans already under consideration. Under Hamilton's plan, the legislature would be a bicameral body, consisting of an Assembly and a Senate (he seems to be the first at the convention consistently to use this term for the second house), which could adopt laws subject to veto. Members of the Assembly would serve terms of three years, whereas senators, to be chosen from state electoral districts, would serve during good behavior.

The executive would be vested in a governor (the use of the term president was not yet in use either) serving during good behavior and selected by electors from senatorial districts. The executive would have a negative—or veto—over all laws, would execute the laws; would direct war; would make treaties; would exercise appointment powers; and would have the power to pardon all offenses, except treason, which would require concurrence by the Senate. The president of the Senate would, like today's vice-president, take over if the executive resigned or were removed until a new one took office. The Senate would have the powers of declaring war, approving treaties, and approving executive officers other than those in finance, war, and foreign affairs.

Under Hamilton's plan, members of the supreme judicial authority would serve during good behavior. Congress would have power to create lower federal courts within each state. All federal officials would be subject to impeachment. All state laws contrary to the national constitution would be void, and, much as under British colonial rule, the general government would appoint a governor or president of each state who could veto any laws there. Hamilton's plan would prevent states from having independent armed forces, and it would subject their militia to U.S. jurisdiction.

RECEPTION OF HAMILTON'S PROPOSALS

People still debate whether a tree makes a noise if it falls in a forest and no one hears it. At least initially, one might wonder whether Hamilton's speech was just like such a falling tree. Delegates must have been entertained; they undoubtedly appreciated his wide erudition, and, in time, some of his ideas would make it into the final document, but how many delegates would be able to take the idea seriously of giving senators and the chief executive life tenure? How many could assent to federally appointed governors with the power to veto state legislation? If the convention did adopt a plan, it was far more likely to be one of the two plans previously on the table. Connecticut's William Johnson would soon observe that although Hamilton "has been praised by every body, he has been supported by none" (1:363).

That does not, of course, mean that Hamilton's plan was without influence. Prior to his plan, delegates had considered one plan that revised the Articles, and another that sought to replace them but retained at least some of its features. Hamilton's plan was far more radical than either. Hamilton had not professed much love for the Virginia Plan, but after he got through speaking, it probably seemed like a more moderate alternative to the New Jersey Plan's proposed revisions than it did before he did so.

MADISON'S SPEECH

On the next day, June 19, Madison gave a lengthy speech of his own. Randolph had taken the lead in introducing the Virginia Plan at the beginning of the convention and in the immediate response to the New Jersey Plan. Madison now clearly took key responsibility for the defense of the Virginia Plan.

He began his speech by observing that, despite arguments that the convention did not have power to veer from the existing federal (today called confederal) form of government, the New Jersey Plan did so in at least two particulars. Thus, he charged that it would, in some cases, operate directly on individuals rather than through the states. Moreover, the plan would do nothing to alter the existing nonfederal arrangement under the

Articles, in which voters in Connecticut and Rhode Island elected delegates directly to Congress without going through the intermediaries of the state legislatures.

Paterson had argued that all the states would have to agree to the dissolution of the Articles before some could establish a new form of government, but Madison could not agree. He thought the situation was analogous to the social compact, where individuals could leave when governments no longer secured their interests. Were one to rely upon compacts among nations, however, a breach on the part of one provided a means of escape for the others. Getting somewhat personal, he noted that New Jersey, which was now calling for state assessments, was among the states that had "*expressly refused* to comply with a constitutional requisition" by Congress (Farrand 1966, 1:315).

Madison argued that if the New Jersey Plan were to succeed, it would need both "to preserve the Union" and remedy its problems (1:315). Madison outlined eight deficiencies of the current system and New Jersey's proposed revision. In examining the first two deficiencies, Madison argued that the proposed revision of the Articles could neither prevent continuing state violations of treaties—that might lead to war—nor "encroachments on the federal authority" (1:316). States had already violated the Articles by launching into wars and making treaties with Indians, by engaging in unauthorized state compacts, and by raising their own troops. Such actions mirrored the problems of earlier confederacies. The New Jersey Plan would be defective in being ratified by state legislatures rather than by the people and in failing to provide original jurisdiction to the federal judiciary in cases where it was needed.

Moving to a third critique, Madison argued that the current system could not "prevent trespasses of the States on each other" (1:317). He was particularly concerned about the ability of debtor states to escape their burdens by printing currency. Nor, in a fourth critique, did he think the system could protect the "internal tranquility" (1:318) of the states. Shays's Rebellion illustrated a major problem that he believed the New Jersey Plan had left unaddressed.

As he continued, Madison drew from research he had gathered for one of the essays that he had penned prior to the convention. He thus charged, in a fifth critique, that the New Jersey Plan would do nothing to provide for better "internal legislation & administration" within the states, which had led to the "multiplicity," "mutability," "injustice," and "impotence" of state laws (1:318), which Virginia's proposed congressional negative of state laws would presumably cure. Madison's sixth critique of the Articles, which he again illustrated by reference to earlier republics, was its inability to secure the government against intrigues by foreign powers with individual states.

Moving to a seventh critique, Madison pointed to the expenses that smaller states were incurring in attempting to pay for their representatives within Congress and noted that, under the Articles, Delaware had relied for a time on representatives from Pennsylvania and New Jersey. Finally, as if to reverse the tables on those who thought that the Virginia Plan was too ambitious, he accused adherents of the New Jersey Plan of pertinaciously adhering to "an inadmissible plan" that might prevent the adoption of any (1:320). If the existing confederation dissolved, or new smaller confederations took its place, smaller states might find themselves to be more vulnerable than they already were. Surely larger states were unlikely to confederate with them again on an equal basis!

As he approached the end of his speech, Madison identified the heart of the problem: "The great difficulty lies in the affair of Representation; and if this could be adjusted, all others would be surmountable" (1:321). Madison believed the dissimilarities among states made it impossible to throw them into hotchpot as some had suggested. Moreover, Madison— whose vision of the United States consistently included both the right to navigate the Mississippi River and that of further westward expansion— observed that continuing state equality would serve as an obstacle to state willingness to admit new states, who would at least initially enter the Union with fewer people.

After all the states except for New York and New Jersey postponed a vote on the first resolution of the New Jersey Plan, Rufus King introduced another motion, which passed by a vote of seven to three, with another state divided. It effectively abandoned the New Jersey Plan and reintroduced the Virginia Plan. As the weeks ahead would show, however, this did not mean that the representatives of the less populous states were willing to abandon their quest to continue their equal representation, and it did not mean that the convention accepted all the details of the Virginia Plan.

SOURCES CITED IN THIS CHAPTER

Farrand, Max. 1966. *The Records of the Federal Convention of 1787.* 4 vols. New Haven, CT: Yale University Press.

Hamilton, John C. 1864. *History of the Republic of the United States.* 7 vols.

4

DELEGATES DEBATE
REPRESENTATION IN CONGRESS

I do not, gentleman, trust you.

—Gunning Bedford (Farrand 1966, 1:500,
emphasis in the original)

The science of policy is the knowledge of human nature.

—Alexander Hamilton, June 22, 1787
(Farrand 1966, 1:378)

As the convention continued its discussion on June 19, both the New Jersey Plan and the Hamilton Plan were off the table. The convention thus began re-examining the Committee of the Whole's report on the Virginia Plan, with its call to establish a new national government.

RENEWED DISCUSSION OF THE REPORT
OF THE COMMITTEE OF THE WHOLE

Contrasting his own views with what he believed were Hamilton's, James Wilson indicated that he did not anticipate that the new government would have to obliterate the states. Indeed he thought that large governments must necessarily be "subdivided into lesser jurisdictions" (Farrand 1966, 1:323). Hamilton indicated that he had not so much favored the obliteration of state boundaries as giving indefinite boundaries to national jurisdiction. His words would not have given much comfort for advocates of states' rights, however, as he agree that "[a]s States, he thought they ought to be abolished. But he admitted the necessity of leaving them, subordinate jurisdictions" (1:323).

Rufus King of Massachusetts was also fairly dismissive of states' rights. He observed that states had already divested themselves of key elements of sovereignty since they could not make war and peace or enter into treaties or alliances. Even under the Articles, "If they formed a confederacy in some respects—they formed a Nation in others" (1:324). It was impractical to "annihilate" the states, but "[m]uch of their power ought to be taken from them" (1:324).

Delegates now recalled the history of the revolution. Luther Martin believed that it had put states "in a state of nature towards each other" (1:324) that would have remained complete had it not been for the confederation. They had entered this confederation as equals, and they were unwilling to part with this status. By contrast, Wilson thought that the states had acted as *"United Colonies"* who were "independent, not *Individually* but *Unitedly"* (1:324). Hamilton concurred with Wilson's analysis and tried to persuade smaller states that they had nothing to fear from the larger ones. Hamilton observed that the three largest states were quite diverse, and that the gradation of states from largest to smallest would allow coalitions of smaller states to protect themselves.

When the convention reconvened on Wednesday, June 20, Connecticut's Oliver Ellsworth proposed dropping the controversial word "national" and replacing it with the words "Government of the United States." Ellsworth was frightened by talk that a breach of the Articles had already created a basis for its dissolution, and he favored offering the convention's work as an amendment of the confederation that states could ratify. He did not like the prospect of state ratifying conventions, because he believed that they were "better fitted to pull down than to build up Constitutions" (1:335). After adopting Ellsworth's resolution for a government of the United States, the convention began to discuss whether Congress should become bicameral.

John Lansing was one of the two New Yorkers whose views were diametrically opposed to Hamilton, and he moved to vest legislative powers in the existing Congress rather than in a new bicameral body (1:336). Lansing argued that the people had not called the convention to draw up a new plan of government, and public opinion would not support such a change. Although Madison had observed that citizens of Delaware directly elected their representatives to Congress, they still represented the state as a sovereign state. While Edmund Randolph had appealed to public dangers, Lansing did not believe them to be that acute. If the convention went beyond its authority, its proposals could "be a source of great dissentions" (1:336). Moreover, if as Hamilton had argued, the larger and smaller states shared similar interests, what was the harm of keeping the existing system of equal state representation?

Lansing next addressed the proposed negative on state laws. How could representatives from one state judge what would be appropriate in another? He thought that such a veto would be "more injurious" than the one that Great Britain had once exercised over the colonies (1:337). Hamilton had not persuaded Lansing either that the general government needed to be able to pass out "offices and honors" (1:337) or that it could do so without completely undermining the states. The system that the Virginia Plan proposed was both "too novel & complex" (1:338).

George Mason was surprised that Lansing was re-agitating an issue that had already been debated. The people had the right to approve whatever the convention proposed. States had already rejected amendments, like Lansing's, simply for increasing congressional powers, and the people of America were unlikely ever to give expanded powers of the purse and sword to a body that they did not choose directly and that was not therefore accountable to them. Whatever could be known about public sentiment, Mason was convinced that the public was both attached to "Republican Government" and to the principle of bicameralism (1:339), with the latter system in ascendancy everywhere in America other than Congress and the state of Pennsylvania. The people's reluctance to entrust increased power to a unicameral Congress explained why Paterson thought that coercion might be necessary to enforce his plan, but Mason reacted "with horror at the prospect of recurring to this expedient" (1:340). It was vital to respect the states, but this should not stop the convention from proceeding ahead and allowing posterity to provide further amendments.

Maryland's Luther Martin accepted the importance of state governments and saw no need to divide Congress into two houses. He believed that the colonies had chosen to establish themselves "into thirteen separate sovereignties instead of incorporating themselves into one" (1:340) and had allied together for security against foreign nations. Martin doubted that the people could reclaim powers that they had already vested in their state legislatures, and he thus opposed the calling of state conventions. The New Jersey Plan would not require the exercise of coercion any more than the Virginia Plan, where the extension of the judiciary into state affairs would prove "ineffectual" (1:341).

Connecticut's Roger Sherman saw no difficulty with a unicameral Congress. Congress had not acted unwisely or unfaithfully; it simply lacked adequate powers, which the convention could supply. The larger states had freely signed onto the Articles and had not suffered from their equality. "If the difficulty on the subject of representation can not be otherwise got over," however, Sherman, who had unsuccessfully called earlier in the convention for an equality of representation in the Senate, was willing to accept a second branch in Congress and allow proportional representation in one and equal state representation in another. This would accommodate the interests of both the large and small states. (John Dickinson had made a similar suggestion on June 1).

Sherman had offered a way to cut the Gordian knot that was preventing the convention from making further progress. Had the convention taken a recess at this point, delegates might have realized that Sherman had presented them with a way out of their biggest impasse, and they probably would have saved an additional two weeks of discord. The fact that they continued to debate indicates that the large states still did not see the growing discord that the introduction of the New Jersey Plan had previously signaled and that they still thought their own arguments for proportional representation, which favored their own interests, would prevail over the interests of the small states that had no more to gain than other states from a new proportional Congress and arguably far more to lose.

Almost as though he had not heard Sherman's partial concession (perhaps he had already prepared his speech or thought that his side would prevail without compromise?), Wilson continued arguing for the advantages of a bicameral Congress. The Articles had succeeded in winning the revolution for reasons other than the construction of its Congress. Larger states had agreed to equality out "of necessity not of choice" (1:343). A state citizen cared more for his own happiness than about which branch of government exercised which powers, whereas a member of a local legislature was likely to view Congress "with the eyes of a jealous rival" (1:344). After Wilson's speech, the convention voted four to six (with one state divided) against Lansing's proposal to keep the existing Congress. Again, the Virginia Plan remained ascendant.

BICAMERALISM AND FEDERALISM

On Thursday, June 21, the convention discussed the provision in the Virginia Plan providing that Congress should be bicameral, but the discussion focused far more on the issue of the proper division between state and general authorities. Connecticut's Dr. William Samuel Johnson thus observed that one of the primary goals of the New Jersey Plan had been "to preserve the individuality of the States" (Farrand 1966, 1:355), and that if that could be assured and they could be guaranteed at least a portion of their sovereignty, then its proponents would be reassured. Wilson thought it was just as important to be able to secure the existence of the national authority against the states, which would be tempted to encroach upon it. Since the current plan called for representing states in the Senate, it was only fair that the national government should also have the power to appoint one of the branches of the state governments.

Madison agreed with Wilson. He believed that the history of past confederacies proved that "the greater tendency in such systems [was] to anarchy than to tyranny, to a disobedience of the members than to usurpations of the federal head" (1:356). Even if the national authority were given "indefinite power" and the states were "reduced to corporations" (a hypothetical that must have frightened as many delegates who were devoted to the small states as it comforted), Madison saw no reason to believe that the general government would have an incentive to take away state powers. It was prudent to give the general government as much authority as was practical, and the inconvenience of going beyond this would serve as its own deterrent. Even if the national government showed a tendency to absorb state governments—another hypothetical that probably continued to confirm small-state fears that more was afoot than advocates of the Virginia Plan were willing to acknowledge—Madison could foresee "no fatal consequence" (1:358). Although bicameralism carried the day, representatives of the small states and the large states appear to have been talking past one another.

Perhaps attempting to address this gap, General Pinckney proposed that state legislatures should be able to decide how representatives to the first branch of Congress should be selected. He believed such a plan would allow for local differences, would help mitigate the influence of larger counties, and would be less likely to result in disputed elections and their associated costs. The fact that Luther Martin seconded the motion suggested that it had small-state support.

Hamilton immediately concluded that the proposal was designed to "vitiate" the Virginia Plan, but his prophecy that if the general government were to survive, "the State Govts. might gradually dwindle into nothing" (1:359) must again have been jarring to small-state advocates. Mason expressed concern that Pinckney's proposal would be undemocratic; Sherman preferred the substitute motion but could live with either plan, and John Rutledge could see little difference between direct election by the people or selection by their representatives. Indeed, he believed that state representatives had probably appointed better individuals to Congress than the people would have elected on their own.

What small-state advocates considered to be a matter of indifference, Wilson believed to be both the "corner Stone" and "the foundation of the fabric" (1:359) of the new proposed government. He recognized that state legislators had interests as members of government that might differ from those of the people. King also thought that state legislatures might select individuals to advance their individual state interests. While General Pinckney argued that his plan was designed to integrate states into the general system, the convention rejected his proposal by a vote of four to six to one.

TERMS OF THE FIRST HOUSE

The Committee of the Whole had recommended setting the terms of the first house at three years, but Randolph now proposed changing this to two. He noted that every state except for South Carolina had annual elections, to which the people were thus partial, but he recognized that the size of the new nation might make such elections of such frequency inconvenient. Dickinson preferred to keep triennial elections while Ellsworth and Wilson spoke out in favor of annual contests. Reflecting a time when governments were involved in far fewer matters than they are today, the latter doubted whether the national legislature would have to sit for more than a fourth of the year. By contrast, Madison worried about the expenses of frequent travel to and from the district to the national capital and feared that a year would be insufficient to give representatives time to learn their jobs.

Although Sherman could accept either annual or biennial elections, he wanted representatives to spend time mixing with the people who elected them. Long before modern commentators began speaking of an "inside-the-beltway" mentality, Sherman feared that if representatives spent too much time in the nation's capital, they might "acquire the habits of the place, which might differ from those of their Constituents" (1:362). Mason introduced yet another consideration by suggesting that annual elections might benefit states nearest to the capital over others. In favoring triennial elections, Hamilton argued that more frequent elections might actually result in voter fatigue—voters might become "listless" to them (1:362). After subsequently voting to strike the three-year term, the convention voted unanimously on a term of two years.

CONGRESSIONAL PAY

On Friday, June 22, the convention considered congressional pay. The Virginia Plan favored paying representatives out of the national treasury, but Oliver Ellsworth wanted states to settle individually on pay for their representatives, according to local circumstances. Hugh Williamson agreed. He did not think that poorer members of western states should have to finance the salaries of those in the East who might be adverse to their interest. Nathaniel Gorham feared that states would be too parsimonious.

A popular aphorism says that "one who pays the piper, calls the tune." Randolph accordingly observed that state pay would foster state dependency and that "The whole nation has an interest in the attendance & services of the members" (1:372). Whereas King thought that the Constitution should specify the amount of pay, Wilson believed that the pay would need to change over time. Madison feared that if Williamson's ideas were followed, western representatives might be treated as inferiors rather than as equals. Hamilton observed that those coming from the greatest distances might end up with the lowest pay.

Wilson proposed that Congress should not only pay, but also set, the pay of its members. Madison (who is recognized as the "father" of the belatedly adopted Twenty-seventh Amendment that later addressed this issue in part) objected that they would be too self-interested and succeeded in blocking the motion. The convention then narrowly voted four to five to two, not to strike the provision allowing members of Congress to be paid out of the national treasury.

MINIMUM AGE FOR MEMBERS
OF THE FIRST HOUSE

After postponing a vote as to whether congressional stipends should be "fixed," or standard, the convention began addressing the minimum age of members of the House. Mason proposed setting the minimum age at 25. Although 21 was the typical voting age, Mason thought that the "political opinions" of most men this age were "too crude & erroneous to merit an influence on public measures" (Farrand 1966, 1:375), and he did not think that Congress was a proper place to provide them with such educations! Although the more democratically inclined Wilson disfavored setting a requirement different than that required for voting, Mason's measure passed by a vote of seven to three to one.

CONCERNS OVER A REVOLVING DOOR

The convention was more closely divided—eventually voting four to four to three—over whether representatives should be ineligible for other governmental offices for a year after they left. Gorham thought the provision was both "unnecessary & injurious" (1:375). Pierce Butler thought it was essential to combat corruption. King feared such a requirement might discourage otherwise meritorious, but presumably otherwise employable, individuals from running. Wilson opined that such a requirement might have kept the Second Continental Congress from appointing George Washington as commander-in-chief. Mixing analogies that Wilson had made earlier in regard to state election of the first branch, Mason thought such a prohibition was essential—"a corner stone in the fabric" (1:376)—to combatting corruption, such as had been exhibited in Great Britain. Hamilton thought both sides had merit but having observed, according to Robert Yates, in words that Madison's notes did not capture, that "The science of policy is the knowledge of human nature" (1:378), Hamilton had insisted on interjecting his own hard-headed realism: "We must take man as we find him, and if we expect him to serve the public must interest his passions in doing so" (1:376). Moreover, Hamilton believed that British "corruption" was one of the factors that kept that system in equilibrium.

Discussion of corruption continued on Saturday, June 23 when Pinckney successfully moved to strike a restriction that would keep members of Congress for serving for a year in offices that had been created by their own states. Sherman had cited the Biblical admonition, later put to even more effective use by Lincoln in the context of slavery, that a kingdom divided against itself could not stand (1:386).

Madison then reintroduced the motion to make members of Congress ineligible for a year not only for federal offices created during their tenures but also for appointments for which the "emoluments," or benefits, had been increased. Apart from Hamilton, who did not regard the issue as significant, the delegates who spoke agreed that corruption was a problem but were divided as to whether the motion at hand would solve it. Appealing to the example of his own state, Virginia's George Mason thus pointed both to "the shameful partiality of the Legislature of Virginia to its own members" (1:387) and to similar partiality in the English Parliament. King noted that Madison's proposed prohibition would not keep ex-legislators from rewarding friends and relatives. Wilson feared stigmatizing those who desired to serve in government offices. Sherman thought that legislatures might evade Madison's prohibition by moving individuals from an existing office (that incumbent legislators would be able to fill) to a new one (that existing legislators could not). Elbridge Gerry saw similar possibilities for intrigue.

Acknowledging that he was pursuing a middle course by permitting legislative appointment to existing, but not to new, offices or those for which the salaries had been increased, Madison noted that states had not only observed legislative partiality but that good men had been reluctant to serve therein. It was important not to erect further barriers to their participation. Although the convention voted against extending ineligibility to a year after a representative served, or for which he was elected, it did prevent sitting members from accepting such offices (1:390).

CHARLES PINCKNEY'S SPEECH

Although its outlines remain uncertain (an uncertainty compounded by Pinckney's own mistaken memory or prevarication, which linked his proposals to many that the Constitution later adopted), Charles Pinckney of South Carolina had apparently introduced an alternative plan of government at the beginning of the convention, which got derailed by the Virginia Plan, but may later have been considered by the Committee of Detail. Perhaps this perceived slight left him eager to distinguish himself; perhaps he envisioned a southern speech that would equal that of Hamilton.

In any event, on Monday, June 25, as the convention prepared to discuss the composition of the upper house, Pinckney delivered a long speech, the first part of which he provided to Madison for his notes. The speech began by noting that Americans constituted a unique people with "few distinctions of fortune & less of rank, than among the inhabitants of any other nation" (Farrand 1966, 1:398). Historian Frederick Jackson Turner would one day argue that the presence of the frontier had a unique democratic effect on America, but more than a hundred years before this, Pinckney was arguing that the "uncultivated lands" of the West already offered opportunities that promised to perpetuate equality and opportunity into the near future.

Some—Pinckney may have had Hamilton in mind—looked to the British constitution, which Pinckney believed to be "the best constitution in existence" (1:398), but it was designed for a very different country that was based on class distinctions. Ignoring the distinctions that slavery had fostered in the South between large plantation owners and both the slaves who worked for them and other white small farmers, Pinckney claimed that such distinctions did not exist in America. The English peerage had unique beginnings and could not be imitated in the New World. Continuing to ignore the effects of slavery within his own region, Pinckney denied that either land or commerce was likely to produce an upper class in America. Nor did ancient examples of government provide adequate examples of alternatives. Pinckney believed that the people of the United States could be divided into three mutually dependent classes that he identified as "professional men," "commercial men," and those with landed interests (1:402). The only institution to which they corresponded in Britain was the House of Commons. The American people would thus reject a hereditary monarch or upper house.

What was the solution? Pinckney continued: "All that we have to do then is to distribute the powers of Govt. in such a manner, and for such limited periods, as while it gives a proper degree of permanency to the Magistrate, will reserve to the people, the right of election they will not or ought not frequently to part with" (1:404). Pinckney believed this could be done by increasing the power of the existing government and "reserving to the States the possession of their local rights" (1:404), rather than by pursuing the Virginia Plan. Madison's notes on the speech end with Pinckney's arguments against abolishing the states, but Yates fills in some details. Pinckney was convinced that the nation was far too extensive to be governed by a single body. He apparently favored allowing state legislatures to choose members of the second house (1:412).

DISCUSSION OF THE SECOND HOUSE

As the delegates continued to debate the Senate, Gorham believed that the smaller states had raised reasonable concerns about proportional representation in both houses and favored compromise on the matter. Delaware's George Read noted that larger states had profited unduly from western lands and that smaller states therefore had reason to believe that they would not be treated fairly in the future. Gorham observed that the convention was in no position to remedy such past inequities.

Wilson again professed to be daunted by "the amazing extent of country" to be governed (Farrand 1966, 1:405). The issue was whether senators should be selected by individuals who voted as citizens of the general government or as citizens of their individual states. The people formed the foundation of both sets of governments. Wilson feared that senators selected by state legislatures "will introduce & cherish local interests & local prejudices" (1:406), but no one seconded his proposal for a system of indirect election for members of the second house.

Ellsworth thought that the Senate would represent state interests, whatever mechanism of selection the convention chose. The key attribute that senators would need was wisdom, and he thought that state legislatures were more likely to select wise candidates than the people themselves. Larger states had already demonstrated the difficulty of governing extensive territories; states would need to be retained for this purpose. Likewise, Johnson and Williamson both reiterated their support for retaining state governments. Mason saw state legislative selection of senators as a necessary means of allowing states to protect themselves.

A flurry of votes followed, some designed to ascertain how the second house would be apportioned. With no recorded debate, delegates decided that thirty would be the minimum age for senators and struck out seven-year terms. Delegates could not agree on whether the term of senators should be four years, five years, six years, or during good behavior, so they resumed this discussion on the following day.

TERMS OF SENATORS

General Pinckney expressed renewed fears that residence in the national capital for long terms would cause senators to lose their state attachments. By contrast, Read proposed a term of nine years, with one-third of the body rotating off triennially.

The motion allowed Madison to explicate one of his favorite themes, that of representation. Madison argued that the proposed bicameral Congress was designed both to "protect the people agst. their rulers" and to protect them against their own "transient impressions" (Farrand 1966,1:421). Interestingly, Yates's notes of this part of Madison's speech are more colorful and detailed than Madison's—he thus noted that Madison had said that "The man who is possessed of wealth, who lolls on his sofa or rolls in his carriage, cannot judge of the wants or feelings of the day laborer" (1:431). Members of the two houses would serve to "watch & check each other" (1:421). Granting one branch of Congress longer terms would give its members greater knowledge; a smaller body might also prevent precipitous actions. Although there was no hereditary class within the United States, the nation was far from a "homogeneous mass" (1:422), and there was always danger from the "leveling spirit" (1:423). A body known for "its wisdom & virtue" could guard against this possibility, and its members would be fortified by longer terms, nine years certainly being appropriate. Reminding delegates that they might be revising a plan that "in its operation wd. decide forever the fate of Republican Govt.," Madison thought it was important not only to safeguard liberty but also to "supply the defects which our own experience had particularly pointed out" (1:423).

Reiterating the need for frequent elections, Sherman thought that terms of four or six years would be adequate for the Senate. Read wondered whether the small states might not profit if the nation were to become one people. According to Madison's notes, Hamilton acknowledged that he was not particularly attached to the idea of republican government but offered thoughts for the consideration of those who were. Liberty led to inequality of property, which needed to be protected, presumably by the Senate. He believed that the tumults in some states were related to the frequency of their elections. Gerry was willing to support Senate terms of four or five years. He did not think the nation would be subject to the same degree of dissension as Great Britain, with its greater class differences.

Wilson added an additional element to the discussion by observing that the new government would not only need to prevent internal oppression but also deal with foreign affairs. To meet the latter challenge, senators needed to be respected abroad. He favored the proposal for a nine-year term, one-third of which would be up for election every third year. The convention agreed to both ideas and then considered senatorial salaries.

Because he hoped that such positions would be occupied by individuals of wealth, General Pinckney proposed that they should serve without salaries. Franklin, who had previously opposed presidential salaries, concurred, albeit this time because he thought that members of the convention might otherwise be thought to have created such positions for themselves. The delegates defeated the measure probably because they questioned the practicality of the proposal.

The convention had decided that members of the first house should be paid out of the national treasury, but what about senators? Ellsworth thought states should pay them. Madison thought this would undermine the stability that the convention had just addressed in raising the length of their terms. Senators should be "impartial umpires & Guardians of justice and general Good" rather than "the mere Agents & Advocates of State interests & views" (1:428).

Mason favored annexing property qualifications to the office but did not introduce a formal motion. The convention rejected a motion to pay senators from the national treasury. Further discussions led to votes to make senators ineligible for federal offices both during their terms and for a year after they left office but not to extend a similar disability to eligibility to state offices. The convention further voted that each house should have the power of originating legislation.

On Wednesday, June 27, the delegates resumed discussion of how to apportion representatives in Congress. Maryland's Luther Martin, who could be desultory even when he was not inebriated (as he often was), led off the discussion, according to Madison, "at great length and with great eagerness" in arguing that Congress was designed "to preserve the State governts: not to govern individuals" and that its powers should be limited (2:437). Madison's summary of this three-hour speech is not nearly as detailed as some of his other notes. According to Madison, Martin himself said that he was "too much exhausted" to finish his remarks (2:438).

Martin observed that once states ceded powers, they would find them difficult to recover, whereas they could always cede additional powers if they proved to be necessary. State failures to comply with congressional requisitions under the Articles were neither the result of disrespect nor because of economic problems brought on by the Articles, but simply because the continuing ravages of the Revolutionary War had made it difficult to comply. Martin did not believe that the examples that Madison had cited of interstate compacts had violated the Articles. Martin proceeded to cite authorities to establish that individuals were equal within a state of nature, and he thought member states of the Articles were equally so. Martin did not know of other confederacies that had a bicameral legislature, and he thought the Virginia Plan of representation would give larger states too free a hand. He was sure that states would never agree to a national negative of their laws. Yates observed that Martin proclaimed that he "would not trust a government organized upon the reported plan, for all the slaves of Carolina or the horses and oxen of Massachusetts" (1:441).

When he resumed his speech the next day, Martin continued to argue that the general government should be for the benefit of its individual governments rather than for the people. He did not think the small states would approve a plan like Virginia's. He further thought that the 10 smaller states would be better off in a separate confederacy by themselves than in an association where the three largest states dominated.

North Carolina's Hugh Williamson was not as concerned about states giving up their equal votes as he was by the possibility that newer and poorer western states might try to lay their burdens on the older states. Professing a willingness to concede all but fundamental principles, Madison did not think that continuing equal state representation was either "just" or "necessary" to protect the small states (1:446). Madison distinguished the equality that was necessary among nations signing a treaty versus jurisdictions that were entering into a compact to deal with the common government among them. He likened this to representing counties within states according to their populations, and further defended his proposal for a national negative of state laws.

Madison surveyed the differences among the large states to show that they would be unlikely to unite against others. The main products of Massachusetts, Pennsylvania, and Virginia were respectively fish, flour, and tobacco. Historically, larger states were more likely to be rivals than allies. Citing a variety of historical examples, Madison argued that larger states were far more likely to oppress smaller ones in weak confederacies than in stronger ones. The large states would only be willing to partition—he seems to have had in mind the formation of western states like Kentucky and Tennessee—if the general government provided adequate security for them.

Perhaps inspired by Madison's own invocation of foreign examples, Wilson noted that granting smaller states the same vote as larger ones was not much different than the widely criticized "rotten boroughs" of England that vested equal votes to districts with meager populations. Sherman, by contrast, did not think it was any more unfair to give small states an equal vote in national councils than to give poor men an equal vote to rich ones.

FRANKLIN SUGGESTS PRAYER

Because Americans are a religious people, it is neither surprising that a delegate might suggest a religious remedy for the deepening divide between the large and small states nor that popular memory might ultimately do more to highlight the proposal than its lack of implementation. On June 28, after noting how little progress the delegates had made over the past month, the venerable Franklin prepared a speech in which he pointed to the way that delegates appeared to be groping in the dark and suggested that they should call upon divine help as they had once done at the beginning of the Revolutionary War. Franklin began citing a variety of scriptural allusions that are more associated with the sermons of his friend the evangelist George Whitefield than with what are generally perceived to be Franklin's own more deistic views. Arguing that "*God governs in the affairs of men*" (1:451), Franklin believed that it would be appropriate for the convention to bring in a local clergyman to lead off each day with prayer.

Hamilton, who would in his later years advocate establishing a religiously based party in the United States, was now among those who feared that beginning such a practice this late in the convention might not only lead to certain "disagreeable animadversions" within the convention (possibly over the choice of clergy?) but might also signal the convention's internal dissentions to outsiders who had been kept in the dark by the convention's commitment to secrecy. Williamson observed that the convention had no money to hire a chaplain. Randolph sought to patch things over by proposing that the convention should commission a sermon for Independence Day celebrations, but the convention appears to have adjourned for the day without adopting a resolution on either.

Franklin had attempted to use prayer to unite delegates. Their failure to accept the solution appears largely to have been based on practical considerations. Was Madison, who had led the fight for religious disestablishment in Virginia and who was deeply aware of the power of religious factions, among those who feared that prayer might divide as much as it unified? Interestingly, neither he nor anyone else appears to have suggested that such prayer violated constitutional norms. No one, of course, could as yet cite the First Amendment, because it had yet to be proposed or ratified. Whatever prayers were to be offered, they would be offered in private rather than by a chaplain paid from the ever-diminishing public fisc.

FURTHER DISCUSSION OF
STATE REPRESENTATION IN CONGRESS

When discussions resumed the next day, Dr. Johnson argued that the difficulty the delegates encountered stemmed from differing ways of viewing the states "as districts of people composing one political Society" and as "many political societies" (Farrand 1966, 1:461). Since both views encapsulated basic truths, the convention should compromise by representing the people in one branch and the states in the other.

Apparently ignoring such a solution, Gorham continued to argue that the smaller states would have little to fear from a stronger Union, which could protect them more effectively than the current Articles. By contrast, New Jersey would find it difficult to protect itself on its own. Read thought that the larger states like Massachusetts—he was almost surely thinking of Shays's Rebellion—needed a stronger Union more than smaller states like his own Delaware. Perhaps seeking to shake things up, Read unexpectedly proposed that Hamilton's plan for abolishing the states should be substituted for the Virginia Plan.

Madison commended Johnson's thoughts on the mixed nature of the proposed government. States were not divided into small and large divisions but fell into a variety of gradations. Under the proposed system, the national government would have the power to tax the people directly, and such taxation would be more fairly apportioned if representation were based on population than on state identity. Moving from interest to principles, Madison designated the current system of representation as "confessedly unjust," and said that its perpetuation would be an obstacle to the duration of the new government. While states were currently weak, if threatened by external danger they would be likely to increase the powers of their executive, which could pose threats to individual liberties. Both a strengthened executive and a standing army could threaten civil liberties. Britain's insular position had somewhat protected it against the fate of other European nations, but either complete dissolution of the Articles or the formation of separate confederacies would be truly "deplorable" (1:465).

Hamilton sought to contrast the rights of individual men with those of artificial states. In his view, the smaller states were contesting "for power, not for liberty" (1:465). The people within each state would retain their liberty under the new system. The primary differences among the states was not the large state/small state divide but the divide between "carrying & non-carrying States" (1:467), that is, between those with harbors and those without them. Hamilton further buttressed Madison's argument by suggesting that if the states broke into separate confederations, European nations would seek to form alliances and pit them against one another. In short, "No Governmt. could give us tranquility & happiness at home, which did not possess sufficient stability and strength to make us respectable abroad" (1:467). The nation faced a critical time, and it was a "miracle that we were now here exercising our tranquil & free deliberations on the subject. It would be madness to trust to future miracles" (1:467). The time to act was now!

Gerry recalled that states were initially granted equal representation despite concerns that this was unfair. Now the states faced a similar situation, but delegates were proceeding not "like a band of brothers" but like "political negociators [sic.]" (1:467). Negotiators or not, a vote of six to four to one reaffirmed apportioning the states in the *first* house differently than under the Articles. Almost immediately, however, Oliver Ellsworth, who had opposed the motion, proposed that the *second* branch should be apportioned like the Congress under the Articles. He expressed hope that this might be the basis for eventual compromise. Such differential representation would recognize that the nation was "partly national; partly federal" (1:468). Without a compromise, Massachusetts was the only eastern (northern) state that would be likely to support the proposal; proposing a plan without equal state representation would thus likely split the Union. A compromise would serve to protect the smaller states, which needed their own means of "self-defence" (1:469). Admittedly, large states were not contiguous and did not share a complete unity of interest, but small states were also diverse and might find it hard to ally in defense. Although Ellsworth professed not to be "in general a half-way man" (1:469), it would be better to only "Half the good we could, rather than do nothing at all" (1:469). According to Yates's notes, Ellsworth suggested that further amendments could be adopted later.

Abraham Baldwin opposed Ellsworth's motion but thought the matter would be much easier to resolve if the convention could decide what powers the new Congress would exercise. Curiously, one has to consult Yates's and King's notes for Madison's response. He pointed out how difficult it had been to adopt amendments under the Articles. He further argued that the greatest division in the country was not between small states and large states but between northern states and southern states (1:477). He further feared that if the two branches were constituted differently, one might counteract the other on key revenue measures.

Whatever the arguments, debate would ultimately be resolved by votes, and the delegates from New Hampshire were still missing. David Brearly, seeking another small state, urged President Washington to implore them to come, but Wilson, who represented a large state, did not want to "spread a great alarm" (1:481), and the motion was defeated.

Ellsworth immediately directed the convention's attention back to the issue of representation within the Senate, and Wilson responded with another erudite speech. Wilson hoped that the proposed plan did not split the Union, but if a split were to occur, it would be appropriate that it split on behalf of majority principles and the "unalienable rights of men" rather than on behalf of "artificial systems" (1:482). Representation should be by majority rule in both houses of Congress. Despite all the talk of an alliance of the three largest states, no one could point to an example of where this had happened. States were a necessary part of the system, but states with a minority of citizens should not be able to prevail over the majority.

Ellsworth responded that it was important not only to protect majorities but also to secure minorities. Delegates had applauded the House of Lords in England without recognizing that it fulfilled such a function.

Accusing fellow delegates of "running from one extreme to another," he observed that they were "razing the foundations of the building" when all they needed to do was to "repair the roof" (1:485). Although noting that he was himself from a medium-sized state, his imagery continued to refer to the "plighted faith" (a term often used to describe marriages) that he thought larger states would be breaking were they to abandon equal state representation in at least one branch of the legislature (1:485).

Madison poked holes in Ellsworth's logic, first by questioning his analogy to the House of Lords and then by citing examples of confederations that had given differential votes to constituent members. If plighted faith were the issue, Ellsworth needed to be reminded that his state of Connecticut had positively refused to comply with a congressional requisition for funds. Continuing state equality in one house would allow them to "*obstruct* the wishes and interest of the majority," to "*extort*" repugnant measures from them, and to "*impose*" upon them (1:486). The central division within the states was not between the small states and the large ones but between those of the North and South. If there were to be a compromise relative to representation, it should represent states according to free inhabitants in one branch and by counting slaves as three-fifths a person in the other!

Ellsworth responded that Connecticut was "completely federal in her disposition" (1:487). If the state had failed to meet its requisitions, it was not for lack of desire but for inability to fulfill it. Sherman wondered how state delinquency pointed to congressional failure; all that was needed was to strengthen congressional power.

North Carolina's William Davie expressed concern over the projected size (90 members or more) of the proposed Senate. There was no reason that the new system, like the nation itself, could not be both "partly federal" and "partly national" (1:488). Wilson suggested giving states one senator for each 100,000 people, with each state having at least one.

Franklin, whose last proposal had advocated prayer, now invoked some homespun wisdom. With small states fearing for their liberties and large states fearing for their money, the delegates needed to imitate a carpenter who crafts a joint when two planks do not match. Franklin favored equal representation in the upper house, which would decide all issues involving possible diminution of state sovereignty. He further proposed that the states should have an equal voice in the appointment of all civil offices, but that salaries should be fixed and paid according to each state's contributions.

King was not initially conciliatory. After arguing that the convention should privilege representation by the people over representation by states, however, he said that he could accept a compromise similar to the one that Franklin had just offered. New Jersey's Jonathan Dayton charged fellow delegates with substituting assertions for proof and terror for argument and viewed the proposed system as "an amphibious monster" (1:490). Yates observed that he thought the Virginia Plan would undermine the 13 "pillars" that supported the Union (1:499). Madison said he could also support Wilson's plan if it could guarantee that the Senate would not simply be another version of the inadequate Articles.

GUNNING BEDFORD'S BOMBSHELL

Delaware's Gunning Bedford thought that there was no "middle way between a perfect consolidation, which he considered to be "out of the question," and "a mere confederacy" (Farrand 1966, 1:490). Whatever they professed, delegates were uniformly seeking to advance what they perceived to be their states' present and future interests. One could not expect smaller states to act with any greater disinterestedness than others. At a time when others were appealing to political theories to justify their positions, Yates noted that Bedford plainly stated "*I do not, gentlemen, trust you*" (1:500). The convention needed to devise a government that the people would approve. Bedford did not believe that the larger states would abandon the confederacy, but if that were their threat, Bedford had one of his own—in such circumstances the small states could seek help from abroad! Almost as if recognizing that he may have crossed a dangerous rhetorical line, he noted that he did not intend "to intimidate or alarm" (1:492), but those who sought to change the existing system rather than simply enlarge federal powers had brought the convention to this impasse.

Ellsworth thought that the states alone could provide for domestic happiness. King thought that making states more subordinate would not prevent this. The Constitution needed to protect states much as laws protected individuals, with the union between England and Scotland serving as a good example. Ellsworth thought that Bedford's intemperance had been unfortunate.

If the convention were to give an award to a hothead, it most surely would have gone to Bedford. Whereas others had speculated that foreign governments might attempt to influence the situation if the confederation were to dissolve or split, Bedford appeared actually to have threatened to seek foreign allies. Delegates must have wondered whether they should have followed Franklin's earlier advice to begin each day's proceedings with prayer! At least some of the delegates must surely have attended church the next day. When they returned to the convention that Monday, they appear to have voted relatively early on Ellsworth's motion for equal state representation in the second house. The convention was now equally divided five to five to one.

Charles Pinckney did not favor equal state representation in the Senate, but he acknowledged that large states would certainly seek to further their own interests both in making appointments and in entering into treaties. Perhaps some proportion could be worked out. Pinckney viewed the situation as pivotal. By his lights, the only circumstance that had prevented the dissolution of the confederation was the calling of the convention, and if it failed, the Articles were likely to fail as well. General Pinckney liked Franklin's proposal better, but suggested the appointment of a committee with a member from each state to come up with a suitable compromise.

A number of delegates agreed, the most loquacious of whom was Gouverneur Morris. Morris doubted that the upper branches of most governments provided a very useful model. If this branch were to check the first, its members must have a personal interest in doing so. This could be brought about by seeing that its members were wealthy and independent. In echoes of Hamilton, Morris suggested that this could be accomplished through life terms. Like Franklin, Morris also disfavored giving senators salaries. He further favored executive appointment. If the group were aristocratic, he did not think it would particularly matter how they were apportioned. The key was to appoint "a select & sagacious body of men instituted to watch agst. them on all sides" (1:514).

Randolph half-heartedly approved the idea of a compromise committee, but he did not think that a branch such as Morris proposed could coexist with a more democratic branch. An "avulsion," or break-up, of the Union would imperil them all (1:515). As delegates weighed in on the propriety of a committee, Wilson observed, perhaps with frustration, that "it would decide according to that very rule of voting which was opposed on one side" (1:515). Madison did not think that a committee would be likely to come up with anything other than the convention as a whole. Gerry counterposed that something had to be done to keep the confederation from breaking apart.

A COMMITTEE TRIES ITS HAND AT COMPROMISE

Shortly thereafter, Gerry was selected to head a Committee of Compromise on Representation in Congress. Fellow members, from north to south, included Oliver Ellsworth, Robert Yates, William Paterson, Benjamin Franklin, Gunning Bedford, Luther Martin, George Mason, William Davie, John Rutledge, and Abraham Baldwin.

While the rest of the convention adjourned, committee members met on July 3, with most everyone celebrating on the nation's independence the following day. When the convention reconvened on July 5, Gerry reported the committee's arguably anticlimactic results. It proposed that each state would have at least one vote and would have one representative for every 40,000 people in the first house. It alone would be able to originate money bills and set the salaries of public officials, which proposals could not be amended by the second house, where each state would be equally represented.

DISCUSSION OF COMMITTEE PROPOSALS

Although it provoked several comments, Madison focused in on what he regarded to be the ineffectiveness of limiting the origin of money bills to the House. The convention should instead focus on pursuing a system of representation that was just. The convention should not pursue harmony over justice.

Gouverneur Morris agreed. As a "Representative of America," and, indeed of "the whole human race," he thought it was important for delegates to look beyond the narrow interests of their states (Farrand 1966, 1:529). Public opinion was unknowable, but smaller states would be unlikely to go it alone for long: "This Country must be united. If persuasion does not unite it, the sword will" (1:530). The proposed system would lead to perpetual conflict. The Articles had been plagued by "state attachments, and State importance"; it was important to "take out the teeth of the serpent" (1:530) and reflect the interest of man as man rather than the interest of the states.

Chalking up his own threats of foreign intervention to his advocacy as an attorney, Bedford noted that Morris's words about uniting with the sword were as provocative as his own had been. Smaller states had shown themselves willing to compromise by limiting money bills to the lower house. Something needed to be done. If the current proposal proved to be insufficient, it could be altered later. Noting that he had not attended the committee meeting, Ellsworth was nonetheless willing to accede to it. Paterson added that talk of "the Sword & the Gallows" were little calculated to produce conviction (1:532). Gerry thought the only real alternative to compromise would be secession. Mason, who might have been thinking of his large family, noted that he had as much desire to be home as anyone but would rather be buried in Philadelphia than return without doing anything (1:533). Gouverneur Morris chimed in with concern that the compromise did not adequately represent property interests. He also desired to see that the current Atlantic states could not later be outvoted by those from the West. The convention voted down a proposal by Rutledge to base apportionment on the basis of the revenue that each state provided.

CREATION OF A SPECIAL COMMITTEE ON ORIGINAL APPORTIONMENT OF CONGRESS

On July 6, the convention discussed referring the provisions related to the first house from a committee of 13 (the "Grand Committee") to a smaller "special Committee" (Farrand 1966, 1:538). Gouverneur Morris questioned the formula that would allocate one representative for every 40,000 inhabitants. Gorham further noted that Virginia and Massachusetts were among states considering division. Gerry feared that the idea of state division could be continued too far. King thought that fixing the ratio of representation at one for every 40,000 would in time result in a Congress that was too large. Butler expressed support for providing some balance between potential new states and existing states as well as between wealth and populations. Pinckney said that contributions of revenue were too changeable; while he would prefer that blacks be counted equally with whites, he could settle for representation by the three-fifths formula.

Shortly thereafter, the convention appointed Gouverneur Morris, Nathaniel Gorham, Edmund Randolph, John Rutledge, and Rufus King to the special committee. The convention then discussed several motions before getting back to the origination of money bills in the first house.

FURTHER DISCUSSIONS OF CONGRESS

Gouverneur Morris thought this would stymie the second branch from coming up with better proposals. By contrast, Wilson thought the concession was inconsequential. Williamson thought the power would be better lodged in the upper house than in the house more directly responsible to the people. Mason feared that if the Senate had such power, it might become too aristocratic, but Wilson responded that this criticism would only apply if it could appropriate money independently of the first house. Gerry thought the power to appropriate needed to be vested in the branch that was closer to the people. Pinckney agreed with Wilson in believing the "concession" was inconsequential. Gouverneur Morris did not think it was possible to have a society without an aristocracy, but that it was important to keep it within check. He wondered whether the president should have the power to dissolve the two houses—the essence of modern parliamentary systems. Franklin summoned the maxim (perhaps from one of his own almanacs?) that "those who feel, can best judge" (1:546) as adequate justification for leaving the initial power in the first house. Wilson pointed to problems that had developed in England when the two houses of parliament were at loggerheads. General Pinckney observed that some of the states that offered this as a concession had previously opposed it as useless. By day's end, the convention approved the provision by a vote of five to three to three.

On the following day, July 7, the convention was back to discussing whether states should have an equal vote in the Senate. Gerry identified this as "the critical question" (1:550) but favored awaiting resolution until the special committee presented its report. Sherman, who may still have anticipated that Congress might have to use force to compel recalcitrant states to do their duty, advanced an argument that equality in the second house would assure that legislation had both the support of popular majorities and a majority of the states. Wilson wanted to be conciliatory but thought that "firmness" was, in this case, "a duty of higher obligation" (1:550). The convention then voted six to three to two to keep this compromise as part of the committee report.

Should the convention focus on the chicken or egg? Gerry thought that the convention should enumerate the powers of the general government before settling definitely on representation. Madison thought that it would be foolish to delineate such powers before knowing whether the new system would be sufficiently representative. Paterson said the small states could not concede their equal representation in the Senate. Gouverneur Morris feared that the compromise would make Congress "a mere whisp of straw" (1:551). Smaller states had used the conflict with Britain unfairly to extort equal representation in the Second Continental Congress, but larger states should now "consider what is right, rather than what may be expedient" (1:552). Whatever their differences, the former colonies shared "a common language, a common law, common usages and manners—and a common interest in being united" (1:553), but their state attachments threatened their harmony.

REPORT OF THE COMMITTEE ON ORIGINAL APPORTIONMENT OF CONGRESS

That Monday, July 9, the Committee of Five delivered a report to the convention in which it recommended a first branch of 56 members. Rhode Island and Delaware would each have one vote; New Hampshire and Georgia two; New Jersey three; Connecticut and Maryland four; New York, North Carolina, and South Carolina five; Massachusetts seven; Pennsylvania eight; and Virginia nine. It proposed granting Congress to augment this number periodically.

Delegates raised questions as to how the committee had arrived at these numbers. Answers suggested that the committee had tried to consider both population and wealth (a likely euphemism for slaves), and after postponing a vote on accepting the proposal, Sherman proposed yet another committee with a member from each state. Gouverneur Morris likely reflected the sentiments of other delegates when he suggested that "The Report is little more than a guess" (1:560). Discussion appeared to indicate that Georgia was given two representatives to Delaware's one, in part because delegates believed that Georgia was growing more rapidly.

Paterson then raised the first real moral objection to counting slaves, albeit because he accepted the southern view that slaves were "property" with "no personal liberty" and "no faculty of acquiring property" (1:561). He questioned why slaves should be counted in national councils when they were unrepresented within their own states. He further feared that such representation would encourage the slave trade, and noted that Congress had been unwilling even to refer to slavery by name!

Madison thought that Paterson's argument contradicted the small-state claim for equality in the Senate, and he suggested that one house should represent free inhabitants and the other, "which had for one of its primary objects the guardianship of property," (1:562) should count both free and slave populations. Butler and King both thought that slaves should count in the balance of the southern states.

THE CONVENTION CREATES ANOTHER COMMITTEE TO RECONSIDER INITIAL REPRESENTATION

The convention then created a new committee of eleven consisting of Rufus King (the chair), Roger Sherman, Robert Yates, David Brearly,

Gouverneur Morris, George Read, Daniel Carrol, James Madison, Hugh Williamson, John Rutledge, and William Houston. On the very next day, the committee proposed adjusting the numbers upward to 65. This gave an extra representative to New Hampshire, Massachusetts, Connecticut, New York, New Jersey, Virginia and Georgia; two extra to Maryland; and left Rhode Island and the Carolinas the same.

Rutledge wanted to reduce the representation of New Hampshire, but King, who argued that North/South differences would be greater than those between small states and large ones, thought this would be unfair to the eastern (northern) states. As if to prove King right, various delegates began to compare northern and southern advantages much as members of Congress would later do in the events leading up to the Missouri Compromise of 1820. Several motions adjusting representation for individual states were then defeated, after which Madison proposed doubling the total number of representatives for all the states so that they would bring adequate "local information" to Congress (Farrand 1966, 1:568). Ellsworth feared that a larger body would delay business; Sherman favored cutting the size of the House to 50; Gerry thought a larger House would be more difficult to corrupt; Mason thought that a quorum of 65 delegates would be far too small to entrust with the nation's business; and Read thought that doubling the size of each state's representation would provide a backup if the single representative from Rhode Island or New Jersey were unable to attend. The convention voted nine to two against Madison's motion.

Randolph called for a periodic census to reallocate representatives, which Gouverneur Morris thought would unduly shackle Congress. He continued to express concern that the seaboard states should assure that they maintained a majority in Congress after the accession of new western states.

Discussion resumed the following day, July 11, on the motion for a periodic census. Sherman argued that it would be unwise to "shackle" Congress in this respect, whereas Mason thought that periodic revisions in representation were essential. Consistent with his own role in crafting Virginia's Declaration of Rights, Mason observed that "From the nature of man we may be sure, that those who have power in their hands will not give it up while they can retain it" (1:578). He was particularly concerned about arguments for keeping power in the eastern states. If western states were to be admitted into the Union, it should be on an equal basis (according to population) with those already in existence. Mason predicted that they might even become wealthier and more populous than those in the East once Spain allowed them access to the Mississippi River. Williamson proposed that the census be specifically designed to measure the number of free whites and three-fifths of other persons, and Randolph accepted this as a substitute for his own proposal. Randolph noted that it was important that the census be conducted by the general government rather than by the states, which would be too self-interested in the results.

Butler and General Pinckney wanted to count slaves on an equal basis, but Gorham noted that Congress had previously settled on the three-fifths ratio in respect to population, and that it seemed to have worked. Butler favored counting slaves equally because he argued that the labor of slaves was just as valuable as that of freemen. Admitting that this would benefit his own state, Mason could not agree. Although slaves raised the value of land and could even be used, if needed, as soldiers (he may have had the Revolutionary War experience in mind), they were not equal to freemen but were a "peculiar species of property" different from that in other states (1:581). Williamson noted that when it came to taxation, northern states had once also argued for equality but considered the three-fifths clause a reasonable compromise. Gouverneur Morris wondered why one species of property should be singled out for special treatment. Debate continued on whether it was wise to tell the legislature how to apportion seats.

As if the divisions between the North and the South were not already apparent, Gouverneur Morris continued to express his fears about new western states and their ability to make equal contributions to those in the East. In his words: "The Busy haunts of men not the remote wilderness, was the proper School of political Talents" (1:583). He also thought that free individuals in northern states would feel degraded if they were put on the same footing as slaves. Congress should be left at liberty in apportioning seats.

Madison marveled that a delegate who had so often spoken of "the political depravity of men" could now be so confident in them (1:584) and, in a line that he must have savored, he accused Morris of determining human character "by the points of the compass" (1:584). Like Mason, Madison anticipated a bright future for the western states once the Mississippi was opened to them and could see no issue with fixing the method of representation. Seemingly ignoring slaves (who were hardly free to follow the dictates of market forces), Madison argued that the states shared more similarities than differences: "Altho' their climate varied considerably, yet as the Govts. the laws, and the manners of all were nearly the same, and the intercourse between different parts perfectly free, population, industry, arts, and the value of labour, would constantly tend to equalize themselves" (1:585). After adopting a provision for a census to count free whites, the convention moved on to the discussion of counting slaves as three-fifths of a person.

COUNTING SLAVES BY FRACTIONS

The three-fifths clause of the Constitution, which would emerge from convention debates and which would be repealed by the Fourteenth Amendment (1868) after a bloody civil war, is today so embarrassing that it is painful to see the delegates debate the formula largely as a matter of interest rather than principle. In the debates, the formula is largely cast as a measure of state wealth. The idea of counting any class of persons as less than full persons is repugnant, although one could certainly argue that being counted as three-fifths of a "person" is better than being viewed simply as property. Wilson showed that delegates had difficulty in justifying what they were doing. Noting that he could "not well see on what principle the administration of blacks in the proportion of three fifths could be explained," he asked: "Are they admitted as Citizens? Then why are they not admitted on an equality with White Citizens? Are they admitted as property? then, why is not other property admitted into the computation?" (Farrand 1966, 1:587). Gouverneur Morris repeated concerns that using the formula would encourage the slave trade—which contemporaries generally condemned as more vicious than the institution of slavery itself. The convention divided on strict North/South lines in rejecting the three-fifths ratio by a vote of four to six. It agreed that the first census should occur the first year after the first meeting of Congress and that this should happen at least every 15 years.

On the following day (July 12), Gouverneur Morris proposed that the three-fifths formula be used for taxation (shortly thereafter modified to apply only to "direct" taxation) as well as representation. Although a number of Southerners agreed (presumably in hopes that this would give them representation according to the same formula), General Pinckney was concerned that southern states, which largely exported agricultural products, might be taxed more heavily on exports and thought that a provision limiting such taxation also needed to be included.

The earlier fault line between large states and small states was now being replicated among free states and slave states with respect to the representation and taxation of slaves. Davie thus observed that North Carolina "would never confederate on any terms that did not rate them at least as 3/5" (1:593). Dr. Johnson suggested that population should be the only standard without regard to whether the population was white or black. Morris saw the developing impasse and suggested that the true standard for representation should be "population & wealth" (1:593). General Pinckney believed this standard was too general and did not give full assurance that slave wealth would be adequately represented. Randolph agreed that southerners needed such "express security" (1:594). Wilson thought it would be less offensive to tie representation to direct taxation. Presumably as a way of encouraging compromise, King suggested that as southern states became more numerous than those in the North (presumably he is referring to population growth rather than the actual number of states), they would be able to take what they wanted. After considerably more wrangling in which Gerry wondered how many occasions there would be where states would be taxed as states, the convention settled on the three-fifths ratio for purposes of both representation and taxation and mandated that Congress conduct a census at least every 10 years. After additional wrangling, the convention decided on the following day to assess direct taxes initially based on the number of representatives each state had in the House of Representatives.

As proposals and counterproposals were offered for representing wealth and numbers, Gouverneur Morris again questioned the coherence of the three-fifths clause, which treated slaves as neither fully human nor fully property. Whereas others were focusing on the differences between North and South (he thought the South was trying to dominate), Morris was more concerned about the difference between maritime and interior states and was beginning to think that equal representation in the Senate might be more important in protecting the former than in protecting the small states. Morris suggested that if the interests of differing regions were simply incompatible, perhaps the sections should recognize this and "take a friendly leave of each other" (1:604). The convention could certainly not satisfy every interest, and northern association with southern and western interests might well involve it in war with Spain over access to the Mississippi River.

Just as Bedford had once expressed distrust on the part of the small states of those that were large, so now Pierce Butler expressed the fears that would, in less than a century, bring on civil war: "The security the Southn. States want is that their negroes may not be taken from them which some gentlemen within or without doors, have a very good mind to do" (1:605). He further predicted that states in the South and West would continue to grow.

Wilson thought that votes should follow population, wherever it was located. Had fellow delegates forgotten that Britain's own unwillingness to give fair representation to the colonies had largely precipitated the revolution? The primary object of society was not securing property but the "cultivation & improvement of the human mind." In achieving this object, "numbers were surely the natural & precise measure of Representation" (1:605).

As discussion resumed that Saturday on the committee report that had proposed using a different basis of representation for the two houses and permitting the origination of money bills only in the first, Gerry renewed concerns about the admission of western states. He wanted the Constitution to guarantee that new states would never outnumber the old. Demonstrating a lack of prophetic powers, Sherman thought this was unlikely ever to happen, certainly not in the near future. More importantly, he observed that the residents of such states were likely to be children and grandchildren who should be provided for fairly. Gerry feared that many such states might instead be populated by "foreigners" (2:3). Wilson continued to press for representation on the basis of population alone. Gerry reiterated the importance of limiting the origination of money bills. Charles Pinckney made a last-minute effort to give states from one to five votes each in the Senate depending on their population. Sensing that it might be this or nothing, both Wilson and Madison agreed.

King proceeded to give a complex speech in which he argued that the new government was to be a general government operating directly on the people rather than a federal (confederal) government, and that as people would be its object, they should also be the basis of representation within both houses. He did not think that equal state representation within the Senate was needed either to honor the existing compact or to protect the small states. He suggested that perhaps the new government should take on all existing state debt. If state governments were to be truly secure, perhaps there should be a third branch that represented states as such. He did not think his state could ever agree to equal state representation in the Senate; in such circumstances, it might be better to do nothing!

Caleb Strong indicated that a report was on the table and that the nation's fate hung in the balance. He observed that the existing government was "nearly at an end" (2:7). Both sides had made concessions, and he thus favored accepting the report.

Madison could feel things slipping away. He thought the Articles were already suffering for having an improper foundation, which the convention now seemed again about to impose in at least one house of the new legislature. If the nation were in fact going to "be partly federal, partly national" (1:8), perhaps the people should be proportionally represented on all matters that affected them directly and states be represented equally on matters that would affect them. However, he did not anticipate that there would ever be a case when the general government would act directly on the states. Summarizing earlier arguments, he found equal state representation in one house to be objectionable for five reasons—giving control to the minority; allowing the minority undue negotiating power; allowing the minority to block necessary measures; allowing inequality to increase with the addition of each new state; and giving an undue prominence to northern states over southern.

Wilson likewise thought that providing for equal representation, even in one house, would repeat the errors of the Articles. State equality under the Articles had led to congressional imbecility. The convention was about to compound "the weakness of the former Governt." with one that was even more complex (2:11)!

Pinckney's measure offered too little, too late and was defeated by a vote of four to six. In his notes of the day, King expressed mortification that his state voted in the negative (2:13).

THE GREAT COMPROMISE

Three committees had reported, and their measures had been debated from every vantage point. On Monday, July 16, the convention faced a revised committee proposal to apportion the first house with 65 members, allow it to originate money bills and take a census every 10 years, and to apportion the second house equally. Five states—Connecticut, New Jersey, Delaware, Maryland, and North Carolina—voted for the compromise; four states—Massachusetts, Pennsylvania, Virginia, and South Carolina—voted against it, and Massachusetts split. Then seeking to entrust Congress with powers "in all cases to which the separate States are incompetent; or in which the harmony of the U.S. may be interrupted by the exercise of individual legislation," (2:17) the convention hit another snag and evenly split over whether this was another matter for a committee to handle.

Some of the delegates were obviously distracted by the earlier vote. Randolph, who had originally introduced the Virginia Plan, noted that the vote "had embarrassed the business extremely" (2:17). Although he wanted to discuss the subject further, he doubted that a re-vote would help; indeed, if the New York delegation were present—or, he might have added, if the New Hampshire delegation had arrived—it would likely vote to affirm. He therefore proposed that the convention adjourn for both sides to consider their options.

Paterson was ready. In what may well have been an intentional distortion, he suggested a sine die, or permanent, adjournment as well as a lifting of the rule of secrecy under which the convention had operated. General Pinckney, who was from one of the more distant states, could not imagine going to his constituents and then coming back to the convention. Randolph clarified. He only wanted to adjourn for the day to consult with other large state delegates to ascertain what they should do if the small states continued to insist on equal representation in the Senate.

This was probably one of those occasions where it must have felt as though one could cut the tension with a knife. The convention equally divided on whether to adjourn! Gerry then proffered that Massachusetts "saw no new ground of compromise" but would be willing to change its vote to give the larger states time to lick their wounds. Rutledge urged that it was important for the convention to do something! On a second vote, the convention adjourned by a vote of seven to two to one.

Madison records that delegates from the large states met the following morning (perhaps for breakfast?) and were joined by some delegates from the small states. Although much of the conversation was "vague," large-state delegates generally concluded that the risks of failure were too great to let the compromise stand in the way. Ruminating that a minority of the states representing a minority of the people had been responsible for the situation, Madison believed that the morning conversation had served to allay the fears of the small states, and he was among the delegates who were resolved to move forward.

The rest of the convention would not be smooth sailing; indeed, Madison would soon suffer another major setback. Still, the mood had changed. Delegates from the larger states had raised just about every conceivable argument for complete proportional representation, but they faced very tangible political interests to which they decided that they had to yield if the convention were to have any hope of success.

It is doubtful that contemporary political scientists, who blithely criticize the Senate for being undemocratic, have either mustered any arguments that delegates to the convention did not raise themselves, or that these political scientists could have done any better (if as well) under the circumstances! The U.S. Constitution is not perfect. It is not a Platonic ideal. It was not imposed from on high. It required the consent of the participating states. While delegates from smaller states were willing to give partial deference to the principle of representation by population, they were not completely willing to part with their existing equality, and the resulting document reflects this. The fact that delegates from the large states were unwilling to allow small-state delegates to take matters back to their constituents at this point probably indicates that they believed the small-state delegates were accurately reflecting sentiments within their jurisdictions.

SOURCES CITED IN THIS CHAPTER

Farrand, Max. 1966. *Records of the Federal Convention of 1787.* 4 vols. New Haven, CT: Yale University Press.

5

FROM THE GREAT COMPROMISE
TO THE COMMITTEE OF DETAIL

> Make him too weak: The Legislature will usurp his powers:
> Make him too strong. He will usurp on the Legislature.
>
> —Gouverneur Morris speaking about the executive
> (Farrand 1966, 2:105)

As the convention resumed business on Tuesday, July 17, 1787, its delegates had spent more than a month focusing almost solely on the issue of representation. Finally, the large states had reluctantly conceded equal state representation in the upper house. Some delegates must have groaned when Gouverneur Morris opened the day with a motion to reconsider the entire resolution that the convention had just adopted. The fact that no one seconded the motion was a clear sign that delegates thought that further discussion of that compromise was useless and that it was high time to move to other business.

The convention returned to the recommendations that the Committee of the Whole had reported after the first two weeks. Now that the nature of the new Congress had been established, it was appropriate to consider what powers it would exercise. The Committee of the Whole had proposed granting the general government power in all cases in which states were incompetent or in which their actions would disrupt national harmony. Perhaps emboldened by the Connecticut Compromise, Roger Sherman wanted to add a proviso designed to protect the rights of states to deal with internal matters, rights often designated, as in Sherman's resolution, as state "police" powers.

Surprisingly, James Wilson, who had been a consistent advocate of the larger states in the prior controversy, seconded the motion. By contrast,

Gouverneur Morris thought that it was precisely such matters—especially related to the issue of paper money—in which the general government should intervene. Sherman then apparently read a list of enumerated powers that he thought Congress should have. Unfortunately, Madison's notes only indicate that these would have included the power to levy taxes on trade but not to engage in direct taxation (Farrand 1966, 2:26). Morris feared that this meant that the government would have to revert to the system of "quotas & requisitions" (2:26), which had proved to be so unworkable under the Articles of Confederation. Perhaps for this reason, the convention defeated Sherman's amendment by a vote of two to eight. The convention went on to ratify an amendment proposed by Delaware's Gunning Bedford granting Congress the power to legislate on general matters and on those in which state legislation would be incompetent.

THE CONVENTION REJECTS THE PROPOSED CONGRESSIONAL NEGATIVE OF STATE LAWS

As the convention proceeded to consider the report from the Committee of the Whole, Gouverneur Morris opposed the provision for a congressional negative of state laws "as likely to be terrible to the States, and not necessary, if sufficient Legislative authority should be given to the Genl. Government" (Farrand 1966, 2:27). Sherman appears neither to have desired nor anticipated the establishment of lower federal courts, and thought that the proposed provision would be unnecessary since state courts would invalidate unconstitutional state laws. Perhaps with the colonial experience in mind, Luther Martin questioned whether, in the presence of a potential congressional negative, states would first have to get permission from the general government before they could enforce their own laws.

Madison thought the congressional veto was one of the lynchpins of the entire system and worried that, by contrast, courts would not get a chance to review disruptive state laws until they had already gone into effect. He further questioned whether "State Tribunals" would sufficiently guard the "National authority and interests" (2:27). Appealing to experience, he observed that the Georgia legislature appointed judges annually and that the Rhode Island legislature had replaced judges who refused to enforce a law they believed to be unconstitutional. Citing the role that the negative placed in supporting the British Empire, Madison conceded that the negative was "sometimes [sic.] misapplied thro' ignorance or a partiality to one particular part of ye. Empire," but anticipated that the proposed new government would be closer to the people. With some recognition of practical difficulties, he further noted that some "emanation" of national power might grant at least "a temporary effect to laws of immediate necessity" (2:28).

Gouverneur Morris remained unconvinced. He feared that the power "would disgust all the States" (I, 29). He further believed that either the judicial system or direct congressional legislation could corral rogue state laws. Sherman further suggested that the veto would implicitly validate any state law that Congress simply failed to veto. Although Charles Pinckney argued for the veto, state delegations rejected it by a vote of three to seven. Almost immediately thereafter, however, the convention voted unanimously to make the new Constitution and all acts and treaties supreme law binding on state judiciaries. It followed with a unanimous vote for a single executive.

SELECTION OF THE EXECUTIVE

The Committee of the Whole had followed the Virginia Plan in proposing to vest the power to select the president in Congress, but Gouverneur Morris thought that such selection, combined with congressional impeachment powers, would undermine the president's independence. He wanted the president to be selected at large "by the freeholders [those who owned a certain amount of property] of the Country" (2:29). New York and Connecticut both had such systems. Morris further suggested that the people would be likely to select men "of continental reputation" (2:29). By contrast, he feared that congressional selection would result in faction and intrigue.

The debate followed a familiar fault line. Sherman, who had worked so hard to get equal state representation in the second house of Congress, thought that its members would make a better choice than the people. He feared that if voters decided the issue, they would vote for candidates within their own state, and only someone from the largest state would have a chance. Apparently anticipating that such general elections would award the prize to the candidate with the highest vote total, albeit not necessarily a majority, he thought that it would be possible to require such a majority within Congress, presumably because it would be in session to continue voting until a single candidate achieved such a vote.

Wilson responded both to this and to objections—perhaps that Madison had failed to record?—based on commotions that such general elections had allegedly caused in Poland. Arguing that the Polish case was dissimilar, he suggested that the convention could follow the example of Massachusetts and vest power in Congress only in those cases where the majority of people did not select a candidate. In such circumstances, the people would effectively serve to nominate candidates, and Congress would choose among them. Wilson repeated Morris's concern that direct legislative election would undermine executive independence.

Charles Pinckney feared that popular elections would "be led by a few active & designing men" (2:30) and would give undue weight to the more populous states. Gouverneur Morris responded that the larger states would be far more likely to combine within Congress than within the general populace. In arguments similar to those that Madison often made in respect to geography, Morris said that the example of New York showed the difficulty that candidates would have in attempting to engage in statewide election intrigue, a welcome obstacle that national size would magnify still further. The people might not know of day-to-day legislative actions, but they would be aware "of those great & illustrious characters which have merited their esteem & confidence" (2:31). By contrast, legislative selection would lead to executive dependence.

George Mason observed that delegates were offering highly contradictory accounts of the trustworthiness of Congress. His main concern was practicality. He thought that vesting the people with the choice of the magistrate was like referring "a trial of colours to a blind man" (2:31). Given the "extent of the Country," he did not think that ordinary voters would have requisite information about those outside their own states (2:31). Gouverneur Morris saw no contradiction between thinking that Congress might be good in some matters and bad in others. He feared that selections of executives invited corruption. By contrast, Williamson thought that one might as soon have selection "by lot" (2:32), that is, by chance as to grant such power to the people. As long as the executive (the delegates were still not using the term president) had a fixed salary and was ineligible for a second term, he would remain independent of Congress.

The convention voted one to nine to leave congressional selection in place and rejected a motion by Martin by a vote of two to eight to add an additional layer of electors. It also unanimously agreed to leave the presidential term at seven years and to allow the executive "to carry into execution the nationl. laws" (2:32). Gouverneur Morris used a homely analogy—the incentive that an executive would otherwise have to "make hay while the sun shines"—to argue for executive eligibility for reelection, and his suggestion was rather surprisingly carried by a vote of six to four.

EXECUTIVE TERM LENGTHS

As delegates resumed the discussion of term lengths, Delaware's Jacob Broom indicated that if the executive were to be re-eligible for election, he favored a term of less than seven years. For his part, Virginia's hitherto silent Dr. McClung, who was probably seeking to avoid the dangers of executive dependency on the legislature, suggested that the executive should serve "during good behavior," or for life (Farrand 1966, 2:33). Hamilton had, of course, advocated something similar in his long speech to the convention. Gouverneur Morris was pleased to second McClung's motion, and Broom said this met his concerns, but Sherman thought that the newly approved eligibility for re-election would provide enough incentive for the executive to exercise good behavior.

In defending McClung, a fellow state delegate, Madison expounded on the necessity of separating powers in the new system. Allowing executives to serve during good behavior would have the same effect as allowing judges so to serve. Madison argued that it was particularly important to prevent the executive and legislative departments from uniting. He expressed doubts as to whether McClurg's motion was practical, but he thought it deserved respectful consideration.

Fellow Virginian George Mason observed that the convention had already rejected a similar proposal by a wide majority. There would be little to distinguish this proposal from "hereditary Monarchy" (2:35), which Mason hoped that no delegate would support. Madison was more fearful of the power of Congress. He noted that state governors had been "in general little more than Cyphers" who were subject to near legislative omnipotence (2:35). Gouverneur Morris thought that a well-devised republican government would be the best antidote to monarchy. McClurg indicated that his primary object had been to keep an otherwise re-eligible executive from becoming unduly dependent on Congress. The convention rejected McClurg's motion by a vote of four to six, and a motion to strike out seven years failed by a vote of four to six.

DISCUSSION OF THE JUDICIARY

After voting to approve a conditional executive veto and to establish a national judiciary, consisting of at least one Supreme Court, the delegates began to discuss the recommendation of the Committee of the Whole that the second branch should select such judges. Nathaniel Gorham thought that it would be better for one house to make such appointments rather than two. Believing, however, that even one house would be too numerous to fix personal responsibility, he favored a system of executive appointment with the advice and consent of the upper house. He noted that his home state of Massachusetts had used this system and found it to work well.

Wilson preferred executive appointment alone, but he thought Gorham's proposal was a good second best. Martin weighed in to favor appointment by the second house, whose members he thought would have wider knowledge of possible nominees, and Sherman agreed. Mason feared that the nation's executive would become too attached to the state where the national capital was located to distribute such appointments fairly. He further questioned whether the executive should be appointing individuals who might determine whether he should be impeached. Gorham responded that senators would be as likely to have personal attachments to the capital as would executives, and that this house of Congress would be more subject to "intrigue & cabal" (Farrand 1966, 2:42) than would a single executive. Gouverneur Morris did not anticipate that judges would form courts for impeachment. Madison suggested allowing presidents to appoint judges and requiring a certain majority in the Senate to confirm them. Sherman believed the collective wisdom of the Senate would be wider than, superior to, and no more subject to intrigue than, that of the executive.

When the Committee of the Whole had recommended senatorial appointment of judges, delegates had not yet determined that the Senate would represent states equally. Although Sherman thus had a new reason to favor appointment by that body, Edmund Randolph also agreed that it would be a better source of appointments than the executive. He focused on the Senate's wider knowledge of individuals throughout the United States. Bedford, perhaps more motivated by the new small-state advantage in that body, agreed. Gorham, by contrast, thought that one person would be more accountable for appointments than would a body of individuals. The convention rejected executive appointment by a vote of two to six (the Georgia delegation being absent). Gorham then introduced a vote on executive appointment with the advice and consent of the senate, and the states split evenly at four to four. By contrast, a motion for service during good behavior passed unanimously.

The convention next discussed a proposal—designed to generate judicial independence—that would prevent increases or decreases in judicial pay during their terms. Gouverneur Morris thought that it was appropriate to protect salaries against cuts but not against needed increases. Franklin agreed that financial circumstances might warrant such increased pay. Madison thought that even this might breed undue judicial dependence but wondered, as he had previously done with respect to legislative salaries, if a commodity like wheat might be chosen as a standard. Delegates decided to eliminate the ban on possible increases in judicial salaries.

The convention turned to the recommendation of the Committee of the Whole that would empower Congress to create inferior judicial tribunals. South Carolina's Butler thought that state courts could do the job, and Martin agreed, pointing to possible jealousies between two sets of courts. Gorham responded that existing national courts dealing with piracies had not had this result. Randolph questioned whether state judges could be trusted to execute national laws. Sherman seemed to favor granting Congress the power to create new tribunals while encouraging it to rely on state courts already in place. Surprisingly, the motion passed unanimously.

The convention next decided to strike the role of judges in sitting as courts of impeachment. Delegates also agreed that judicial jurisdiction should "extend to all cases arising under the Natl. laws: And to such other questions as may involve the Natl. peace & harmony" (2:46), and they agreed to the proposal to allow for the admission of new states. By contrast, they decided that they did not need to provide specifically for the continuance of Congress until the creation of the new government.

GUARANTEEING STATE GOVERNMENTS

The Committee of the Whole had proposed that the new government should guarantee "a Republican Constitution" to each state. After Gouverneur Morris expressed his unwillingness to support laws such as the inflationary policies being adopted in Rhode Island, Wilson suggested that the provision was designed to guard against "dangerous commotions, insurrections and rebellions" (Farrand 1966, 2:47). Perhaps with the example of Shays's Rebellion in mind, Mason thought it would be odd if the government had to "remain a passive Spectator of its own subversion" (2:47). Madison, seconded by Dr. McClurg, proposed making the objective clearer.

Georgia's William Houston feared perpetuating the existing government in his home state and wondered how the national government would distinguish "between contending parties" (2:48). Martin thought that states should suppress rebellions on their own. Gorham wondered whether, without a guarantee of republican government, a state might establish a monarchy; the national government would not have to intervene in mere verbal disputes, but if one or both sides resorted to force of arms, it would surely have to act. After some additional discussion, the convention unanimously voted both to guarantee a republican form of government and to protect against both domestic and foreign violence.

RENEWED DISCUSSIONS OF THE EXECUTIVE

When the convention resumed the next day, it reconsidered whether the executive should be re-eligible for office. Gouverneur Morris began a long speech. Pointing to the difficulty of administering republican government over a large nation, he favored an executive of "sufficient vigor to pervade every part of it" (Farrand 1966, 2:52). Morris expressed particular concern over the aggrandizement of legislative powers and suggested that the executive might often have to protect the people against the wealthy interests that were represented there. While the second house would check some unwise policies, "It is no check on Legislative tyranny" (2:52). The executive, by contrast, should "be the great protector of the Mass of the people" (2:52). He would do so in part by appointing officers to administer and dispense justice. Preventing the executive from serving for more than a single term would have three dire consequences. It would take away a "great incitement to merit public esteem" that was prompted by the "love of fame" (2:53); it would encourage executives to take advantage of the time they did have in office; and it would tempt executives to violate the Constitution. Morris feared that the power of impeachment would also sap presidential powers and suggested that if it were to be kept, it be kept for major cabinet officers, without which the executive would find it difficult to act. Morris favored election of the executive by the people to two-year terms as a way to transcend the effects of intrigue on such elections.

Randolph did not favor presidential re-eligibility. Anticipating a system where either both houses of Congress would select the president by joint ballot or where one nominated and the other selected, Randolph feared that it would destroy the executive's power over Congress, particularly his willingness to use his veto power. He did not believe a president would seek an unconstitutional second term unless the people were corrupt enough to allow this to happen.

Rufus King opposed ineligibility and favored entrusting the people with the power of election, perhaps by choosing electors for this purpose. William Paterson suggested that the people of each state could choose from one to three electors, depending on the state's size. Wilson liked the idea of popular participation. Madison reiterated the necessity of providing each branch with separate and independent powers. Although he liked the idea of direct election in theory, he noted that elections in the South did not include slaves. He therefore favored a system of electors to represent voters there, which would thus indirectly count slaves in the electoral power that whites would wield—in later years, Jefferson would be called "The Negro President" because his historic election in 1800 rested in part on the additional votes that the three-fifths clause gave to the southern states (see Wills 2003).

Gerry did not think that Congress should choose an executive who was subject to re-election, but he disfavored popular elections. Consistent with earlier speeches, he feared that the people would be "misinformed" and "misled by a few designing men" (Farrand 1966, 2:57). He suggested that state executives should appoint electors who would choose the president, thus giving the executive and members of both houses of Congress separate electoral bases.

Consistent with Paterson's early suggestion, Oliver Ellsworth moved instead to grant to each state from one to three electors. After further discussion the convention agreed to use electors chosen by state legislatures but postponed a decision—reminiscent of the one that had so divided them on the issue of congressional representation—as to what ratio each state would have. The decision to select the executive independent of Congress apparently provided the impetus, however, for a decision to allow for executive re-eligibility and to settle on a term of six, rather than seven, years.

When the convention resumed on Friday, July 20, to consider granting each state from one to three presidential electors depending on whether they had populations of under 100,000, from 100,000 to 200,000, or above 300,000, delegates reverted to examining everything from an individual state perspective. After Madison noted that, as population grew, in time all states would be entitled to three electors, Gerry proposed an initial allocation that was, after several suggested tweaks, rejected. North Carolina's Williamson then proposed apportioning electors according to state representation in the first house of Congress, which states accepted by a vote of six to four.

IMPEACHMENT

The delegates next considered the provision for impeachment and conviction for "malpractice and neglect of duty" (Farrand 1966, 2:64). Charles

Pinckney and Gouverneur Morris disfavored such a clause whereas North Carolina's Davie thought that it was essential to prevent the executive from using questionable means to be reelected and Wilson concurred. In sentiments that seem almost to mirror the impeachment controversy that would later surround President William Jefferson Clinton, Morris suggested that re-election could vindicate an executive against charges against him. He further wondered who would do the impeachment.

Mason emphasized that no man should be above the law. He feared that if electors chose the president, he might seek to corrupt them and get by with it. Franklin observed, presumably with a wry sense of humor, that, without a system of impeachment, individuals might be tempted to resort to assassination! Impeachment would provide not only for conviction of the guilty but also for the exoneration of the innocent. Fellow Pennsylvania delegate Gouverneur Morris now backtracked to argue not against impeachment per se but to require a more particular enumeration of impeachable offenses. Madison suggested that it was important to have a means to deal with "incapacity, negligence or perfidy" (2:65). Thinking especially about the possibility of incapacity, he noted that impeachment would be particularly important for an office like the executive that was to be occupied by a single individual.

Charles Pinckney feared the legislature would use the impeachment mechanism to control the executive. Gerry thought that good executives would have nothing to fear. King questioned whether impeachment would be consistent with separation of powers. He thought that impeachment was only appropriate for individuals holding office during good behavior, but advised that "under no circumstances" should such power be vested in Congress (2:67). By contrast, Randolph argued that impeachment was a way to subject the executive to the rule of law but thought that Hamilton's idea of using a forum of state judges might work, as might some kind of "preliminary inquest" (2:67), to decide whether there were proper grounds for it. Franklin thought that impeachment might have worked in a situation in Holland involving the Statholder [Governor], but King disputed the relevance of this example since it involved an individual who served in the position for life. Wilson wondered whether if the convention provided for impeachment of the chief executive, it should also have to provide it for members of congress. Pinckney questioned whether the president would have adequate powers to require an impeachment mechanism.

Gouverneur Morris said he now recognized the need for executive impeachment. He believed charges could be connected to "treachery," corrupting electors, or incapacity (2:69). In the latter case, impeachment should result only in removal from office. The people, rather than the executive, would be "the King" (2:69). Still, the impeachment mechanism should not leave the executive at the mercy of Congress.

Quick votes followed accepting an impeachment mechanism for the executive, fixed compensation, and payment from the national treasury. Gerry and Morris also received unanimous consent to a resolution preventing executive electors from being members of Congress, officers of the United States, or candidates for the office. Dr. McClurg further suggested that sometime before a Committee of Detail was created to draft a final document, the convention should decide on what forces would be at the executive's disposal. As the delegates reconvened on Saturday, July 21, they also unanimously decided that executive electors should be paid out of the national treasury.

THE COUNCIL OF REVISION

That same Saturday, James Wilson reintroduced the proposal to ally the judiciary with the executive in the exercises of the veto power. As a future Supreme Court justice, his views have special relevance because they continue to illumine modern ideas respecting the power, known as judicial review, that courts exercise to strike down unconstitutional legislation. Wilson cited earlier arguments indicating that judges would exercise such a power, but he recognized that this power would necessarily be limited to laws that were unconstitutional rather than those that were also "unjust," "unwise," "dangerous," or "destructive" (Farrand 1966, 2:73). Wilson believed that judges should have broader powers, and Madison agreed.

Gorham questioned whether judges' knowledge of such policy matters would be better than anyone else's. Ellsworth thought allying judges with the executive would give the latter "more wisdom & firmness" (2:74), and he anticipated that judges would also be competent on matters involving international laws. Madison saw the alliance as a means to protect both departments and the people against the legislative "vortex," a term that refers to a strong whirlwind or whirlpool. Mason also thought that the council would help buck up the executive.

Gerry, by contrast, expressed surprise that the issue was being revised because he thought the proposal improperly mixed the functions of those who should be expositing the laws with the jobs of those who ought to be writing them. Caleb Strong of Massachusetts concurred on like grounds. Gouverneur Morris thought that English judges, who served as part of the Privy Council, exercised powers similar to those being proposed but acknowledged that the British situation was quite different because the monarch had plenty of means to protect his prerogatives. Like Madison, Morris feared the power of the new Congress. He hoped that a free press would help mitigate abuses, but he did not think it was fully capable of preventing such abuses.

Martin thought that the Council of Revision would constitute "a dangerous innovation" (2:76). Since judges would already have the power to invalidate unconstitutional laws, this council would grant them "a double negative" (2:76). If judges had to oppose popular measures, judges might lose the confidence of the people.

Madison again denied that the proposal violated the maxim of separation of powers. He viewed the council as a defensive mechanism. It would be no less appropriate for judges to participate in the veto of legislation than for the executive to do so. Mason further believed that such a check might discourage demagoguery that would lead to unwise legislation within Congress. As to charges that this would constitute a double negative, he observed that the power of judicial review would not apply to laws that were unwise but only to those that were unconstitutional.

Gerry preferred an absolute executive veto over an alliance between the executive and the judiciary. Gouverneur Morris saw the alliance as purely defensive and formulated a rather homey example of three neighbors who made a pact in which one had the power to make, one to execute, and yet another to interpret the laws. Gorham advanced the case against the council by suggesting both that participation on the council would likely predispose judges to favor or disfavor laws that later came before them, and that judges might so overbalance the executive as to allow them to "sacrifice" rather than defend him (2:79). Wilson suggested that this might be remedied by somehow adjusting the votes that each would have, although he did not explain how. After Rutledge weighed in against the council, the convention rejected it by a vote of three to four to two. By contrast, the states unanimously approved a qualified presidential veto.

JUDICIAL SELECTION

The convention next considered a proposal that Madison had previously advanced to allow the executive to appoint judges subject to rejection by two-thirds of the upper house. This mechanism has particular contemporary relevance because it works much like a legislative veto (in which Congress vests the president with power subject to a veto by one or both houses of Congress). In the absence of explicit constitutional support, the U.S. Supreme Court ruled this legislative veto to be unconstitutional in 1983 in what is commonly called the Chadha Case.

Madison argued that such a mechanism would secure executive responsibility while providing a check "in case of any flagrant partiality or error, in the nomination" (Farrand 1966, 2:80). In light of equal state representation in the second house, Madison also praised his proposal as a mechanism that would provide adequate representation to the states. He feared that if the Senate exercised this power on its own, judges could be appointed by individuals who did not represent a majority of the American people.

Charles Pinckney believed that the second branch alone was likely to have better knowledge of potential nominees and greater popular confidence. Randolph preferred Madison's proposal to senatorial appointment but thought the Massachusetts plan for executive appointment and legislative confirmation was better. He feared that bodies with multiple members were far more likely to engage in cabal than a single executive. Ellsworth preferred allowing the second branch to nominate and the president to veto. He did not think that a two-thirds confirmation majority would block many nominations.

Gouverneur Morris favored Madison's motion over senatorial appointment for three reasons. First, he thought that the Senate would reflect state interests as to which judges were appointed. Second, he thought senators would be less informed than the president. Third, he wondered how one could trust the president with control of the military and not with judicial appointments.

Gerry wanted a system that would satisfy both the people and the states, and he did not think Madison's proposal would satisfy either. Gerry believed that the Senate would be better informed than the executive, and he thought the two-thirds majority was too high. Madison offered to allow rejection by a majority, but his colleague Mason feared that such a mechanism entrusted too much power to the executive, which might result in undue influence over the judicial department. Mason did not think senatorial appointment would accentuate differences between the North and the South. The convention then rejected Madison's proposal and stuck with the recommendation of the Committee of the Whole for senatorial appointments by identical six to three votes.

OATHS

At long last, July 23 marked the arrival of the two New Hampshire delegates. The convention unanimously affirmed the need to provide an amending process before debating whether state officials should take an oath to support the new government. North Carolina's Williamson wondered if national officials should also pledge to support governments within the states.

Wilson considered oaths to be what he described as "a left handed security" (2:87). Good governments did not need them, and bad governments were unworthy of support. He also wondered how the oath would relate to cases in which officials favored constitutional amendments. Perhaps with a view to the delegates' work at the convention, Gorham saw no inconsistency between adhering to the current constitution and favoring changes. After Gerry argued that such oaths would help members of the states recognize that they were no longer distinct from the general government, the convention agreed unanimously to the resolution.

RATIFICATION OF THE CONSTITUTION

The Virginia Plan had proposed that conventions within the states should ratify the proposed Constitution. Ellsworth now proposed that this task should be performed by state legislatures, and Paterson agreed. Mason, however, thought that ratification by convention was one of the Committee of the Whole's most important proposals. Power flowed from the people, whereas state legislatures were "mere creatures of the State Constitutions, and cannot be greater than their creators" (Farrand 1966, 2:88). Moreover, if one legislature could approve, another could reverse such action. The new Constitution should be grounded in "the clear & undisputed authority of the people" (2:89).

Randolph had a more practical objection. The new Constitution would weaken state power and would thus likely encounter opposition from "local demagogues" (2:89) who would also lose power. Gerry, by contrast, thought that state ratification would carry with it the authority of the existing Articles. Consistent with earlier fears of popular rule, he thought that resort to the people would result in "[g]reat confusion" (2:90).

Gorham mustered five arguments in favor of popular convention ratification. First, convention delegates would be chosen for a specific task and would not, like legislators, have something to lose. Second, it would be easier to get ratification from unicameral conventions than from bicameral state legislatures. Third, more able men—including clergymen who were helpful in formulating the Massachusetts Constitution but who were sometimes barred from state legislatures—would be available to serve in conventions. Fourth, conventions would not be subject to other business that might delay deliberations. Fifth and finally, the method for ratifying amendments through state legislatures under the Articles required unanimous consent, which seemed unlikely either from Rhode Island, which had not sent delegates to the convention, or from New York, which was reaping the advantage of being able to tax neighboring states. Ellsworth would not object to states choosing other modes, but he expected better results from state legislatures than from the people.

In responding to Mason, Ellsworth observed that approval by popular conventions constituted a relatively new mechanism that he did not think was superior to legislative approval. If a new confederacy were to be formed among consenting states, it would matter little whether it were approved by conventions or state legislatures. Williamson thought the intent of the resolution under discussion was to allow approval by either means. By contrast, Gouverneur Morris argued that if the letter of the Articles were to be followed, only unanimous state legislative ratification would work. Morris did not think the convention was proceeding under the confederation.

King agreed with Ellsworth that legislative approval would be sufficient, but he thought that "a reference to the authority of the people expressly delegated to conventions" would provide stronger authority. Madison was more emphatic. He did not think that "a Legislature could change the constitution under which it held its existence" (2:92–93). The difference was that "between a *league* or *treaty*, and a *Constitution*" (2:93). While both would carry "*moral*" obligations, the latter would have greater "*political*" obligations (2:93). Popular approval of the Constitution would enable judges to use it to invalidate conflicting legislation that they might leave in place if state legislatures approved the document. Treaties could be voided by a breach by a single party, but a constitution approved by the people could not.

The convention rejected Ellsworth's proposed legislative substitution by a vote of three to seven. The convention also rejected Gouverneur Morris's subsequent proposal to send the plan to "one general Convention," with apparent ability to amend (2:93). All the states present except Delaware then voted for the proposal for convention ratification.

REPRESENTATION IN THE SENATE

Morris and King next moved to give each state an unspecified, but equal, number of senators and to allow them to vote "per capita" (Farrand 1966, 2:94), that is, individually, rather than as a single delegation. Morris subsequently proposed giving each state three senators, so that the body would be numerous enough to prevent it from being governed by too small a quorum. Gorham preferred two senators per state, because he thought a smaller number could more easily deliberate about matters of war and peace, which he thought would be entrusted to that body. He further anticipated the addition of Kentucky, Vermont, Maine, and Franklin (Tennessee) and the division of some of the larger states. Mason also opposed three senators per state and anticipated that two would be cheaper. Williamson thought it would be more difficult for distant states to find more senators.

After a motion rejecting three senators per state, the convention settled on two. It subsequently approved per capita voting. After some other issues, including General Pinckney's observation that southern states needed some guarantees preventing the emancipation of slaves or taxes on exports, the convention decided to create a Committee of Five to begin drafting a document.

LEGISLATIVE SELECTION OF THE EXECUTIVE RECONSIDERED

By prior agreement, the convention resumed the next day (Tuesday, July 24) with a discussion of executive electors. Houston proposed, and Spaight seconded, a motion to return the function of selecting presidents to Congress; Houston feared that distant states would find it difficult to find "capable men" (2:99) to serve as electors. Gerry did not think this would be a problem and suggested that many governors might want to serve. He also noted that if Congress were to make the selection, the convention would need to reconsider executive re-eligibility. Strong thought that intervening elections would solve this problem and that a system of electors would make the new system too complex.

Williamson suggested returning to the original plan of selecting executives for a single seven-year term. He did not think electors would be men of sufficient consequence. He further favored a plural executive of three, one from each of the nation's major geographical divisions, rather than a unitary executive who might favor one area over others. Williamson also feared that a single executive would consider himself "an elective king" (2:101) and attempt to perpetuate himself in office.

Dispute bred complexity. Gerry proposed: that state legislatures should cast votes in the same proposed portion as electors; that the first house of Congress should choose two from among the top four vote-getters; and the senate should decide between them. After this was voted down by voice vote, the convention voted to approve Houston's motion for congressional selection, and Martin and Gerry again attempted to make the executive ineligible for more than one term.

EXECUTIVE RE-ELIGIBILITY AND TERM LENGTHS

The arguments were becoming familiar. Ellsworth thought that an executive would be more likely to rule better if he could be re-elected. Gerry was willing to increase the executive term to 10, 15, or 20 years. It was as though an auction had commenced! Martin proposed a term of 11 years; Gerry of 15; King of 20, and Davie—here the auction analogy breaks down—of 8. The fact that King identified 20 as "the medium life of princes" (Farrand 1966, 2:102), indicates that he was probably highlighting what he considered to be the absurdity of the proposals rather than raising the "bids."

Wilson believed these votes all proceeded from the vote to vest executive selection back in Congress. He cited examples of individuals, including popes, who had ably served at advanced ages, and suggested that if the minimum age of the executive were to be set at 35 (as it later would be), an individual serving a 15-year term would still have to resign in the prime of life. After Gerry proposed entrusting this issue to committee, Wilson suggested using lots to select up to 15 legislators who would resign and then choose the executive.

Gouverneur Morris thought that legislative selection was the worst possible mechanism. Correctly anticipating that there would be two major parties within Congress, he feared that party interests would rule over the common good and would breed intrigue. He posed the dilemma that he thought a chief executive raised: "Make him too weak: The Legislature will usurp his powers: Make him too strong. He will usurp on the Legislature" (2:105).

After Wilson then advanced his proposal to select legislators to choose the president by lot, Gerry observed that this would leave too much to chance. King noted that the lot might select delegates from the same state, who would reward one of their own. By day's end, the convention voted to postpone the matter.

Carroll and Morris then questioned the proposal for apportioning state taxation on the basis of the three-fifths clause, and Gouverneur Morris suggested that it had served as a bridge to reach compromise on the issue of state representation but was no longer needed. The convention ended the day by choosing John Rutledge, Edmund Randolph, Nathaniel Gorham, Oliver Ellsworth, and James Wilson to a committee to incorporate existing resolutions into a complete document.

When discussions resumed the next day, Ellsworth sought to combine two methods of presidential election, that is, legislative selection in the first instance and election by electors chosen by state electors in the case of incumbents. Gerry continued to oppose any form of legislative selection and proposed that state governors and presidents should do the selecting, with help from their councils or electors chosen by the state legislatures.

Madison pointed out the obvious: there were arguments that could be raised against every method that had been proposed. *Someone* had to make the selection! He thought that judges were out of the question. Legislative selection was likely to "agitate & divide the legislature" (2:109), and could lead both to domestic and foreign intrigue. After illustrating with foreign examples, Madison turned to state authorities. Since the new government was being formed in part to work against state propensities, it would be unwise to invest states with the responsibility. The choice was ultimately between selection by the people directly or indirectly by electors. The advantage of electors was that they would meet immediately, proceed to their business, and disperse. Believing the convention had decided against such a mode, however, Madison believed popular election would be the best. He did recognize that the proposed government might need a mechanism to guard against the preference of each state to select one of its own. He also feared that there might be more qualified northern voters than southern voters, but he anticipated greater population growth in the latter region. Although Ellsworth thought that the argument for state preference for its own candidate was insuperable, by a vote of four to seven the convention defeated his motion for selecting incumbents and non-incumbents by different mechanisms.

Charles Pinckney then proposed that no person would be eligible for the executive office for more than six of twelve years. Mason supported the proposal as did Gerry. Gouverneur Morris objected that such "rotation" (2:112) would breed governmental instability, similar to that which his own state had experienced. Given human nature, immediate ineligibility would not prevent intrigue for future office. Election by the people would be far better than by Congress, but he approved Wilson's proposal for mixing the two methods. Williamson suggested that each elector should vote for three candidates, at least two of which were from states other than his own. Morris suggested voting for two. Madison thought something like this might work.

Gerry still believed that popular election would be "radically vicious" (2:114). He feared that elections would be subject to undue organized influence, perhaps like that of the Society of Cincinnati. Dickinson, however, thought the people were "the best and purest source" (2:114). He suggested that the voters of each state should choose their best citizen, and that either Congress or electors selected by Congress should choose among them. The convention rejected Pinckney's motion to prevent an executive from serving for any more than six of twelve years.

Colonel Mason began the next day, July 26, with a speech reviewing seven different modes that had been proposed for selecting the executive and showing problems with each of them. This review suggested to him that the best mode proposed was that of legislative election, that, in turn, required a single term. Citing "the pole star of his political conduct" as "the preservation of the rights of the people" (2:120), Mason thought that this could best be secured by having office holders return from time to time to take their station with the people. He thus reintroduced the provision of the Committee of the Whole that the executive serve for a single seven-year term. After Franklin added that by republican principles, returning to the people one was serving was actually a promotion, Mason's motion to restore the resolution was adopted. Gouverneur Morris wondered why the principle of returning to the people had not been applied to the judicial branch, but his comments did not prevent adoption of the renewed proposal by a vote of six to three to one.

PROPERTY AND ANTI-DEBTOR QUALIFICATIONS FOR LEGISLATORS

Mason next suggested that the Committee of Detail should be asked to add a property qualification for legislators. He thought that debtors sometimes ran for office in order to "promote laws that might shelter their delinquencies" (Farrand 1966, 2:121). After Charles Pinckney seconded the motion, Gouverneur Morris suggested that if qualifications were to be added, they should apply to voters. As to debtors, many were in that condition because they had lent money to the government that it had not repaid! Madison wondered whether the restriction should apply to those who had received public monies for which they had not properly accounted. Morris responded with the ancient maxim that "we should not be righteous [or wise] overmuch" (2:122). He feared that the principle that Madison had introduced was to be used as an excuse to exclude suitable individuals from office. As if ignoring Morris, the Pinckneys proposed applying similar restraints on members of the other two branches, and Gerry wondered even if this went far enough. King observed that requiring "landed property" might end up discriminating against "the monied interest" (2:123).

Dickinson opposed listing any such qualifications within the Constitution. He feared that such "veneration for wealth" (2:123) was inconsistent with republican principles. Madison proposed, and Morris seconded, a motion to strike the word "landed" (2:123) and launched into an extended speech on how representatives should represent the landed, commercial, and manufacturing classes. The convention agreed by a vote of ten to one and then voted to approve Mason's proposal eight to three.

What about electing those with unsettled accounts? Wilson feared that this would "put too much power in the hands of the Auditors" and observed that "We should consider that we are providing a Constitution for future generations, and not merely for the peculiar circumstances of the moment" (2:125). Despite Gerry's fear that Congress might end up consisting of "public debtors, pensioners, placemen & contractors" (2:125), the convention rejected the proposal by a vote of three to seven to one, as, after further comments from Gouverneur Morris, it also struck out disabilities for those with unsettled accounts. After Ellsworth proposed eliminating the rest of the clause, and Charles Pinckney raised objections to excluding debtors, the convention ended up deleting the entire provision by a vote of two to nine.

LOCATION OF THE CAPITAL

Mason next introduced a motion, seconded by Martin, to keep the new capital from being situated in the same city as any existing state capital. He reasoned that such a prohibition would prevent jurisdictional disputes and would serve to discourage giving "a provincial tincture" to national deliberations (2:127). Gouverneur Morris feared this might alienate individuals from New York and Philadelphia. Langdon wanted to know what would keep a state from moving its capital after the national government constructed buildings there; Gorham suggested the national government could simply delay building! Gerry did not want the capital located in any major commercial center. Mason withdrew his motion for the moment, and the convention adjourned until August 6 to await the report of the five-man Committee of Detail.

SOURCES CITED IN THIS CHAPTER

Farrand, Max. 1966. *The Records of the Federal Convention of 1787.* 4 vols. New Haven, CT: Yale University Press.
Wills, Garry. 2003. *"Negro President": Jefferson and the Slave Power.* Boston: Houghton Mifflin.

6

DEBATES OVER THE REPORT OF
THE COMMITTEE OF DETAIL

Likewise To insert essential principles only, lest the operations
of government should be clogged by rendering those provisions permanent and unalterable, which ought to be accommodated to times and events.

—Edmund Randolph's explanation of how the
Committee of Detail proceeded in drafting
a document (Farrand 1966, 2:137)

Experience must be our only guide. Reason may mislead us.

—John Dickinson (Farrand 1966, 2:278)

Once the convention agreed to the Connecticut Compromise, it made
considerable progress as it reviewed and refined the earlier resolutions
from the Committee of the Whole. Having largely completed this task, delegates thought that it was once again time to compile existing resolutions
into a single coherent document that could serve as the source of further
discussion. The convention committed this task to John Rutledge, Edmund
Randolph, Nathaniel Gorham, Oliver Ellsworth, and James Wilson.

PRINCIPLES APPLIED BY
THE COMMITTEE OF DETAIL

The break that the convention took from Thursday, July 26 to Monday,
August 6 to give the Committee of Detail time to do its work was the
longest during the course of the convention. One of the most fascinating

documents from this period is a set of notes in Edmund Randolph's hand-writing, with some changes by Rutledge, that describes how committee members went about drafting a constitution. In what probably represents the sentiment of the entire committee, the notes cited two maxims. One was "To insert essential principles only, lest the operations of government should be clogged by rendering those provisions permanent and unalter-able, which ought to be accommodated to times and events" (Farrand 1966, 2:137). The second focused on using "simple and precise language, and general propositions," patterned on the constitutions of the states (1:137).

As valuable as these precepts proved to be, they did not provide an absolute template for the final document. At this stage, at least, the committee had decided against proposing a preamble. According to Randolph's notes, there was no need to designate the ends of government since "we are not working on the natural rights of men not yet gathered into society, but upon those rights modified by society, and *interwoven with* what we call the rights of states" (2:137; note some emendations). The committee was thinking instead of pointing to the inadequacies of the Articles and advanc-ing a government of three branches, a mechanism that corresponded to the idea of separation of powers, as the only cure. The first resolution of the committee report began with the words "We the people of the States," which, like the Articles of Confederation, it then individually enumerated, "do ordain, declare, and establish the following Constitution for the Gov-ernment of Ourselves and our Posterity" (2:177). Twenty-three articles, similar to Roman numerals within an outline, followed.

AN OUTLINE OF THE REPORT
FROM THE COMMITTEE OF DETAIL

There were relatively few surprises, but the committee had filled in many details, which the delegates debated in the following weeks. Article I pro-posed that the new government should be called "The United States of America" (2:177). Like the original Virginia Plan, Article II provided for dividing this government into legislative, executive, and judicial branches.

Article III vested legislative powers in a bicameral Congress and specified that it would meet each year on the first Monday in December. Article IV designated a House of Representatives whose initial 65 members would be chosen every two years by voters qualified to select members of the most numerous branch of their own state legislatures. The article outlined minimum age (25 years), citizenship and residence requirements, and specified that money bills would originate there. It granted the House "the sole power of impeachment" (2:178–79) and provided for filling vacancies. Article V designated the second house as the Senate. Each state legislature would choose two members who would serve six-year terms. Senators would have to be 30 years or older and, like members of the House, would choose their own officers.

Article VI provided for state legislatures to set times and places for congressional elections subject to congressional oversight. Congress would have power to set uniform property qualifications for members. Thirteen sections further detailed legislative operations.

Article VII may have been the most innovative of the document, and the one that most influenced the final Constitution. The Article delineated eighteen powers that Congress would exercise. These ranged from control over foreign and interstate commerce, to appointing a treasurer, to the power to make war, to the final power "to make all laws that shall be necessary and proper for carrying into execution the foregoing powers" (2:182). Further sections of this article defined treason, introduced the three-fifths formula into that for direct taxation, limited taxation of imports or of the slave trade, and required a two-thirds vote for the adoption of any navigation acts. Article VIII provided for a supremacy clause. Article IX vested the senate with power to appoint ambassadors and judges and provided for a complicated mechanism, not unlike that under the existing Articles of Confederation, for resolving controversies among the states.

Article X designated the executive as the president. Congress was to choose him for a single seven-year term. His powers included most of those, including the power to be commander in chief of military forces, which would make it into the final document.

With a vagueness that would also be reflected in the final document, Article XI proposed vesting the judicial power in a Supreme Court and in such other inferior courts as Congress might create. Judges would serve during good behavior. Section 3 outlined federal jurisdiction, and subsequent sections provided for trial by jury in criminal cases and for judgments in cases of impeachment.

The next several articles (most of which would be incorporated into Article I, Sec. 10 and in Article IV of the final Constitution) addressed the states. Articles XII and XIII provided for limits on them. The following article provided for the privileges and immunities of all state citizens. Article XV provided for extradition of suspected criminals; Article XVI provided for full faith and credit to the acts of other states. Article XVII provided for the admission of new states and Article XVIII for a national guarantee of state republican governments. Additional articles: allowed two-thirds of the state legislatures to call a convention to amend the Constitution; provided for judicial oaths; specified a process for constitutional ratification that required the approval of the existing Congress; and provided for the implementation of the new document and the beginning of a new government.

The committee had gone beyond the work of simple compilation. A new frame of government was taking shape. The convention adjourned and set aside the next day for delegates to examine the work on their own. During this time, James McHenry's notes indicate that delegates from Maryland met to discuss whether voters there would be likely to approve such a system. Martin was convinced that they would not and berated Jennifer for not voting with him. Carroll, Mercer, and Jennifer did not think mere amendments to the Articles would prove adequate; McHenry thought they might. They remain divided. What would the rest of the delegates think?

PROVISIONS RELATIVE TO CONGRESS

After accepting the first two proposed articles, Mason objected to giving each house of Congress a veto of acts by the other house "in all cases," and Gouverneur Morris suggested modifying this provision to refer only to "legislative acts" (Farrand 1966, 2:196). Gorham further wanted Congress to choose the president through a "joint ballot," which he thought would help minimize "delay, contention & confusion" (2:196). The convention ultimately followed a proposal by Madison to strike out the words "in all cases" altogether, since he thought that subsequent provisions already delineated those cases in which the consent of both houses was necessary.

CONGRESSIONAL MEETING TIMES

Madison also questioned whether the Constitution needed to set the meeting date of Congress each year. Gouverneur Morris, and later Rufus King, wondered whether Congress would even need to meet annually. Gorham said that such provisions had not presented problems in his own state. Madison favored providing for one annual meeting, as did Mason. Perhaps somewhat anticipating later congressional investigations, Mason said that if Congress were to have both "*inquisitorial*" and legislative powers, then it "can not safely be long kept in a State of suspension" (2:199). Sherman observed that most state legislatures met annually and that Congress would have plenty to do. The convention then voted to set an opening day that Congress could subsequently vary.

The Committee of Detail had suggested that the annual meeting should be in December, but Gouverneur Morris and Madison preferred May, the month in which the Constitutional Convention had begun. Morris thought this would be more likely to correspond with the time that the United States was hearing of plans that European powers hatched during the winter. Madison thought that travel would be easier in May, but Wilson thought that December was more convenient for business. Consistent with the predominantly rural nature of the country, Ellsworth observed that many legislators would be farmers who needed to be home during the summers. Randolph noted that Congress could change the time once it met, and the convention left the provision as it was proposed, with the stipulation that Congress would meet at least once a year.

VOTING QUALIFICATIONS

Discussion switched to the provision tying the qualifications to vote for members of Congress to those required to vote for members of the most numerous branch of state legislatures. Wilson explained that the committee had found it difficult to devise a single uniform national rule and argued that it was reasonable to link individual state and national qualifications together. Gouverneur Morris said that many states had variable requirements for different offices. Ellsworth thought that "[t]he right of suffrage was a tender point" that states would not want the national government to dictate (2:201). Mason agreed that it was dangerous to vest such power in Congress. Dickinson, by contrast, thought both that it was important to limit the vote to freeholders, and—in an argument that seems to undercut this perceived necessity—that the people would not object to such a requirement since most individuals already fell into this category. Ellsworth wondered how to identify freeholders, especially when it came to merchants whose primary wealth would not be in the form of land.

Addressing concerns that the new government might create an aristocracy, that is, a rule by wealthy elites, Gouverneur Morris speculated that such an aristocracy might actually spring from the House of Representatives. At a time when people cast votes publicly rather than by secret ballot, Morris feared that people without property would sell their votes to the rich. He pointed to the increase of "mechanics & manufacturers who will receive their bread from their employers" (2:202), as people who were not independent enough to vote. He believed, however, that nine-tenths of the people were freeholders and that merchants and others could become freeholders if they chose to do so. Mason suggested that the proper qualification for voting was not the freehold, a concept that had developed in Great Britain, but "every man having evidence of attachment to & permanent common interest with the Society" (2:203). He thought that it was absurd to question the interests of merchants, monied men, and parents! Madison certainly did not think that the convention should entrust Congress with the power to set standards for who should vote. Some states already limited the vote to freeholders, who were its safest depository. By contrast, the landless poor might combine with others to threaten liberty and property.

Dr. Franklin composed an eloquent speech arguing against demeaning "the virtue & public spirit of common people" (2:204). He observed that they had demonstrated considerable courage during the Revolutionary War. He feared that setting a national standard would produce unease among them. Mercer, by contrast, had little faith in the people's judgment and noted how people within towns often outvoted those in the country. Rutledge feared creating distinctions among the people, and the convention overwhelmingly agreed.

Once again, McHenry's notes give some insight into at least one state delegation's thinking. After they discussed a number of proposals that they hoped to change, McHenry openly questioned whether he could consent to ratification of the new Constitution by conventions, rather than by the method specified under the Articles. Consistent with what he would say in the convention the next day, Mercer indicated that he thought the new system was too weak, although he also indicated that he might be willing to "go with the stream" (2:212).

QUALIFICATIONS FOR
THE HOUSE OF REPRESENTATIVES

The Committee of Detail had proposed that members of the House of Representatives should have to be 25 years of age, state residents, and citizens for at least three years. After Mason said that he favored "opening a wide door for emigrants" without, however, allowing "foreigners and adventurers [to] make laws for us & govern us" (2:216), the convention agreed to change the three-year citizenship requirement to seven years. Sherman thought that the word "inhabitant" would be a better term than state "citizen." Morris noted that voters would rarely choose a nonresident. In an eerie premonition of the controversy between advocates and opponents of slavery that would later take place in Kansas prior to the U.S. Civil War, Mason feared that, without a sufficient residence requirement, men in one state might corrupt men from other states to vote there. After voting down several alternatives, the convention voted to keep the section as written. It also voted for an amendment by Williamson to apportion the House according "to the rule hereafter to be provided for direct taxation," which would count each slave as three-fifths of a person (2:219).

SLAVERY AND RELATED ISSUES

Despite Williamson's efforts to gloss over the slavery issue, Rufus King of Massachusetts detonated a rhetorical land mine. He had not, he said, previously objected to the formula to count slaves as three-fifths of a person toward representation in the House of Representatives, but it now appeared as though the new government would both allow for continuing slave importation and prohibit the taxation of exports. The government needed to be able to protect the nation from both foreign and domestic threats, but continuing to add slaves simply increased the latter, since, under the new system, free states would be responsible for protecting slave states against insurrection by those whom they were enslaving. Undercutting the moral force of his argument against slavery by expressing his willingness to trade it for a northern interest, however, King concluded that "either slaves should not be represented, or exports should be taxable" (2:220).

Although Sherman thought that the "slave-trade" was "iniquitous," or sinful (2:220), he did not think this was time to revisit the issue. Similarly, Madison expressed greater concern over the formula (one for every 40,000 people), which he thought would eventually result in too many representatives. Gorham openly scoffed at whether it was likely that the new nation with large western territories could last 150 years or more, but the other delegates were hopeful enough to insert words making the 1-to-40,000 formula a floor rather than fixed requirement.

Gouverneur Morris was next to raise the slavery issue by proposing that the formula for representation in the first house should count only "free" inhabitants. He delivered a withering critique of slavery. It was "a nefarious institution"; it was "the curse of heaven on the States where it prevailed." Where slavery began, "prosperity & happiness" was replaced by "misery and poverty" (2:221). If slaves were men, they should be permitted to vote! If they were property, they should count for no more than other forms! Morris explained his reaction to the three-fifths clause: "the inhabitant of Georgia and S.C. who goes to the Coast of Africa, and in defiance of the most sacred laws of humanity tears away his fellow creatures from their dearest connections & dam[n]s them to the most cruel bondages, shall have more votes in a Govt. instituted for protection of the rights of mankind, than the Citizen of Pa or N. Jersey who views with a laudable horror, so nefarious a practice" (2:222). And then, in perhaps the greatest lost opportunity of the convention, Morris proclaimed that "He would sooner submit himself to a tax for paying for all the Negroes in the U. States. than saddle posterity with such a constitution" (2:223).

One can only imagine what might have happened had several delegates begun discussing this possibility seriously (and the result may well have been fruitless or even counterproductive), but they had assembled to reform a governmental structure rather than to free the slaves, and Morris's words appear to have been little more than a rhetorical flourish. Sherman did not think slave representation was a major issue. Pointing to issues that spotlighted other regions of the country and that were often tied together in navigation treaties, Charles Pinckney thought "the fisheries & the Western frontier" (2:223) were far more burdensome than slaves. The convention rejected Morris's motion, and it further tweaked the 1-to-40,000 ratio by guaranteeing each state at least one representative in the House.

Next on the agenda was the restriction limiting the origination of money bills to the House of Representatives. Although Mason "was unwilling to travel over this ground again" (2:224), other delegates were not as reluctant, and after several objections to the proposal, including one by Madison, the convention voted to strike this limitation, which had originally been part of the Connecticut Compromise. This vote did not end the matter; the very next morning, delegates announced that they wanted a re-vote.

FILLING SENATORIAL VACANCIES

After they made this intention clear, Wilson objected to the provision in Article V proposing that state executives should fill vacancies in the U.S. Senate. He thought this mechanism was too far removed from the people since in most states the legislators were responsible for choosing governors. Randolph, by contrast, thought that this provision might be needed, especially in cases where the legislatures only met once a year. Ellsworth argued that, as written, the provision could be interpreted to allow the state legislatures to make such appointments when they were in session. The convention left the provision in place with some explanatory words that Madison suggested, and voted for per capita voting only after it was clear that the convention would return to a discussion of the origination of money bills.

DURATIONAL CITIZENSHIP REQUIREMENTS

Discussion followed on senatorial qualifications. Gouverneur Morris proposed a citizenship qualification of fourteen years instead of four. Ellsworth feared this would discourage the migration of "meritorious aliens" (Farrand 1966, 2:235). Charles Pinckney argued that extra precautions were needed for a body that dealt with foreign affairs. Were it not for the contributions that foreigners had made to the U.S. Revolution, Mason said that he would have favored excluding the non–native born from the body altogether. Madison feared the proposed emendations would "give a tincture of illiberality to the Constitution" by discouraging "the most desirable class of people from emigrating to the U.S." (2:236). He thought that "men who love liberty and wish to partake [of] its blessings," would "feel the mortification of being marked with suspicious incapacitations" (2:236). By contrast, Butler feared that individuals who were born abroad would not only feel continuing attachments to their countries of origin but would also import dangerous political ideas. Franklin, who in addition to having spent numerous years abroad, had also written a letter of introduction for Thomas Paine when he had immigrated to America, sided with Madison in fearing the introduction of "illiberality" (2:236) into the Constitution. After reminding fellow delegates of the contributions that foreigners had made to the patriot cause, Randolph said he would not favor a requirement of more than seven years.

Wilson pointed out that he had been born abroad. He thought it would be odd if individuals like him could be trusted to help formulate a constitution but not to serve under it! He repeated Madison's and Franklin's fear that this would lend an "illiberal complexion" to the system (2:237). Indeed, he noted that when he had moved to Maryland, he found himself under a similar incapacity, which he had found to be both "grating, and mortifying" (2:237).

Perhaps attempting to undercut Wilson's personal appeal, Gouverneur Morris counseled fellow delegates to be "governed as much by our reason, and as little by our feelings as possible" (2:237). He further counseled moderation—through the use of an illustration far more likely to appeal to passion than to reason—by observing that delegates should not emulate certain unspecified Indian tribes whose hospitality reputedly extended to offering their wives and daughters to visitors! Although earlier in the convention, he had described himself as a representative of "the whole human race" (1:529), Morris now professed not to trust "citizens of the world." He explained that "The men who can shake off their attachments to their own Country can never love any other" (2:238). Safeguards were needed.

After rejecting Morris's proposal for a minimum citizenship of 14 years, the convention began a kind of reverse bidding. It rejected 13 years and 10 years before finally settling on 9, which was two years longer than the minimum years of citizenship that it had accepted for House members.

CONGRESSIONAL OVERSIGHT OF FEDERAL ELECTIONS

The delegates next discussed whether Congress should have the right to oversee federal elections. Fellow South Carolinians Charles Pinckney and John Rutledge both thought such matters should be purely left to the states. Madison followed Gorham in suggesting that federal oversight was needed. He noted that members of Congress would themselves be accountable to those who elected them for such oversight. King thought such a congressional power was a concomitant to judging the election returns of its members, and after Sherman concurred, while professing confidence in the states, the convention voted to retain this proposed oversight.

PROPERTY QUALIFICATIONS FOR MEMBERS OF CONGRESS

On Friday, August 10, delegates discussed the proposal in Article VI allowing Congress to establish property qualifications for its members. Charles Pinckney favored listing the specific qualification in the Constitution rather than leaving them to congressional determination. Opposing an "undue aristocratic influence in the Constitution," he still thought that it was important that members "be possessed of competent property to make them independent & respectable" (Farrand 1966, 2:248). He believed that a president should be worth at least $100,000 and judges and legislators at least half of that, although he was willing to leave the specific amount blank for the moment. Fellow delegate Rutledge concurred.

Ellsworth thought that regional differences would make it difficult to fix such an amount and favored leaving the matter to "legislative discretion" (2:249). Franklin again stood up for "the common people"—"Some of the greatest rogues he was ever acquainted with, were the richest rogues" (2:249). Scripture warned against covetous rulers. "Partiality to the rich" would demean the United States (2:249). The convention rejected Pinckney's motion by voice vote.

Madison thought that, if there were to be qualifications, it would be better for the Constitution to specify them than to leave them to legislative discretion. He argued that it would be just as improper for members to establish their own qualifications as to set their own wages! Ellsworth did not see a similar danger, but Williamson thought that, absent some guidelines, legislators might seek to limit offices to members of their own kind, for example, fellow lawyers. The convention voted to delete this section, after which it moved to reconsider a three-year, instead of a seven-year, citizenship requirement for members of the House of Representatives on the following Monday.

QUORUMS AND OTHER CONGRESSIONAL MATTERS

The Committee of Detail had proposed in Article VI that a majority of members should constitute a quorum of each house. Gorham thought that the bar was too high and might result in delay. Mercer feared that members of Congress might be able to stymie business by absenting themselves.

By contrast, Colonel Mason feared that without a majority quorum, western states that would have to send their delegates longer distances might arrive at the capital only to find that delegates from eastern states had conducted business in their absence. If the legislature had too much discretion, a junto, or faction, might rule! King pointed to difficulties on the other side of the issue. Gouverneur Morris proposed setting the number at 33 of 65 in the House and 14 of 26 in the Senate, which was amended to leave this as a base. Ellsworth and Wilson thought this number was too low. The convention ultimately settled on a remedy that Madison suggested of keeping a quorum at a majority but allowing Congress to compel attendance through the use of penalties.

What about votes to expel members? Madison thought this should require a vote of two-thirds of the members, and Randolph, Mason, and Carroll agreed. Although Gouverneur Morris managed to divide his state, all the others agreed to Madison's modification.

Professing concern for the small states, Gouverneur Morris wanted to empower any member to call for a recorded vote rather than requiring one-fifth or more to make such a request. Sherman questioned the value of such recorded votes since they were not accompanied by explanations. Gorham said that such a motion should require support by more than one member, and the convention agreed, but it limited requests for recorded votes to legislative matters, apparently in an attempt to exempt the Senate in cases where it was dealing with diplomatic issues.

On August 11, delegates began discussing the provision that required Congress to keep records of its proceedings. After some discussion of whether this should include matters relative to military affairs, Ellsworth suggested that the provision should be deleted altogether. Although the delegates were participating in secret debates, Wilson responded, with no apparent sense of irony, that "the people have a right to know what their Agents are doing or have done," and publication should not be optional (2:260). Wilson observed that since the Articles already had such a publication provision, individuals would notice and might question a change. The convention adopted the motion but then watered it down by adding a proviso allowing secrecy when Congress thought it necessary.

The convention next considered a provision allowing houses to adjourn to another place. King feared this might result in undue changes in the location of the capital, and Madison agreed to his suggestion that such a change should require adoption of a law. This led to a discussion as to whether the capital would remain permanently in New York. Madison, who would continue his efforts when he was elected to the new Congress, effectively began lobbying for "a central place" (2:261)—undoubtedly Virginia!—where the new government could be located.

Delegates had already announced an intention to reconsider the decision deleting the requirement that money bills originate in the house. Randolph presented this provision as important both in honoring the Connecticut Compromise and for soliciting popular support. He believed it would give somewhat more power to the House of Representatives. Although Charles Pinckney thought that reconsideration would waste time, the convention voted overwhelmingly for it.

YEARS OF CITIZENSHIP FOR
MEMBERS OF THE FIRST HOUSE

As agreed, on the following Monday, August 13, the convention began by reconsidering the years of citizenship required for members of the House. Randolph favored changing seven years to four, and Wilson seemed to favor leaving the time to legislative determination rather than constitutional stipulation. Gerry wanted to confine membership to native-born citizens, largely because he feared that those born abroad might be subject to influence by foreign powers. Williamson favored extending the time from seven years to nine, and commented negatively on the "luxurious examples" that some immigrants were bringing with them (Farrand 1966, 2:268). Hamilton, who had—like Wilson—been born abroad, did not favor any such constitutional provision but was willing to allow Congress to impose such restraints. Madison seconded Williamson's motion, likely as a means of foreclosing more draconian measures. Wilson noted that his home state of Pennsylvania had largely prospered because of its openness to immigrants. The convention voted against alternatives, including proposals for nine years and four years. Gouverneur Morris then proposed exempting any current citizens. Rutledge did not think they needed an exemption any more than individuals who were under 25 and would no longer be eligible to run for the House; the nation needed the same security against all of those who were born abroad, whether they were currently citizens or not. Sherman did not think that the national government owed immigrants anything; states had invited immigrants from abroad and should be free to set or change such requirements at their pleasure. Gorham did not want to distinguish between natural-born and naturalized citizens.

Madison then attacked the "peculiarity of the doctrine of Mr. Sherman" (2:270). Madison feared that Sherman's argument might become the basis of future evasions of public debts. The national government had an obligation to honor faith pledged by states on all such matters. Backing away from such pledges would "expose us to . . . reproaches" (2:271). Morris attempted to distinguish the age and citizenship requirements. No assurances had even been given to people under 25 that they could run for office. Charles Pinckney noted that the United States could not be bound to respect widely differing state naturalization requirements. Mason was impressed not by the "*peculiarity*" but by the "*propriety*" of Sherman's reasoning (2:271). A new government needed to take proper precautions "in the outset" (2:271). Wilson read the provision within his state's constitution guaranteeing full rights to immigrants after two years and thought that foreign princes would make hay out of any alteration of this pledge. Mercer agreed. Baldwin saw no difference between age and durational citizenship requirements. After the convention defeated Morris's motion and a proposal for five years, it affirmed the section with its specification of seven years.

THE ORIGINATION OF MONEY BILLS

The convention next returned to the provision limiting the origination of money bills to the House of Representatives. Randolph proposed modifying the proposal so as to apply only to laws passed "for the *purpose of revenue*" and observed that this provision had been part of the essential Connecticut Compromise. Mason agreed that the change was desirable. He observed that only the people's branch should be able to tax them, and the Senate did not directly represent the people but the states. Mason believed that the chief danger in republican government was the danger that demagogues would arise who would help the majority oppress the minority. Serving for six-year terms, senators might be able to appropriate money for themselves if given the chance. He did not necessarily oppose the Senate's terms, but "the pursestrings should be in the hands of the Representatives of the people" (Farrand 1966, 2:274).

By contrast, Wilson feared that the provision at issue would lead to disputes between the two houses for which the proposed constitution provided no mediator. He feared that the House would insert other matters into money bills, make them interdependent, and thus destroy the Senate's deliberative powers. As to Mason's analogy, "the purse was to have two strings" (2:275), one in each house, and the house should not be denied it proper role in such matters.

Gerry believed that the provision for originating money bills had been essential to the Connecticut Compromise and that the people would not permit anyone, other than their immediate representatives, from originating such bills. Gouverneur Morris thought that the Senate could just as easily prevail against the House by withholding consent as by originating its own bills. Madison thought the Senate should at least have the power to "*diminish* the sums to be raised" thus "checking the extravagance of the other House" (2:276). Noting how one of the "greatest evils incident to Republican Govt. was the spirit of contention & faction" (2:276), he thought this provision would perpetuate it. He observed that the term revenue was ambiguous, and illustrated by pointing to disputes prior to the Revolutionary War as to what British measures were for taxation and which were for trade. He feared that the unequal status of the two houses in relation to such bills would result in greater inflexibility.

One of the most refreshing aspects of the Constitutional Convention is that it reveals a group of serious men who were committed to making the best arguments to come up with the best possible document. In this respect, the Constitution is a tribute to the eighteenth-century view of itself as an age of reason. Some decisions at the convention were the product of deductive, or syllogistic, reasoning. As he spoke, however, Delaware's John Dickinson observed that facts, the components of inductive, or scientific, reasoning, should also play a major role. In his words, "Experience must be our only guide. Reason may mislead us" (2:278). In his mind, such experience demonstrated the utility of "restraining money bills to the immediate representatives of the people" (2:178). England restricted the origination of money bills to the House of Commons. Eight of the existing states limited the origination of money bills to the lower house, but most of these allowed the upper house to amend. That is what he favored. By adopting such a provision, the convention would undercut arguments that the new Constitution was too aristocratic. Randolph agreed with this class analysis. He also believed that the right to declare war should originate in the more popular branch.

Rutledge came down on the other side. He believed that the Senate's right to amend would be "a mere tub to the whale" (2:279), or distraction. If the right to originate money bills were to be limited to one house, he would prefer that it would be the senate. As to state experience, much of it had followed in "blind adherence to the British model" (2:279). Within his own state, the mechanism had proved to be divisive. Carroll said that Maryland had expressed similar difficulties. Several succeeding votes to add or amend a money bill provision failed.

ELIGIBILITY OF MEMBERS OF CONGRESS TO OTHER JOBS

On the following day, August 14, Charles Pinckney questioned the proposed provision making members of Congress ineligible for jobs that had been created during their terms or for one year afterwards. In his view, the stipulation was "degrading," "inconvenient," and "impolitic" (Farrand 1966, 2:283). He expressed hope that the Senate might "become a School of Public Ministers, a nursery of Statesmen" (2:283), and he favored allowing them to take such jobs as long as they resigned from Congress. Observing that Mason was speaking ironically, Madison records that Mason then proposed to strike the whole section in favor of an aristocracy, or rule of elites, which most delegates believed was inimical to republican government. Mercer said that a "first principle in political science" was "that whenever the rights of property are secured, an aristocracy will grow out of it" (2:284). In an argument that tracked Hamilton's earlier defense of English "corruption," Mercer argued that in the absence of force, the executive would need influence, which his ability to make appointments would further. Mercer also wanted to reconsider allying the president with a Council of Revision.

Gerry said that his instructions from his state forbade him from allowing members of Congress to hold other offices under the new government. He did not think the provision at issue was "degrading." Rather, he argued, "Confidence is the road to tyranny" (2:285). He did not favor the establishment of multiple ministries, and, unlike Pinckney, he did not want the two houses of Congress to serve as their "nurseries" (2:285). If legislators were to be so rapacious as to serve in the hope of such offices, it would be better to have "a single despot" (2:285). To Gerry, Mercer sounded as though he thought government was based on "plunder" (2:285). Gerry feared that the Senate, with longer terms and smaller state delegations, could degenerate into a junto. He would prefer to prevent members of either house from taking government jobs for at least a year after they left the body.

Gouverneur Morris thought it was just as undesirable to create a class of persons who were ineligible to appointments as it was to exclude members of the armed forces from such jobs. Williamson feared that the convention had created a House of Lords. He traced most instances of corruption within his own state of North Carolina to "office hunting" (2:287). Sherman thought the delegates should do all that they could to reduce the temptation to corruption. Charles Pinckney noted that state constitutions had not imposed a disability on members. Gouverneur Morris feared that imposing a disability on legislators would deprive the nation of needed talent. Pennsylvania had not found such an expedient necessary for its own officers. Ellsworth did not think a one-year disability would have much impact. Mercer reiterated that the new government needed both "force" and "influence" on its side (2:289). A disability on federal offices might drive the best men into positions at the state level. Wilson and Morris renewed fears that a disability might disqualify men of merit, the latter focusing on the need for military commanders. The convention split evenly on the matter and then postponed whether to make a special exception for those chosen to serve in the military.

PAY FOR MEMBERS OF CONGRESS

The Committee of Detail had suggested that *states* should pay their members of Congress. Ellsworth objected that this would lead to undue dependence on them. Gouverneur Morris added that this burden would fall more heavily on distant states but then asserted that members of Congress would not be tempted to overpay themselves. While Ellsworth feared dependency, Butler thought that members of Congress, especially in the Senate, should be reminded of whom they were serving. Langdon reiterated Morris's fears that this would burden distant states. Madison pointed to a possible disconnect between members of Congress who were elected biennially and state legislatures that met annually. Expressing his continuing faith in "[t]her enlargement of the sphere of the Government" (Farrand 1966, 2:291), which he would later elaborate in Federalist No. 10, he suggested that perhaps the convention should set a minimum and maximum salary to be ascertained by the states. Gerry noted the possibility that states would reduce salaries in order to rid themselves of their senators. Mason observed that, as worded, members of both houses would be beholden to the states. Broom did not think state legislatures had abused the power to set their own salaries. Sherman feared that legislatures would set salaries so low that only those who were rich would be able to serve. He suggested that the national government pay five dollars a day and let states who wanted to do so add more. Carroll said that this provision compounded the problem caused by not disabling members of Congress from resigning and accepting state jobs. Using a catchy analogy, he observed that "The new Govt. in this form was nothing more than a second edition of Congress in two volumes, instead of one, and perhaps with very few amendments" (2:292).

Dickinson emphasized "the necessity of making the Genl. Govt. independent of the prejudices, passions, and improper views of the State Legislature" but thought there were difficulties in setting congressional pay based on the price of a commodity like wheat (something Madison had suggested on an earlier day) and proposed that Congress adjust salaries every 12 years (2:292). The convention voted nine to two to pay members of Congress from the national treasury, and rejected a proposal to fix their pay at five dollars a day plus five dollars for every 30 miles traveled. Dickinson subsequently withdrew a motion that would have required the same pay for members of both houses, because arguments had convinced him that senators might have to stay longer, especially during times of war.

Delegates must have been wearied to return on August 15 to a discussion of whether the origination of money bills should be left to the House. Strong and Mason wanted this provision restored. Mason was already concerned that the Senate "could already sell the whole Country by means of Treaties" (2:297). Given the division of opinion as to whether the Senate might threaten liberty, Williamson wondered what harm such a provision could do but suggested postponing a decision until after the powers of the Senate had been established. Mercer did not think the Senate should have power over treaties, and the convention voted to postpone further action on money bills.

COUNCIL OF REVISION AND VETO POWERS

Madison had still not abandoned his cherished idea of a Council of Revision. He proposed, and Wilson seconded, a motion submitting all laws to the executive and the Supreme Court and requiring two-thirds votes to override if one objected, and a three-fourths vote if both did. Charles Pinckney objected that involving members of the judiciary in legislation would bias their future judgments. Mercer favored the measure, but stated his opinion that judges should not have the power to declare laws to be unconstitutional; "laws ought to be well and cautiously made, and then to be uncontroulable" (2:298). Delegates defeated Madison's motion by a vote of three to eight.

Gouverneur Morris, who was particularly concerned about state inflationary policies, suggested substituting three-fourths majorities of both houses of Congress for the two-thirds that the Committee of Detail had recommended to override a veto. Dickinson agreed with Mercer about the dangers of judicial review. Morris then suggested an absolute executive veto as a way to check legislative usurpations. Sherman wondered why the people should trust one man over the others. Carroll wanted to postpone a vote, and Wilson reiterated the danger of legislative usurpation. He observed that although it was more common to associate the words "*King* and *Tyrant*," a legislature could act in similar fashion, and it was important to give the executive and judiciary a "defensive power" (2:301). The convention voted six to four to two to change the size of the congressional majority to override vetoes from two-thirds to three-fourths, a move it would later reverse. The convention also voted to give the president ten days, instead of seven, to exercise his veto. The following morning the convention also widened the kinds of legislation that the president could veto.

CONGRESSIONAL POWERS

That same day, delegates began examining the proposed congressional powers to levy duties and imposts. Delegates disputed whether the terms duties and imposts had different meanings. Mason thought the South would require some prohibition against the taxation of exports. Rutledge wanted similar security for the importation of slaves, and Gouverneur Morris objected that one of these provisions (it is not altogether clear which one, although he had earlier given a strong speech against slavery) was "so radically objectionable, that it might cost the whole system the support of some members" (Farrand 1966, 2:306). Madison did not share Mason's sentiments. He thought that it was proper to tax exports, that the power should be vested in the national government, that it might be particularly useful with respect to products like tobacco, that it would be unfair to allow states to tax the exports of other states, that the South could not complain because it would require more naval protection, and that delegates should remember that they were legislating not simply for the moment but for a time when states would be more equalized in respect to such matters.

Delegates joined in the debate over taxing exports. Gerry feared that such taxation "might ruin the Country" (2:307) whereas Gouverneur Morris thought they might prove to be "a necessary source of revenue" (2:307). Mercer argued that Madison had things backward—the South was saddled with promoting the vessels of the North, without which they could hire foreign ships. Most speakers did agree that states had abused the power to tax the exports of neighboring states. Ultimately, only Gerry voted against the proposal.

Today's Congress exercises most of its powers under the interstate and foreign commerce clause, but the convention, which may well have been more focused on existing state abuses than on future exercises of national power, unanimously accepted this and other powers with no recorded discussion. Delegates did discuss whether Congress should be able to emit (issue) bills of credit and/or print paper money. Mason was among those who "had a mortal hatred to paper money" (2:309) but was unwilling to tie the legislature's hands completely. Randolph would express similar sentiments. Mercer, by contrast, favored paper money and did not want the convention to alienate others who agreed with him. Ellsworth thought this was an appropriate time to stop paper money altogether, and Read, who did not hide his own emotions, compared paper money to the mark of the beast in the Biblical book of Revelation! The convention approved the congressional power to borrow but rejected the power to emit paper money.

Some delegates raised questions over whether Congress or the president should have power to appoint the treasurer, but ended up leaving the appointment to a joint vote of both houses. Delegates tinkered with provisions related to piracies and counterfeiting. They then discussed whether Congress should have to wait to subdue rebellion in a state until state legislatures requested such help. Luther Martin thought that such a request was critical, but Ellsworth proposed that either elective branch should be able to request help. Gerry observed that federal intervention in Shays's Rebellion within his own state would have made matters worse than they were. In regard to the executive, Gouverneur Morris accused fellow delegates of first forming "a strong man" and then tying his hands (2:317)! The convention agreed to a modified power that provided federal help in cases where the legislature was not in session.

The convention next examined the congressional power to make war. Charles Pinckney had a number of objections. He thought that Congress acted too slowly to wield such a power effectively. He thought the House would be too large. By contrast, the Senate would be more equipped to act and would more fairly represent all the states. Madison and Gerry then moved to change the word "make" to "declare" and grant the executive the power to repel unexpected attacks. Sherman liked the change. Gerry feared it would increase executive power unduly. The convention nonetheless voted for this change while rejecting an additional power to declare peace.

On Saturday, August 18, a number of new powers that James Madison and Charles Pinckney had devised were referred to the Committee of Detail for consideration. Mason was interested in giving Congress power to regulate the militia in hopes that it could avoid large standing armies during times of peace. The militia of individual states would require some coordination that Congress could provide. Other delegates mentioned other powers. Mason thought that it was important to limit the period during which new taxes would be levied. Rutledge wanted to create a committee to consider whether the national government should assume state debts; Sherman suggested that it would be better simply to give Congress permission to do so.

Instead, the convention formed a Grand Committee on State Debt and Militias (also to be known as the Committee of Eleven) consisting of a delegate from each state present (New York delegates had gone home), namely John Langdon, Rufus King, Roger Sherman, William Livingston, George Clymer, John Dickinson, James McHenry, George Mason, Hugh Williamson, Charles Cotesworth Pinckney, and Abraham Baldwin. After Rutledge observed that the length of the convention was making both delegates and members of the public impatient, delegates also accepted a motion to begin work each day at 10:00 a.m. and to stay until 4:00 p.m.

Ellsworth still wanted to create a presidential council. He suggested that it might include the president of the Senate, the chief justice, and cabinet ministers. Charles Pinckney thought it would be better for the president to consult advisers on his own than to bind him with a council. Gerry disfavored giving department heads or justices anything to do with legislation.

Gerry wanted a provision against standing armies in times of peace and suggested, with Martin's concurrence, limiting the number to 2,000 to 3,000. Washington, who had some real-world experience in this area, is reputed facetiously to have suggested, as a countermotion, that "no foreign enemy should invade the United States at any time, with more than three thousand troops" (Hutson 1987, 229)! The convention rejected the proposal.

Mason then introduced his proposal to allow national regulation of the militia subject to state appointment of its officers. Dickinson proposed allowing the general government to regulate only one-fourth of the militia at once, while Mason proposed either establishment of, or regulation of, only a "select militia" (2:331). Madison questioned whether the power over militia could be divided between two sets of governments. Sherman said that states would never give up their defense against possible "invasions and insurrections, and for enforcing obedience to their laws" (2:332), which, like taxation, he considered to be a concurrent, or mutually exercised, power. Gerry continued to express his distrust of the national government. In the end, the convention entrusted such issues to the Grand Committee.

On Monday, August 20, the convention further submitted a list of proposals advanced by Charles Pinckney to the Grand Committee. Interestingly these included provisions: for a writ of habeas corpus (used to release individuals from custody in cases where the government did not file formal charges); for liberty of the press; against religious tests; and for a great Seal of the United States. Gouverneur Morris, in turn, proposed consideration of a Council of State that would include the chief justice and secretaries of Domestic Affairs, Commerce and Finance, Foreign Affairs, War, the Marine, and State.

Mason, who had hired an architect to design his own Gunston Hall both inside and out in the best colonial tradition, further proposed enabling Congress to enact sumptuary laws, regulating food, drink, and clothing. Delegates defeated the measure after several objections including Gerry's sage observation that "the law of necessity is the best sumptuary law" (2:344).

There are times when the convention seemed to strain at a gnat and swallow a camel. Thus, the provision granting Congress the power to make all laws that were "necessary and proper," like the provision granting it powers over commerce, sailed through without recorded objection. By contrast, Madison thought that the definition of treason as levying war against the United States or adhering to their enemies was too narrow and favored an English definition outlined in a statute under Edward III, with which other delegates seemed familiar. After several delegates joined the fray, the convention settled on a rather minor revision, only to confront the question as to whether it was possible to commit treason against the national government only or also against the states. Language allowing for punishing either but requiring the testimony of two or more witnesses to an overt act was followed by additional discussion, much of which still centered around the difficulties connected to the idea of dual sovereignty. Further votes followed. By contrast, when King asked a fairly consequential question about the meaning of "direct taxation," Madison reported that no one answered (2:350)!

FIRST REPORT FROM THE COMMITTEE ON STATE DEBTS AND MILITIA

On Tuesday, August 21, Livingston reported that the Committee of Eleven was recommending that Congress would have power to fulfill obligations for debts that had been incurred under the Articles, and to make laws to regulate militiamen, whose officers would be appointed by the states. Gerry thought that the first provision would undermine public faith by "giving the power only, without adopting the obligation" of existing debts (Farrand 1966, 2:356). Sherman said it offered no more or less than the existing government under the Articles, and the convention tabled the proposal.

Several motions, most of which were withdrawn, delayed, or negated, followed before the convention considered a provision prohibiting congressional taxation of exports or on the importation of slaves. New Hampshire's

Langdon feared that this would still allow individual *states* to enact taxes on exports, which he thought would be unacceptable, but Ellsworth thought that Congress would be able to prevent such taxes under its authority to regulate commerce. Ellsworth further favored the ban on congressional taxation of exports, because he thought such taxes would "discourage industry," result in unfairness, and "engender incurable jealousies" among the states (2:360). Williamson said it would be unacceptable to allow one state to tax goods coming in from another state. Gouverneur Morris thought that there would be times when the government might need to tax exports. Dickinson also thought the power was needed, although he thought it might be possible to list some exceptions to it. Sherman disfavored such discrimination and wanted the power prohibited altogether.

Madison observed that delegates should "be governed by national and permanent views" (2:361), which he thought might in time require some taxes on exports. Long before he would advocate embargoes against Great Britain as secretary of state and president, he further observed that "An Embargo may be of absolute necessity, and can alone by effectuated by the Genl. Authority" (2:361). He favored allowing Congress to tax both imports and exports. Ellsworth did not think the section prohibited an embargo, and McHenry thought that the government could declare an embargo as part of its war powers. Wilson favored national regulation over state taxation of exports whereas Gerry feared that such a power "will enable the Genl Govt to oppress the States, as much as Ireland is oppressed by Great Britain" (2:372). Mason thought that those who favored "reducing the States to mere corporations" (2:362) would favor taxing state exports, but he feared that the majority would oppress the minority at every opportunity and saw distinct differences in interest between the North and South on this matter. He specifically cited tobacco. Clymer noted that other states would have their own unique crops. His proposal to amend the clause by limiting taxation to matters of revenue failed, as did a measure that Madison introduced to require congressional majorities of two-thirds to enact such measures. The convention voted instead to prohibit taxes on exports, with the five southern states all in agreement, though Madison observed that both he and Washington did not so concur.

IMPORTATION AND TAXATION OF SLAVES

Luther Martin then proposed to alter the report by the Committee of Detail so as to allow either the prohibition or taxation of slaves. He feared that otherwise the three-fifths clause would encourage further importation, which he believed would weaken the union by increasing the chances of domestic insurrection and would be "inconsistent with the principles of the revolution and dishonorable to the American character" (Farrand 1966, 2:364). Rutledge denied either that the section would encourage importation or that slave insurrections were a serious problem. As to morality, he responded somewhat cynically that "Religion & humanity had nothing to do with this question—Interest alone is the governing principles with Nations" (2:364). Northern states should recognize that increasing the number of slaves would increase the number of goods that they would ship. Ellsworth also suggested that "the morality or wisdom of slavery are considerations belonging to the States themselves" (2:364). What enriched one section would serve to enrich all. Charles Pinckney added that South Carolina would never agree to a plan that prohibited the slave trade, although he thought his state might eventually suppress it as Virginia and Maryland had done.

The following day, Sherman proposed leaving the section as it stood. He "disapproved of the slave trade" (2:369) but noted that states already possessed the right to import slaves, and restricting it might pose an additional obstacle to ratification. What followed was almost surreal. George Mason, who was one of the convention's largest slaveholders, began a tirade against the institution, which he linked to "the avarice of British Merchants" (2:370). He pointed to the way that the British had further encouraged slave insurrection during the Revolutionary War and said that allowing South Carolina and Georgia to import slaves undercut prohibitions by Maryland and Virginia. He further feared that these states would be a conduit for the introduction of slavery into the western states. His attack on the institution was every bit as dramatic as Gouverneur Morris's had been: "Slavery discourages arts & manufactures. The poor despise labor when performed by slaves. They prevent the immigration of Whites who really enrich & strengthen a Country. They produce the most pernicious effect on manners. Every master of slaves is born a petty tyrant. They bring the judgment of heaven on a Country" (2:370). He further implicated "our Eastern [northern] brethren" (2:370) in the trade. He thought the national government should be equipped to discourage its spread.

Connecticut's Ellsworth seemed put off by what he probably considered to be Mason's hypocrisy. Noting that "As he had never owned a slave [he] could not judge of the effects of slavery on character" (2:371), he said that if a moral course were to be followed, then slaves already in the country should be freed! Further identifying what he believed to be the financial interest behind Mason's rhetoric, he suggested that slaves multiplied faster in Mason's state and Maryland than in the swampier states to the South. Then, in a statement that might explain why even those with strong moral objections to slavery did not demand more, Ellsworth (who, in fairness, could hardly have anticipated Eli Whitney's invention of the cotton gin, which increased the value of slave labor in the South) made a stunningly inaccurate prediction, at least for the time period up to the Civil War: "As population increases; poor laborers will be so plenty as to render slaves useless. Slavery in time will not be a speck in our Country" (2:371). He noted that Massachusetts had already abolished it, and Connecticut was beginning to do so. He further somewhat optimistically hypothesized that the threat of insurrection would provide "a motive to kind treatment of the slaves" (2:371).

The South Carolinians followed. Charles Pinckney said that slavery was "justified by the example of all the world" (2:371). He believed South Carolina would eventually vote to stop the trade, but he also thought that the state would resent being told that it must do so. General Pinckney hazarded that he and his colleagues did not have sufficient influence to carry South Carolina and Georgia unless the Constitution included protections for slavery. Seeking to undercut Mason's argument, he further distinguished between Virginia's desire for the value of their slaves to rise so that they could sell them and those of South Carolina and Georgia in needing to obtain them cheaply to work them. He repeated Rutledge's early argument that more slaves would result in more production and greater commerce for all.

Baldwin said that he thought the convention had been called to deal with national issues rather than local ones, and Georgia would not look kindly on "an attempt to abridge one of her favorite prerogatives" (2:372). Although he believed his state "may probably put a stop to the evil" (2:372), he arguably highlighted the racism underlying the institution (and its incompatibility with the principles of the Declaration of Independence) by comparing opponents of slavery to those, presumably Hindus, who wanted to extend the idea of the "*equality of men*" to "the whole animal creation" (2:372).

Wilson logically questioned why the southernmost states were so adamantly attached to a practice that they claimed they would probably eliminate. He further questioned why slaves should be the only import exempt from an import tax. Although Gerry did not believe that slavery was a national concern, he also did not think the convention should approve it. Dickinson thought it was "inadmissible on every principle of honor & safety" to authorize further importation (2:372), and he thought the problem was a proper matter for national authorities to address.

Williamson said that his state of North Carolina did not prohibit, but that it did tax, imported slaves, putting a higher tax on those from states where slavery had been abolished. He did not think northern states should force their view on southerners. King could see no reason to exempt slave imports and not others. Langdon did not think delegates should rely on assurances from southern states that they might abolish the slave trade. General Pinckney affirmed that he did not expect his state to stop the trade permanently but, perhaps as a way to appeal to northern interests, he suggested that he would not oppose having slaves taxed like other imports. Gouverneur Morris, who had earlier spoken in terms of morality, now suggested striking a "bargain" between North and South (2:374). Sherman justifiably feared that permitting an import tax might be thought to confirm that the nation regarded slaves as property. With recognition of the feelings of Quakers and Methodists in free states, Randolph wanted to seek "some middle ground" (2:374). Despite Ellsworth's fears that the convention was widening options when it should be narrowing them, delegates voted to send this and related matters to a new committee on Slave Trade and Navigation. It included John Langdon, Rufus King, William Johnson, William Livingston, George Clymer, John Dickinson, Luther Martin, James Madison, Hugh Williamson, Charles Cotesworth Pinckney, and Abraham Baldwin.

PROTECTIONS FOR CIVIL LIBERTIES

Gerry and McHenry next moved to prohibit Congress from adopting bills of attainder (legislative punishments inflicted on specific individuals without trial) or ex post facto laws (retroactive criminal laws). This generated considerable discussion. Morris thought that it was essential to prevent bills of attainder but not ex post facto laws. Ellsworth thought that the latter were void even without such a prohibition. Wilson agreed. Carroll pointed out that some legislatures had passed ex post facto laws whether they were illegal or not! Williamson further noted that judges in North Carolina had used an ex post facto clause to overturn bad laws. Ultimately, the convention added both prohibitions. After further discussion, the convention also agreed that the new government would pay the debts and fulfill the other engagements entered into by the government under the Articles.

GOVERNING THE MILITIA AND
NEGATING STATE LAWS

When the convention reconvened on August 23, the committee appointed on August 18 to deal with regulation of the militia reported its recommendation. It proposed granting the power to organize, arm, discipline, and govern the militia to Congress while reserving the rights to appoint officers and train militiamen to the states. Gerry said he was more willing to disarm militiamen than to subject them to the "despotism" of national control (Farrand 1966, 2:385). Two counterproposals were offered and rejected.

Perhaps in part because he had not been present during earlier debates over state representation, Langdon professed to be surprised by the "jealousy" expressed by some: "The General & State Govts. were not enemies to each other, but different institutions for the good of the people of America" (2:386). Gerry, who consistently defended states' rights, had an answer that others probably shared. He did not think liberty would be "as safe in the hands of eighty or a hundred men taken from the whole continent, as in the hands of two or three hundred taken from a single State" (2:386). Madison thought that states would be more likely to neglect their militia under a stronger national government than they were already doing under the Articles. Martin did not think that states would give up this power. Randolph did not see the danger from national regulation, and the committee report was accepted.

The convention further rejected a motion by Madison limiting state appointment to junior officers. Indeed, the primary effect of Madison's proposal seemed to have been that of inflaming Gerry even further. He apparently included Madison among those who "will support a plan of vigorous Government at every risk" and, despite Gerry's own comments at the convention fearing popular control, himself among those "of a more democratic cast" who "will oppose it with equal determination" (2:388). More ominously, he feared the conflict between the two views could lead to a "civil war" (2:388). The delegates then voted to support a provision prohibiting U.S. citizens from accepting titles of nobility from foreign governments without congressional approval as well as a revised version of the supremacy clause.

General Pinckney then reintroduced a proposal to give a two-thirds majority of both houses of Congress to veto state laws. Sherman thought the supremacy clause made such a provision unnecessary, and Madison was not comfortable with the proposed language. Mason wondered whether Congress would have to approve every local road project. Wilson thought it was "the key-stone wanted to compleat [sic.] the wide arch of Government we are raising" (2:391). By contrast, Rutledge thought this provision would, or should, "damn the constitution" (2:391). Pinckney withdrew the proposal. Tempers seemed unusually short. When the convention agreed that Congress would fulfill the debts under the Articles, Butler suggested—in a debate that would soon dominate the first Congress—discriminating against "the Blood-suckers who had speculated on the distresses of others," in favor of "those who had fought & bled for their country" (2:392).

TREATIES

In examining the provision for the Senate to make treaties and appoint ambassadors, Madison said that, since senators now represented the states, it was proper to include the president in this process. Gouverneur Morris suggested that Congress should ratify treaties, presumably after the president negotiated them. Madison wondered how practical this would be. Morris actually wanted to impede treaty-making. He observed that "The more difficulty in making treaties, the more value will be set on them" (2:393). Wilson said that Britain required parliamentary approval of treaties negotiated by the monarch. After further discussion, the convention defeated Morris's motion, although Madison suggested that perhaps different kinds of treaties might be treated differently.

On August 24, the convention's first discussion centered on the proposed mechanism that the Committee of Detail had proposed for dealing with disputes among the states. Rutledge, who would later serve as one of the first U.S. Supreme Court justices, said that the elaborate mechanism that the Committee of the Whole had proposed would be unnecessary with the establishment of a national judiciary. Wilson, who would also serve on the Supreme Court, was among those who persuaded the convention to strike the provision.

THE EXECUTIVE BRANCH

The delegates next agreed to vest executive power in a single individual, but they were divided as to whether he should be selected individually or jointly by both houses of Congress. Earlier supporters of the New Jersey Plan feared that the influence of the smaller states would be negated by a joint ballot. Carroll and Wilson's proposal to entrust the president's election in the people failed. After Madison observed that the ratio between the smallest and largest states in joint balloting would be one to four, rather than to the one to ten ratios in population, the convention voted for a joint ballot, and rejected a proposal to give each state a single vote. It did require that the winner should have a majority of the votes cast, but rejected the idea of giving the president of the Senate the deciding vote in case of a tie. Gouverneur Morris continued to object to legislative selection of the president, which he associated with "cabal & corruption" (Farrand 1966, 2:404), but his proposal to have the president chosen by state electors was narrowly defeated by a vote of five to six, with a more "abstract question" producing four in favor, four opposed, two divided, and one absent!

As the delegates examined presidential powers, Wilson feared that the president's responsibility to appoint military officers should not apply in times of peace when it might lead to corruption. Dickinson proposed one modification in language that the convention accepted and another that it did not.

On Saturday, August 25, Mason objected to mandatory language ("shall") that, he feared, when applied to debt obligations would "beget speculations and increase the pestilent practice of stock-jobbing" (2:413). Recognizing the difference between those to whom governmental securities had been issued and those who later bought them at a fraction of their original price, Mason did not want to preclude an attempt to distinguish between them. Langdon wanted to leave the status quo in place. Gerry affirmed that someone needed to be paid, and suggested that for all the criticism of "Stock-jobbers," they had kept up "the value of paper" (2:413). Randolph suggested a motion making the debts contracted by the Articles equally binding on the new government. Johnson did not think that changing a government would alter such obligations, and Gouverneur Morris weighed in on using obligatory language. All the states except Pennsylvania then voted to adopt Randolph's motion.

IMPORTATION AND TAXATION
OF SLAVES RECONSIDERED

William Livingston had presented the report from his Committee of Eleven the previous day. It had proposed prohibiting Congress from ending the slave trade until 1800 but permitting a tax on the trade that did not exceed the average of other items. General Pinckney wanted to extend the first deadline until 1808, and Gorham agreed. The amendment passed despite Madison's opinion that the change, which he probably did not think was essential to support from the southernmost states, was "dishonorable" both to the national character and the new Constitution (2:415). Gouverneur Morris wanted more specifically to use the word "slaves" and identify the culprits by listing the states of North Carolina, South Carolina, and Georgia as the miscreants, but Colonel Mason wisely opposed both measures as likely to provoke offense. After Williamson said he opposed slavery but thought it better to allow the Deep South states to enter the union than to exclude them, Morris, who probably felt that he had already made his point, withdrew his motion. Dickinson proposed, and the convention ratified, an amendment making it clear that the clause only applied to states that wanted to continue importation. After wrangling over what the tax on imported slaves should be and over whether the presence of such a tax would imply—as Madison feared—that slaves were mere items of merchandise, the majority of state delegations gave at least a hint of their overall opinion on the subject by voting to permit a tax "for each *person*" of up to ten dollars (2:417, italics added).

TREATIES RECONSIDERED

As the convention considered treaty-making provisions, Madison proposed, and the convention adopted, a provision clarifying that the new government was accepting treaties that had been negotiated under the Articles of Confederation. After delegates expressed fears that Congress might discriminate among states in collecting duties, the convention entrusted this issue to a Committee on Commercial Discrimination consisting of John Langdon, Nathaniel Gorham, Roger Sherman, Jonathan Dayton, Thomas Fitzsimons, George Read, Daniel Carroll, George Mason, Hugh Williamson, Pierce Butler, and William Few. The convention voted on several other matters, at one point rejecting a proposal by Sherman that would have allowed the Senate to decide on the appropriateness of presidential pardons.

PARDONS AND MILITIA

On the following day, Martin proposed limiting the president's pardon power to cases where individuals had been convicted of crimes. He withdrew the proposal after Wilson argued that a pardon might sometimes be necessary to elicit testimony about accomplices. Sherman then moved, and the convention accepted, an amendment allowing the president to control state militia only when they were in actual service.

The Committee of Detail had designated the president of the Senate as the provisional successor to the president, but Gouverneur Morris suggested that this was a proper function for the chief justice, and Madison feared that the Senate might attempt to keep power in its own hands on such occasions. Dickinson observed that the term disability was vague, and this was postponed while the convention voted to add a now-familiar provision to the presidential oath requiring that he "preserve[,] protect[,] and defend the Constitution of the U.S." (2:427).

JUDICIAL POWERS

The convention next voted to accept a motion by Dr. Johnson to extend judicial powers not only to cases in law but also to those in "equity," that is, cases that, in English law, involved more flexible remedies. Dickinson wanted to add a provision saying that judges could be removed on application of both houses of Congress. Gouverneur Morris objected that this was contradictory; Rutledge feared that it would undermine judicial judgment; and similar expressions of the need for judicial independence combined to defeat the proposal. Delegates then debated whether to strike the provision allowing Congress to increase judicial pay during their terms of office, but neither this nor a three-year delay proposal carried. After Johnson moved to widen judicial jurisdiction to cases arising under the Constitution, Madison said that such intervention should be limited to cases of a judicial nature, but the convention voted for it apparently with the understanding that this limit was already implicit in the language. It further debated and settled a number of other matters related to judicial jurisdiction.

Similar discussions carried over into business on August 28. The most important provision provided for jury trials in criminal cases. The convention also voted to approve the habeas corpus clause. It then accepted the provision prohibiting Congress from emitting bills of credit after Sherman observed that this was "a favorable crisis for crushing paper money" (Farrand 1966, 2:439).

PROHIBITIONS ON THE STATES

King next proposed a prohibition on state interference with private contracts. Gouverneur Morris thought this prohibition was taking things too far, but Madison thought such a prohibition would be useful, albeit not as effective as his own proposed negative of state laws. When Mason objected that a prohibition was too drastic, Wilson noted that it only applied to retrospective alterations, and the convention voted to prohibit both bills of attainder and retrospective laws. Madison further wanted to prohibit states from engaging in embargoes, but Mason thought they might sometimes be necessary, and Morris thought that Congress would retain overall control over state laws through its power over commerce. The convention approved a provision prohibiting states from taxing imports or exports, despite George Clymer's fears that this would sacrifice the interests of the East to those of the West. Pierce Butler and Charles Pinckney proposed adding a clause requiring the return of fugitive slaves to that dealing with extradition in criminal cases, but the issue was delayed.

On August 29, the convention resumed discussion of what is today known as the full faith and credit clause. The delegates committed this provision, and another proposal dealing with bankruptcies, to a Committee on Interstate Comity and Bankruptcy, to which John Rutledge, Edmund Randolph, Nathaniel Gorham, James Wilson, and William Johnson were appointed. Perhaps hoping the committee would take up an additional issue, Dickinson noted that his study of the law indicated that prohibitions on ex post facto laws applied only in criminal cases, and that some "further provision" (2:449) might be needed.

SUPERMAJORITIES AND COMMERCIAL REGULATIONS

Although the convention had earlier accepted congressional power over commerce with no recorded debate, Pinckney, who observed the diverse commercial interests among different states, now wanted to require a two-thirds vote for such regulation. General Pinckney, by contrast, said that his own suspicions of those from other states had been relieved by their willingness to forgo the taxing of exports, and he therefore thought his cousin's proposal was unnecessary. Sherman argued that the very diversity of interests that Charles Pinckney had cited was likely to serve as a restraint on unwarranted legislation. Charles Pinckney responded that the nation would still have distinct northern and southern interests. Williamson still favored a two-thirds vote, but thought that if northern shipping rates got too high, southern states could build their own ships. Mason still feared that southerners would need special protections against northerners. Madison feared that a two-thirds requirement might obstruct necessary retaliatory measures against other countries. He further thought that the proposed government already provided each section with numerous defenses. Rutledge also argued for a larger view that would lay "the foundation for a great empire" (2:452).

Edmund Randolph, who had originally introduced the Virginia Plan, then proceeded to say, somewhat ominously and perhaps unexpectedly, that certain features of the new system were "So odious in the Constitution as it now stands, that he doubted whether he should be able to agree to it." He added that "A rejection of the motion would compleat [sic.] the deformity of the system" (2:452). Gorham feared overly fettering Congress and thought that the South would face greater dangers from disunion than would the North. The convention rejected Pinckney's motion thus affirming the committee's decision to delete the two-thirds requirement in the report of the Committee of the Whole. Perhaps partly to allay the minds of the South, the convention immediately approved a fugitive slave clause.

THE ADMISSION OF NEW STATES

The convention next debated whether to approve the provision admitting new states on an equal basis with those already existing. Gouverneur Morris wanted to delete a provision admitting new states on an equal basis with those in existence, whereas Madison thought equality was absolutely essential, and Mason thought such equality would keep westerners firmly attached to the union. For the moment, at least, Morris won. An additional clause prohibiting the formation of new states without the consent of the state being divided as well as of Congress provoked considerable discussion, some of it generated by the anticipated application for statehood by Vermont, which was seeking independence from the claims of New Hampshire and New York, as well as of Franklin (Tennessee) from North Carolina, and Kentucky from Virginia. This discussion continued on August 30 with a solution eventually worked out that would not require New York's consent for New Hampshire's application. Martin still feared that eastern states might seek to obstruct the independence of their western territories. He accused Wilson and other large state representatives of inconsistency in previously arguing that states as states were not that important but now trying to secure their interests.

Discussion then commenced as to whether to detail congressional control over vacant lands. Madison thought this was covered by the judicial provision. After considerable discussion, the delegates adopted a clause giving Congress power to make rules respecting U.S. territories. The convention further refined the provisions relative to intervention in state domestic controversies by allowing the state executive to apply for such aid. Delegates also voted to allow Congress to call amending conventions at the requests of two-thirds of the states and to prohibit religious tests as a condition to public office.

STATE RATIFICATION OF THE CONSTITUTION

Wilson proposed that the convention should allow the new government to go into effect when seven states ratified it. Gouverneur Morris suggested that different numbers might be required depending on whether or not ratifying states were geographically contiguous. Sherman thought that a minimum of ten states should be required to initiate a new government, and Wilson favored eight. Dickinson wondered whether congressional concurrence would be required. In a timely metaphor, Wilson noted that "The House on fire [an obvious reference to the Articles of Confederation] must be extinguished, without a scrupulous regard to ordinary rights" (Farrand 1966, 2:469). Butler proposed nine, but Carroll thought that an agreement unanimously entered into by the states would require unanimous consent to dissolve.

Delegates partially resolved the issue on the next day (August 31) by voting to specify that the new government would only apply to consenting states. Madison then proposed that the new union should require both a majority of states and of the people. Delegates from Maryland said that they were obligated to follow the method of state legislative ratification outlined in the Articles. Gouverneur Morris wanted to allow states to decide how they wanted to ratify. By contrast, King thought that "conventions alone" would serve. Morris clarified that he was attempting to make ratification easier rather than harder, but Madison thought conventions were essential: "The people were in fact, the fountain of all power, and by resorting to them, all difficulties were got over. They could alter constitutions as they pleased. It was a principle in the Bills of rights, that first principles might be resorted to" (II, 476). Martin incorrectly predicted that both the people *and* the legislature of Maryland would oppose such a new plan, and that the only thing that might change this was if they were stampeded into such a decision. The Convention ultimately settled on ratifications by conventions in nine or more states. It further deleted reference to the "approbation," or approval, of Congress.

As the Convention approached the end of the Committee of the Whole's report, the discussion was getting testy. Gerry affirmed Martin's view that the proposed system was "full of vices" (II, 478). Mason, who had previously declared that he would rather be buried in Philadelphia than go home to Virginia without a plan, now used similar hyperbole to say that "he would sooner chop off his right hand than put it to the Constitution as it now stands" (II, 479). Gouverneur Morris suggested that another convention was needed "to provide a vigorous Government, which we are afraid to do" (II, 479). Approaching the discussion from another angle, Randolph thought that states should be free to propose amendments, which would then be considered in yet another convention.

MORE COMMITTEES

After finally getting through the report of the Committee of Detail, the Convention accepted that part of the report of the Committee of Eleven prohibiting preference for the ports of one state over another. It also accepted a provision prohibiting a state from requiring vessels to clear or pay duties in another.

The Convention ended the day by creating a Committee of Postponed Matters or Committee on Unfinished Parts. It consisted, North to South, of Nicholas Gilman, Rufus King, Roger Sherman, David Brearley, Gouverneur Morris, John Dickinson, Daniel Carroll, James Madison, Hugh Williamson, Pierce Butler, and Abraham Baldwin.

That Monday, the delegates continued to tinker with the document before them. They approved an earlier proposal to allow Congress to establish a uniform rule for bankruptcies. Charles Pinckney tried unsuccessfully to eliminate the provision limiting the appointment of congressmen to offices created (or the pay for which was increased) during their tenure to a simple incompatibility clause but stimulated a renewed round of spirited discussion on the topic. Mason saw the proposal not as a way of "excluding merit," but of avoiding "corruption, by excluding office-hunters" (II, 491). Wilson was among those who argued that exclusion might increase the powers of the executive. Anticipating that the first Congress would be filled with able men, he did not want them excluded from offices created by the new government. The Convention ultimately settled on both an emoluments clause and an incompatibly clause.

REPORT BY THE COMMITTEE
ON POSTPONED MATTERS

On Tuesday, September 4, David Brearly reported from the eleven-man Committee of Postponed Matters that the Convention had created the previous Friday. It proposed nine measures. They dealt with issues: (1) relating to taxing and borrowing; (2) expanding congressional power to regulate commerce with Indians; (3) giving the Senate the power to try impeachments and requiring a two-thirds majority for conviction; (4) proposing selection of the president and a vice president, who would serve four-year terms, through an electoral college that gave each state a number of electors equivalent to its total members of Congress, and with each elector casting two votes; (5) limiting the presidency to natural-born citizens; (6) granting the vice president the power to preside over the Senate except in cases of presidential impeachment; (7) granting appointment powers to the president with the advice and consent of the Senate and requiring confirmation of treaties by a two-thirds vote; (8) granting the president the power to request opinions from executive department heads; and (9) providing for removing the president for conviction of impeachable offenses.

DEBATE OVER PROPOSALS BY THE
COMMITTEE ON POSTPONED MATTERS

While the convention immediately approved the first two proposals, it spent considerable time on others. The committee's most innovative proposal was an electoral college, whose electors, chosen from individual states during each presidential election, would each cast two votes. The individual with the highest number of electoral votes would be president and the person with the second highest vice president, but the Senate would choose from among the top five candidates when no presidential candidate got a majority. Gorham feared that the person who got the next highest number of votes might be "a very obscure man" (Farrand 1966, 2:499). Sherman explained that the committee had sought to find a way to allow for presidents to be re-eligible for election without making them dependent on Congress. Madison and Gouverneur Morris feared that Senate selection would be difficult, but after a request to explain the changes that the committee had proposed, Morris went on to cite six somewhat overlapping reasons for it that seemed to offer something for everyone. They included the following: (1) the fear that legislative selection would lead to intrigue; (2) the desire to alleviate issues caused by presidential re-eligibility; (3) the desire to have an impeachment body without conflicts of interest; (4) the dissatisfaction with legislative selection; (5) the pressures for more popular input; and (6) the desire to lessen executive dependency on the legislature.

Mason thought the new plan remedied "the danger of cabal and corruption," but he feared that the Senate, which he did not think was a proper body to make such decisions, would end up too frequently resolving such elections. Charles Pinckney agreed in part because the Senate would also be the body that presided over impeachment trials. After a number of other delegates spoke, Wilson, who seems to have temporarily forgotten the earlier impasse over congressional representation, said that the issue was "the most difficult of all on which we have had to decide" (2:501). Although he thought that the plan marked a significant improvement over earlier ones, he argued that it would be better to assign the choice among candidates without a majority to the legislature (he seems fairly clearly to have meant the House of Representatives) rather than to the Senate, and to limit the body to a choice among the top three candidates rather than the top five. Randolph had similar concerns, and the matter was postponed along with preparation of a plan to defray convention expenses.

FURTHER PROPOSALS AND DEBATES RELATIVE TO THE COMMITTEE ON POSTPONED MATTERS

The following day, Brearly offered five further proposals from his committee. They included provisions: (1) granting Congress power to declare war and grant letters of marque and reprisal, or (as was common in the late eighteenth century) authorizations to private individuals to raid enemy ships; (2) limiting military appropriations to no more than two years; (3) allowing the Senate to alter or amend money bills; (4) allowing Congress to make rules for the national capital and other national facilities; and (5) granting Congress power to issue copyrights and patents.

After the convention unanimously approved the first proposal, Gerry raised fears that the second might make standing armies more likely. Sherman noted that the provision did not prohibit shorter military appropriations, and the convention approved this clause as well. The convention postponed the provision on money bills, but voted unanimously to grant Congress authority to govern the capital. After an objection by Gerry, the convention somewhat modified congressional authority over other facilities so as to require state legislative consent. Delegates approved the copyright and patent proposal without recorded debate.

Williamson raised renewed objections to the number of representatives that states had in Congress, and Charles Pinckney fired several rhetorical broadsides into the proposed electoral college plan. He feared: that electors would have insufficient knowledge of the most eminent men; that the system would leave the president unduly dependent on the Senate; that the president and senate would join forces against the House; and that presidential re-eligibility would lead to life terms. Rutledge also had objections, but the convention voted down his proposal to vest presidential election in a joint body and to limit a president to a single seven-year term. Mason also feared that the plan would vest too much power in the Senate and ally the president and the Senate against the House of Representatives. Williamson argued that vesting electoral powers in the Senate could lay "a certain foundation for corruption & aristocracy" (Farrand 1966, 2:512).

The convention rejected motions to limit the role of the Senate. Madison wanted to keep presidential selection out of the Senate as much as was possible. Randolph feared that having already "made a bold stroke for Monarchy" (2:513), the convention was about to make a similar stroke on behalf of aristocracy. The convention rejected motions: by Madison, to limit the choice to the Senate only to cases where candidates did not get one-third or more of the electoral votes; by Gerry, to vest six senators and seven members of the House chosen by lot with the choice; by Madison, to limit selection to the top three candidates; and by Spaight, to allow choice among 13 candidates. Mason, however, saw aristocratic elements creeping into the plan and said, with apparent hyperbole, that he would prefer the Prussian government to that being proposed.

On September 6, the convention accepted a proposal by King and Gerry prohibiting members of Congress and other office holders from serving as electors. Gerry proposed vesting the choice among top electoral vote-getters to the legislature, a term that delegates were still using to refer to the first house. Sherman said that in such a case, each state delegation within the House should have a single vote. Wilson feared that the new plan had "a dangerous tendency to aristocracy" (2:522) in the Senate. He feared that the new proposal would make the president "the Minion [puppet] of the Senate" rather than "the man of the people" (2:523). Gouverneur Morris disputed this conclusion, but Williamson thought it was obvious that the electoral proposal increased the power of the Senate.

Hamilton said that he continued his dislike of the convention's work but planned to support it over the even more objectionable current system.

He favored allowing the top electoral vote-getter to win the presidency, whether he had a majority or not. The convention then rejected a motion setting the president's term at six years before approving the proposal that it be for four. The convention subsequently: voted to provide for presidential election on a uniform day; agreed that at least two-thirds of the Senate would have to be present for the selection of the president; but then decided to vest selection power in the House. The convention had finally cut yet another Gordian knot, leaving only a few details to be complete.

The following day, Randolph proposed, and the convention agreed to, vesting legislative power in Congress to determine what officers would be next in line in case of presidential and vice presidential death or disability. In a decision for which there is no recorded debate other than that raised earlier in the proceedings in connection with citizenship of members of Congress, the convention next voted to require the president to be a natural-born citizen, of 35 years, and having at least 14 years of U.S. residency.

Gerry opposed a resolution to make the vice president the president of the Senate, or, indeed, even to have a vice president. Whereas Gerry feared undue executive influence in the Senate, Gouverneur Morris responded that "The vice president then will be the first heir apparent that ever loved his father" (2:537)! Sherman thought the office would give the vice president something to do, and Williamson remarked that the committee had largely created the vice presidency as a consequence of giving each elector two votes. Mason, however, thought that giving the vice president a role in the Senate would violate separation of powers and then suggested that the power of appointment should be vested in "a privy Council of six members" (2:537). The convention nonetheless affirmed the provision making the vice president head of the Senate.

In addressing the resolution to grant the power to make treaties with the advice and consent of the Senate, Wilson proposed vesting the latter power in both congressional houses. Sherman objected that this would be inconsistent with the need for secrecy. The motion was defeated.

Wilson did not like combining the president and the senate in the appointment power because he feared it would undercut presidential responsibility. He preferred the use of Mason's proposed privy council for this purpose. Gouverneur Morris responded that the proposal would provide both for presidential "responsibility" and for senatorial "security" (2:539). Gerry did not think the president would have extensive enough knowledge to make such appointments, whereas King claimed that the privy council that Mason had proposed would share in most of the inconveniences that would accompany senatorial confirmation. King also feared the expenses that would accompany "an unnecessary creation of New Corps" (2:539). The convention not only voted for president appointments with senatorial consent but also for granting the president power to fill vacancies during Senate recesses.

Madison proposed that the Senate should not be able to approve treaties without the consent of two-thirds or more of its members present. Wilson feared this could lead to minority control. Madison proposed exempting treaties of peace from the two-thirds requirement, but the convention defeated the motion in part out of fears that Gerry raised that this might permit one area of the continent from sacrificing another one.

As the convention proceeded to discuss whether the president could request written opinions from his principal officers, Mason renewed his objection that it was novel to create an executive without a privy council. He proposed allowing a committee to examine the possibility of a six-man Council of State with two members from each geographical area of the nation to be selected by one or both houses of Congress. Franklin seconded the motion, arguing that such a council "would not only be a check on a bad President but be a relief to a good one" (2:542). Wilson favored using a council to involving the Senate in confirmations. Dickinson thought such a council would encourage presidential deliberation. The convention, however, rejected the proposal.

On Saturday, September 8, the convention resumed examination of proposals by the Committee on Postponed Matters. King wanted two-thirds majorities to ratify all treaties, including those negotiating peace. Wilson wanted the two-thirds requirements for any treaty stricken. Gerry thought a two-thirds vote was necessary to outweigh foreign influence on the Senate. A series of inconclusive votes and discussions followed.

The convention then began examining the proposal giving the Senate the power to try impeachments of the president for treason and bribery. Mason thought the charges should include "maladministration" (2:550). Madison, who had earlier in the convention proposed incapacity as a grounds for impeachment, now objected that Mason's term was too vague, and Mason substituted the words "other high crimes & misdemeanors" (2:550) to which the committee agreed, without any debate that might, in turn, explain the still-disputed meaning of the new phrase. Madison suggested that the Supreme Court would be a better body to try impeachments. Gouverneur Morris thought the Court would be too small to do this. Charles Pinckney feared that senate trials would undermine executive independence. Sherman noted that the president would have appointed the justices, and the convention voted not to involve the Court in impeachments.

Returning to one of its favorite chestnuts, the convention finally accepted a provision that limited the introduction of money bills to the House while permitting the Senate to "propose or concur with amendments as in other bills" (2:552). It further provided that it would require a two-thirds vote of the Senate to convict of impeachable offenses. After dealing with some other minor matters, the convention created a Committee of Style consisting of William Johnson, Alexander Hamilton, Gouverneur Morris, James Madison, and Rufus King. It then narrowly defeated a motion advanced by Williamson, seconded by Madison, opposed by Sherman, and supported by Hamilton, to increase the size of the House of Representatives.

CONSTITUTIONAL AMENDMENTS AND THEIR RATIFICATION

Although delegates had appointed a Committee of Style, there were still some matters to clear up relative to the Committee of Detail. On September 10, Gerry asked to reconsider the provision granting two-thirds of the states the power to petition Congress under the proposed government to call a convention to amend the Constitution. Perhaps with a view to the unanimity required under the Articles of Confederation, he feared that the two-thirds majority might not be adequate to provide protections to states of their sovereignty. Hamilton seconded Gerry's motion but expressed a different fear. He thought that "an easier mode" (Farrand 1966, 2:558) needed to be considered. He thought that there would be times when Congress more readily perceived the need for change than the states, and wanted two-thirds of each branch to be able to call a convention on their own.

Sherman proposed, and Gerry then seconded, a motion allowing Congress to propose amendments but requiring consent—presumably unanimous—"by the several States" (2:558). After the convention narrowly voted against this, Wilson proposed allowing two-thirds of the states to ratify amendments. The convention narrowly voted against this before unanimously agreeing to another Wilson motion setting the ratifying majority at three-fourths. Madison then proposed, Hamilton seconded, and the convention approved a proposal that two-thirds of the states could apply for a convention, or two-thirds of both houses could propose amendments that would require three-fourths of the state legislatures, or conventions, to ratify them. Rutledge managed to protect his state's interest by attaching a clause prohibiting amendment of the slave importation clause prior to 1808.

The most immediate amendment on most delegates' minds was the one that proposed replacing the Articles of Confederation with a new Constitution. Gerry thought that the existing Congress needed to be included in this process. Somewhat surprisingly, Hamilton agreed and thought that Congress should then send the document on to the states for ratification by conventions. After Thomas Fitzsimons of Pennsylvania noted the difficulty that members of the existing Congress would have in dissolving the government under which they were operating, Randolph indicated that although he had arrived at the convention convinced "that radical changes were necessary" (2:560), he thought that the "Republican propositions" within the original Virginia Plan had "been widely, and . . . irreconcileably departed from" (2:561). He thus wanted to leave states free to propose alterations when they ratified, and submit these to "a second General Convention, with full power to settle the Constitution finally" (2:561). Gerry pointed to "the indecency and pernicious tendency" of dissolving the Articles with the consent of only nine states. Hamilton offered a motion, seconded by Gerry, providing for congressional approval and ratification by nine or more states.

Wilson strongly opposed the provision for congressional ratification. He thought such congressional approval would threaten months of "the laborious & arduous task of forming a Government" (2:562). George Clymer thought the whole matter would "embarrass" Congress (2:563), and the convention voted it down.

LINGERING CONCERNS

As delegates focused on ratifying their handiwork, Randolph, who as a sitting governor may well have been thinking of voters back in Virginia, was having second doubts about the convention's work. He opposed: the Senate's role as a court of impeachment in trying the president; the provision allowing three-fourths, rather than two-thirds, of both houses to override a presidential veto; the small size of the House of Representatives; the failure to restrict a standing army; the breadth of the necessary and proper clause; the lack of restraint for navigation acts; the power to tax exports; the right of Congress to quell domestic disturbances at the request of state governors; the lack of a definite boundary between state and national powers; the president's power to pardon treasons; and the lack of control on the salaries that members of Congress might give themselves. Faced with a government that he thought might end in tyranny, he favored sending the results to Congress, then to state legislatures, then to conventions with power to amend, and then to "another general Convention with full power to adopt or reject the alterations proposed by the State Conventions" (2:564). Franklin seconded this motion, but Mason suggested leaving it on the table until the Committee of Style returned its report.

SOURCES CITED IN THIS CHAPTER

Farrand, Max. 1966. *The Records of the Federal Convention of 1787.* 4 vols. (New Haven, CT: Yale University Press.

7

WRAPPING UP BUSINESS, SIGNING, AND RATIFYING

> The people were in fact, the fountain of all power, and by re-
> sorting to them, all difficulties were got over. They could alter
> constitutions as they pleased. It was a principle in the Bills of
> rights, that first principles might be resorted to.
>
> —James Madison speaking at the Convention on
> August 31 (Farrand 1966, 2:476)

> it [the Constitution] is now a Child of fortune, to be fostered
> by some and buffeted by others. What will be the General
> opinion on, or the reception of it, is not for me to decide nor
> shall I say any thing for or against it: if it be good, I suppose it
> will work its way good; if bad, it will recoil on the Framers.
>
> —George Washington in a letter to the
> Marquis de Lafayette, September 18, 1787
> (St. John 1990, unnumbered page)

The convention skipped its session on Tuesday, September 12 in order to give the Committee of Style more time to do its work, but members of the convention must have wondered whether their work would end in a new government or in yet another convention. Randolph had hinted that he had objections to the document, but he had been silent about some of these perceived weaknesses prior to his last speech. How many other delegates had similar reservations? Would the long summer of work be in vain?

On September 13, Dr. Johnson presented two documents to the convention on behalf of the Committee of Style and Arrangement, which he chaired. One was a letter to Congress that explained that the convention had concluded that a new system was needed to "Promote the lasting Welfare of that Country so dear to us all and secure her Freedom and Happiness" (Farrand 1966, 2:584). The other was a revision of earlier deliberations by the Committee of Detail that the committee had condensed from 23 articles to today's familiar 7.

CONGRESSIONAL MAJORITIES NEEDED TO OVERRIDE AN EXECUTIVE VETO

Perhaps taking a cue from one of Randolph's stated objections, Hugh Williamson suggested changing the congressional majority needed to overturn a presidential veto from three-fourths to two-thirds, so as not to give the president too much power. Delegates lined up on both sides of the issue, with proponents of three-fourths arguing that it would reduce the number of unnecessary laws, and opponents fearing that it would vest too much power in the hands of too few congressmen. Madison pointed out that the delegates had agreed to the three-fourths majority requirement when they anticipated that Congress was going to select the president for a seven-year term. The veto was designed to enable the executive to defend himself and to "prevent popular or factious injustice" (2:587). Although Madison thought that there was greater "danger from the weakness of 2/3" than "the danger from the strength of 3/4" (2:587), the convention adopted the two-thirds substitute.

PROPOSAL FOR A BILL OF RIGHTS

Williamson next proposed that the new document should provide for jurors in civil cases. During this debate, Colonel Mason suggested that the proposed Constitution should be "prefaced with a Bill of Rights" that, he thought, "would give great quiet to the people" (Farrand 1966, 2:587). Perhaps thinking back to his halcyon days writing the Virginia Declaration of Rights, Mason said that such a bill could be drafted "in a few hours" (2:588). Gerry favored the idea, but Sherman observed that the new Constitution was not repealing *state* declarations, which should be sufficient to protect individual rights. In a little-debated move that many delegates undoubtedly came to regret, state delegations voted unanimously against adding such a bill of rights.

Tinkering with the Constitution from the Committee of Style and Arrangement, Mason next suggested that states should retain power to enact incidental duties on exports that states found it necessary to inspect. A number of delegates approved of the change although some feared that it might be used to discriminate against the commerce of other states. Madison did not miss the opportunity to remind his colleagues that they had turned down his proposal for a congressional negative of state laws, but he believed that the Supreme Court could address such abuses. The following day the convention adopted the proposal permitting incidental duties.

That same day, Mason renewed an earlier plea to give Congress authority to enact sumptuary laws. He thought that this would result in a greater simplicity of manners consistent with republican government. Dr. Johnson agreed. The convention created a committee consisting of Mason, Franklin, Dickinson, Johnson, and Livingston to draft such a proposal, but the convention records provide no further information on the committee's work, and the Constitution avoided such regulations until the adoption of the Eighteenth Amendment in 1919, which provided for national alcoholic prohibition. The fact that the amendment was widely evaded, and brought about numerous unintended consequences, before being repealed in 1933 by the Twenty-first Amendment suggests the limitations of such laws.

The convention then proceeded to examine the Constitution as proposed by the Committee of Style. Most motions were fairly trivial, but a number of major issues arose. On September 13, the committee revised its earlier suggestions on ratification of the Constitution, now proposing that the convention should send the document to Congress, which would then submit it to state conventions for approval.

On Friday, September 14, the convention considered a proposal that would have suspended individuals who were impeached from office until their trial was held, but Madison was among those who feared that this would make the president too dependent on Congress, and the delegates defeated the measure. That same day, the convention also struck down the provision in the proposed Constitution that would have granted *Congress*, which was most closely associated with the power of the purse, rather than the president, the power to appoint a treasurer by a joint ballot.

That same day, Franklin wanted to grant Congress the power to cut canals where they were needed. Madison preferred to go still further and allow Congress to create corporations "where the interest of the U.S. might require & the legislative provisions of individual States may be incompetent" (2:615). Rufus King feared this would create controversy over whether

Congress could establish a bank. In another prediction by a delegate that proved wide of the mark—the controversy was one of the major issues in Washington's first term and resulted in the creation of the Federalist Party, led by Hamilton, who favored the bank, and the Democratic-Republican Party headed by Madison and Jefferson, who opposed it—Wilson doubted that this "would excite the prejudices & parties apprehended" (2:616). He believed that Congress could control banks under its power to regulate trade. Mason expressed his fears of "monopolies of every sort" (2:616), and the motion was defeated. The convention also defeated a motion to grant Congress power to establish a secular university—one "in which no preferences or distinctions should be allowed on account of religion" 2:616). This vote was somewhat inconclusive since Gouverneur Morris argued that Congress could establish such an institution under its power to regulate the seat of government.

Mason next suggested adding a specific amendment opposing the establishment of standing armies in time of peace. It was defeated along with another motion to strike the provision against ex post facto laws. Charles Pinckney and Elbridge Gerry then proposed to add protection for freedom of the press. As with the previous motion for a bill of rights, the majority of delegates thought that such a national provision was unnecessary in view of state protections. The convention did add a provision that Mason suggested and Madison modified, which required Congress to give accounts of its expenditures from time to time. The convention did not accept Gerry's proposal to apply a restriction on impairing the obligation of contracts to Congress as well as the states.

On September 15, the convention decided not to prepare an address to the people to accompany the proposed Constitution. Delegates were concerned over the propriety of such a speech and the possible delay that might result from composing it. The convention rejected several last-minute appeals to change the initial representation of individual states within the House of Representatives. A motion by McHenry and Carroll would have given states the power to levy duties to clear harbors and erect lighthouses. After Gouverneur Morris said he thought they already had this power, Madison finally directed attention to the little-discussed congressional powers over interstate commerce. Observing that the clause was vague, he correctly anticipated its potential by saying that "He was more & more convinced that the regulation of Commerce was in its nature indivisible and ought to be wholly under one authority" (2:625).

Delegates then voted to require congressional assent to any such duties. Delegates once again rejected a proposal by Rutledge and Franklin that would prohibit Congress from paying the president. A motion by Randolph to prevent the president from granting pardons in cases of treason was eventually defeated, in part because of lingering republican fears that the alternative of giving the president such power with Senate approval might encourage an aristocratic alliance between the two institutions.

The convention voted against adding a provision for jury trials in civil cases and began reexamining the amending provisions. Seeing the power inherent in this clause, Sherman moved to add a provision, like that protecting slave importation, which would guard continuing equality of state representation in the Senate against future amendment. Mason expressed a more general concern that the proposed amending process was both "exceptionable & dangerous" (2:629) because it relied on congressional action, which that body would be reluctant to take. Gouverneur Morris and Elbridge Gerry proposed allowing two-thirds of the states to apply for a convention to propose amendments. Madison did not think this was a major change, although he thought Mason's proposal left many questions—which remain unanswered to this day—about "the form, the quorum &c which in Constitutional regulations ought to be as much as possible avoided" (2:630). The motion to provide for the calling of such conventions carried.

Sherman renewed his call for a provision limiting interferences in state police powers and for a guarantee of continuing state equality in the Senate. Madison feared the proliferation of such provisions, and the measure was voted down, after which Sherman dramatically moved to strike the amending provision altogether. Although delegates rejected this proposal, it probably provided the impetus for a motion by Gouverneur Morris to consider the motion for entrenching the provision for state equality by itself. Madison observed that this continuing testament to the issue that had led to the Great Compromise was unanimously adopted "being dictated by the circulating murmurs of the small States" (2:631). The convention rejected a measure, introduced by Mason and similar to the restraint on slave importation, that would prevent the adoption of any navigation laws without a two-thirds majority before the year 1808.

RESERVATIONS ABOUT THE DOCUMENT

After commenting on his own concerns about the new Constitution, Randolph introduced another motion "that amendments to the plan might be offered by the State Conventions, which should be submitted to and finally decided on by another general Convention" (Farrand 1966, 2:631). He then raised the stakes by saying that, without such a provision, he did not anticipate that he could sign the document, although he might support it when it reached his state. Mason seconded Randolph's motion. Not only did Mason fear that the new system might degenerate "either in monarchy, or a tyrannical aristocracy," but he observed that, as this convention had been secret, another might better reflect popular sentiments (2:632). Like Randolph, he could not sign without giving state conventions the right to propose amendments.

Noting that such reservations "give a peculiar solemnity to the present moment," Charles Pinckney could anticipate nothing "but confusion & contrariety" stemming from state conventions (2:632). He did not anticipate that delegates to a new convention would be likely to come to any better agreements. Moreover, "Conventions are serious things, and ought not to be repeated" (2:632). Despite his own reservations about the plan before the convention, he intended to support it. Not surprisingly, Gerry did not. He listed a host of objections that included:

> 1. the duration and re-eligibility of the Senate. 2. the power of the House of Representatives to conceal their journals. 3. the power of Congress over the places of election; 4. the unlimited power of Congress over their own compensations. 5 Massachusetts has not had a due share of Representatives allotted to her. 6. 3/5 of the Blacks are to be represented as if they were freeman. 7. Under the power over commerce, monopolies may be established. 8. The vice president being made head of the Senate. (2:633)

He was even more concerned about what he considered to be the insecurity of individual rights, which he thought were especially threatened by the necessary and proper clause, by the lack of controls on legislative power over the military, and by trials without juries in civil cases. Despite dissention within the ranks, the states present unanimously rejected Randolph's proposal and ordered the Constitution to be engrossed, or transcribed onto vellum parchment, a job that delegates assigned to Jacob Shallus, the Assistant Clerk of the Pennsylvania Assembly.

THE SIGNING OF THE CONSTITUTION

On Monday, September 17, the proposed Constitution was read, after which Benjamin Franklin rose to get Washington's attention and have Wilson deliver what probably proved to be the single most important speech in the ratification debates that would follow. Acknowledging his age, Franklin indicated that while there were provisions in the new Constitution that he did not favor, he recognized that he was not always right. Men, like religious faiths, tended to think that they were infallible, but experience demonstrated otherwise. Franklin would support the proposed document because a new general government was needed, and because Franklin doubted "whether any other Convention we can obtain may be able to make a better Constitution" (2:642). Assemblies of men brought together not only "their joint wisdom," but also "their prejudices, their passions, their errors of opinion, their local interests, and their selfish views" (2:642). Given such qualities, Franklin was astonished "to find this system approaching so near to perfection as it does" (Farrand 1966, 2:642). Franklin would sacrifice his own opinions to the common good and pleaded with other delegates to do the same. If delegates left the convention and immediately began focusing on their own objections to the plan, it would be unlikely to gain popular support. Franklin therefore introduced a resolution, indicating that the Constitution had been "Done in Convention, by the unanimous consent of *the States* present the 17th. Of Sepr. &c."

Madison indicated that Gouverneur Morris had drafted the resolution but that the more popular Franklin had proposed it to garner greater support. By referring to the states "present," the resolution would minimize Rhode Island's absence and New York's lack of a quorum of its members. By emphasizing the unanimous approval of the "states" present, the resolution would not reflect disharmony within some states' ranks.

In what seems to be a fairly unusual move, Nathaniel Gorham then proposed "lessening objections to the Constitution" (2:643) by altering the provision for representation within the House of Representatives by allowing up to one representative for every 30,000 residents rather than for every 40,000. After George Washington, who may have heard similar concerns in private conversations, gave a rare speech in support of the proposal, the convention adopted it unanimously. All the *states* present subsequently approved the document, but some delegates still wanted to have their say.

Edmund Randolph spoke first. He thought that Franklin had singled him out and apologized for not signing the document but indicated again that he was not necessarily committed to opposing it "without doors" (2:645), that is, during ratification debates. Gouverneur Morris said that he too had reservations but that, like Franklin, he thought the document was the best that the convention could obtain under the circumstances. Hugh Williamson suggested that perhaps reluctant delegates could instead sign the letter that would accompany the plan to state legislatures. Hamilton pleaded for unanimity, noting that he planned to sign despite having as many or more reservations than most delegates. William Blount said he was willing to sign, not in full support of the document, but to attest that states had unanimously adopted it!

Franklin indicated that he had not intended to single out Randolph, whose efforts at the convention he appreciated. He nonetheless hoped that Randolph, and any other delegate with objections, might put them aside for the common good. Randolph did not think the form of the resolution made signing the document any more palatable, but he reiterated that he might support the plan at the state level.

Gerry also rose to express "the painful feelings of the situation, and the embarrassment under which he rose" (2:646) but to reiterate his concern that civil war might erupt out of the current crisis. Given sentiments within his own state of Massachusetts, he had hoped for a document "proposed in a more mediating shape" (2:647). Gerry did not find Franklin's proposed resolution made it easier to sign, and would not do so.

General Pinckney agreed that the resolution was unlikely "to gain many converts" (2:647), but said that, for his part, he planned both to sign and support the document. In a curious turn, Franklin said that it was too soon for delegates to pledge support prior to approval by Congress and by state conventions, whereas Jared Ingersol viewed his own signature "as a recommendation, of what, all things considered, was the most eligible" (2:647).

After King suggested that the journals of the convention should be either destroyed or deposited in Washington's safekeeping, Wilson proposed the second option, and all the states but Maryland, whose delegates felt bound by instructions to report the proceedings to the state, approved. Thirty-eight delegates signed the Document including George Read of Delaware who also signed on behalf of John Dickinson who had left. Randolph, Mason, and Gerry did not sign.

Perhaps asserting the prerogatives of age, Franklin had led off discussions of the day, and he planned to have the last word, which Madison managed to capture in his notes. Turning to the colleagues nearest him, Franklin pointed to one of two existing objects that today's historians can definitively track to the room on that day—the other is a silver inkstand make by Philip Syng, Jr. of Philadelphia, that was also used in the signing of the Declaration of Independence. Franklin observed that the Chippendale chair in which Washington had been sitting as he presided over the convention had a painted sun at the top of the back facing the conventioneers.

Although artists "had found it difficult to distinguish . . . a rising from a setting sun," Franklin expressed confidence that the sun was rising over a new American nation (2:648).

OUTLINE OF THE CONSTITUTION

The Constitution that the convention proposed is an elegant document that owes much to Gouverneur Morris, its chief stylist. Morris wrote a letter to Timothy Pickering on December 22, 1814, in which he said that "That instrument [the Constitution] was written by the fingers, which wrote this letter. Having rejected redundant and equivocal terms, I believed it to be as clear as our language would permit" (Farrand 1966, 3:420). Madison later affirmed that "The finish given to the style and arrangement of the Constitution fairly belongs to the pen of Mr. Morris" (3:499).

The most notable feature of the preamble of the Constitution—which Patrick Henry would argue was impertinent—is that it does not, as the Articles of Confederation had done, list states individually as originators of the document but rather speaks in the name of "We the People of the United States." The introduction, or Preamble, elegantly identifies the goals of the Constitution "to form a more perfect Union, establish Justice, insure domestic Tranquility, provide for the common defense, promote the general Welfare, and secure the Blessings of Liberty to ourselves and our Posterity." In so doing, it looked both backward to the less perfect union that the Articles of Confederation represented and forward to the generations that it hoped would enjoy the "Blessings of Liberty" that the delegates who drafted the new Constitution hoped to secure.

Articles I through III of the Constitution delineate the respective organization and powers of the three branches of government. Article I outlines a bicameral Congress, with a variety of enumerated powers, including the necessary and proper clause. The House of Representatives, whose members serve two-year terms, was apportioned by state population and elected by the people. The Senate had six-year terms. Each state legislature (the Seventeenth Amendment changed this to popular election in 1913) would select two senators. Article II created a unitary president, serving as chief executive and as commander in chief of the armed forces and selected by an electoral college, that was independent of Congress, to renewable four-year terms. Article III allowed for, but did not mandate, the creation of a system of lower federal courts and provided that they would be headed by a Supreme Court whose members would be appointed by the president and confirmed by the advice and consent of the Senate to service "during good behavior." Section 3 defines treason as "levying war" against the United States or giving aid or comfort to their enemies.

Article IV is essential to the federal system. It delineates the various powers and responsibilities that the states have to one another and that the state and national governments have to one another. It provides, for example, that states must provide "full faith and credit" to acts and proceedings in other states, that state citizens must be given full "privileges and immunities" when in other states, and that states must return, or extradite suspected criminals (and prior to the adoption of the Thirteenth Amendment, fugitive slaves) to other states. The article also provides for the admission of new states, for national authority over its territory, and for the national guarantee of "a Republican Form of Government" to the states.

Article V outlines the amending process, which involves a two-step process of proposal and ratification involving supermajorities of both houses of Congress and the state legislatures, as well as the still-unused convention mechanism. Article VI contains the Supremacy Clause, the oath requirement of office holders, and the prohibition against religious tests for national offices. Article VII wraps up the document by grounding the new Constitution in the consent of the people by specifying that the new document would go into effect when ratified by conventions in nine or more states.

Many printings of the Constitution note that it was "[D]one in Convention by the Unanimous Consent of the States present the Seventeenth Day of September in the Year of our Lord one thousand seven hundred and Eighty seven and of the Independence of the United States of America the Twelfth In Witness whereof We have here unto subscribed our Names." This is the document's only reference to God. The reference to the Declaration of Independence is meant to show that the delegates still valued natural rights and that they viewed the Constitution as a way to translate these rights into constitutional language. Some delegates were fairly enthusiastic about the proposed Constitution, others signed because they humbly deferred judgment to others, some had left the convention by the time the document was signed, and three delegates who remained refused to sign at all.

In a quotation long falsely attributed to Robert Morris, Gouverneur Morris noted in a letter of January, 1788 that "This paper has been the subject of infinite investigation, disputation, and declamation. While some have boasted it as a work from Heaven, others have given it a less righteous origin. I have many reasons to believe that it is the work of plain, honest men, and such, I think, it will appear" (3:242–43). Writing to Lafayette the next day, Washington observed that the Constitution was to be "a child of fortune," with no one able to foresee its outcome.

RATIFICATION OF THE CONSTITUTION

When the Constitution emerged from the convention, it was only a proposal. Although the delegates had refused to follow procedures under the Articles of Confederation by requiring unanimous consent of the state legislatures, they arguably set a fairly high bar by requiring that conventions within nine or more states would have to approve the document before it could go into effect among them. When the convention had discussed the issue of roll-call votes in Congress, Sherman had observed that such votes were of little value without the explanations behind them (Farrand 1966, 2:255). Similarly, as newspapers published, and citizens read, the proposed new document that had emerged from closed-door proceedings, they were not privy to all the arguments and compromises that went into its making.

FEDERALISTS AND ANTIFEDERALISTS

In the ensuing months, those who supported the Constitution became known as Federalists, and those who opposed it, as Antifederalists. By claiming the Federalist moniker, supporters of the Constitution were patching over the manner in which the federalism of the new Constitution significantly differed from that under the Articles. The early federalism under the Articles of Confederation, which today's scholars call confederalism, left states sovereign and did not permit the central authority to act directly on individual citizens. By contrast, the new federalism made the U.S. Constitution the supreme law of the land and allowed both national and state authorities to act directly on individuals. It is no wonder that, consistent with convention debates, Madison described the new government in Federalist No. 39 as being "partly national and partly federal."

When the convention reported the Constitution to the states for their approval, Federalists had several advantages. First, there was general agreement that the Articles of Confederation were a failure and that some change was needed. Antifederalists could point to flaws, or perceived flaws, within the proposed Constitution, but Federalists were advocating a positive remedy to evident flaws in the existing government. Second, Federalists could claim that the system they were advancing had the approval of the continent's leading men. Surely, Federalists argued, Washington and Franklin would not have attended the convention and signed a document that they believed threatened the nation's peace or liberties! Third, Federalists were generally better organized and better informed about the new Constitution, in part because many of them had spent the summer together writing it. Although no one had direct access to the official records, which were in George Washington's possession, delegates who attended were in a better position to answer arguments about particulars within the document based on arguments that they had heard at the convention. Fourth, and finally, one might argue that while they had no monopoly, Federalists ultimately had the better arguments; they certainly dominated the press, which was overwhelmingly in favor of the new document.

Antifederalists were not, however, without advantages of their own. While the Articles of Confederation were far from perfect, its consequences were far better known than those of the new government. Neither large nor small states had achieved all that they wanted under the new system since highly populated states were denied proportional representation in the Senate, and less-populated states were denied equality in the House. The new executive was far stronger than any that the states or nation had previously ever known and might have a tendency toward monarchy, particularly during times of war. Similarly, judges, who served during good behavior, might lend an overly aristocratic element to the new government. Historically, a democratic-republican government had never operated on a land area the size of the United States (the Baron de Montesquieu, a highly respected French philosopher, had associated such nations with monarchies), and many thought it highly problematic that this one could do so. Moreover, whereas most state constitutions had prefatory declarations of rights, the national Constitution did not.

STATE CONVENTIONS MEET

Whereas the Constitution was drafted by a single body, its adoption required the ratification of many. During debates at the convention, delegates had often speculated as to whether the public would approve or disapprove of individual measures, but in the absence of publicity about the convention proceedings or of modern scientific polling, most such predictions were little more than guesses. The true test would come in the state ratifying conventions.

Delaware's convention was the first to ratify the Constitution on December 7, 1787 and its vehicle license plates accordingly proclaim it to be "The First State." Its unanimous vote was a reassuring sign that the Connecticut Compromise was acceptable to less-populated states. Pennsylvania's ratification, which followed two days later, was more problematic. Federalists had achieved a quorum in the Pennsylvania legislature, which had to call a ratifying convention, by rounding up opponents and forcing them to attend, which led outsiders to question why Federalists were attempting to railroad ratification so quickly. The convention was also divided, with 46 delegates agreeing to the new document but 23 voting to oppose it. Although the methods Federalists used tarnished their reputations, James Wilson emerged during his state's ratification as a forceful advocate for the new document, and his arguments on behalf of the Constitution were widely printed and reprinted.

New Jersey followed Delaware's example by unanimously ratifying on December 8. This was a particularly portentous ratification since New Jersey delegates had fought so hard for equal representation within the Senate. Georgia, which appears to have been motivated by hope of getting national help to control its Native American population, followed with a similar vote on December 31. Connecticut, whose representatives had been so influential in forging the Great Compromise relative to congressional representation, ratified 128 to 40 on January 9, 1788.

Massachusetts indicated that all would not be smooth sailing. Initially, both John Hancock, who had so prominently signed the Declaration of Independence, and Samuel Adams, who has been one of the state's most vocal opponents of British rule, chose to stay on the fence rather than support the new proposal. Federalists finally persuaded delegates at the convention that while they could not ratify the Constitution conditionally, they could vote for the document and suggest amendments for the new Congress to consider—a tactic that Federalists would also pursue in other states. On February 6, 1788, delegates voted to ratify by a vote of 187 to 168.

In Maryland, the legislature published a negative broadside against the Constitution authored by Luther Martin called *The Genuine Information,* but, in what some Federalists must have considered to be an act of Divine Providence, he got laryngitis during the debates. Fellow delegates followed the example of other small states by voting 63 to 11 to ratify the Constitution on April 28, 1788.

May 23, 1788 marks the date that South Carolina ratified the Constitution by a vote of 149 to 73. Delegates were relieved to find a provision that counted each of their slaves as three-fifths of a person for representation in the House and another that allowed for their continuing importation for 20 years.

Provisions protecting slavery and prohibiting religious tests for national offices aroused opposition in New Hampshire, which had its own official state church, but the state ultimately had the honor of being the ninth state when its delegates voted 57 to 47 to approve the Constitution on June 21, 1788. This apparent finish line was somewhat deceptive, however, since it was doubtful whether the new union could survive without its largest member, Virginia, which at the time included most of the current states of West Virginia and Kentucky, or New York, which had a major port and had not yet given its consent.

George Washington did not attend the ratifying convention in Richmond, but James Madison and John Marshall were among those who had to battle the bombastic Patrick Henry, the onetime revolutionary who was now a strong proponent of states' rights, had refused to attend the Constitutional Convention in Philadelphia, and raised almost every single imaginable objection to the Constitution, including the fear that the national government would attempt to eliminate slavery. He also cited a private letter from Thomas Jefferson, which Henry believed opposed ratification—in fact, Jefferson had expressed his hope that the required number of states would ratify and that the others should then hold out for a bill of rights before ratifying. Working in favor of Virginia's ultimate 89 to 79 vote on behalf of the Constitution was the fact that Washington approved ratification wholeheartedly and that Edmund Randolph, who had refused to sign the Constitution but had left his options open at the convention, now decided to support it. When the delegates voted, they had not yet gotten word of New Hampshire's ratification, and many undoubtedly wanted the honor of being the state whose ratification made the critical difference.

Given the division of New York's delegation at the Constitutional Convention, it is not surprising that its vote on ratification by 30 to 27 on June 16, 1788, was the closest of any state in the nation. Although there were hundreds of newspaper articles both in favor of and in opposition to the new Constitution, none proved to be more influential than the 85 Federalist essays that were later compiled into a book. Alexander Hamilton led the effort to solicit these essays, which were written under the pen name of Publius. Hamilton wrote most of the essays defending the presidency and the judiciary. James Madison authored among the most thoughtful of the Federalist essays, including No. 10, wherein he portrayed the new republican government over a large land mass as a cure for the mischiefs of faction. John Jay, a New Yorker who had served as a diplomat and would become the first chief justice of the U.S. Supreme Court, wrote a handful of essays that dealt largely with issues of foreign policy.

North Carolina chose to take a wait-and-see attitude when on August 2, 1788, its delegates decided by a vote of 184 to 84 to wait for the adoption of a bill of rights. A second convention voted to accept on November 21, 1789. Rhode Island had been the only state that refused to send delegates to the convention, so it is hardly surprising that it was also the last state to ratify the Constitution, which it did on May 29, 1790. By this time, the other states had already elected members of Congress, had inaugurated George Washington as their first president on April 30, 1789, and had begun exerting not a little pressure on it.

ADOPTION OF THE BILL OF RIGHTS

Some of the arguments that Antifederalists raised were based on unlikely fears of the unknown, but others reflected a deep-seated distrust of a strong national government that might oppress the people. The argument that ultimately had the most resonance with voters and delegates was based on the absence of a bill of rights. Initially, Federalists argued that such a bill would be unnecessary both because states would retain their own constitutional protections and because the new government was one of enumerated, or listed, powers that would prevent it from wandering into areas where it did not belong. Hamilton argued in *The Federalist* that the entire Constitution was a bill of rights because it was structured so as to keep any single branch from dominating. Others argued that a bill of rights might even prove to be dangerous because, if it inadvertently omitted any right, officials might use this as an argument that they did not value it. This argument was more problematic than others because, as a matter of fact, the existing text of the Constitution did include a number of explicit protections for human rights, including the prohibitions against ex post facto laws and bills of attainder contained in the last two sections of Article I, which respectively limited the states and Congress.

Although Madison was among those Federalists who were adamant in arguing that states could not conditionally ratify the Constitution contingent upon the adoption of a bill of rights, he eventually came to believe (in part because of correspondence on the subject with Thomas Jefferson, who was still in France) that the adoption of a bill of rights would do no harm and might even serve as a valuable resource by which judges could uphold individual rights. Although Governor Patrick Henry attempted to gerrymander Madison's district with Antifederalists to favor the election of James Monroe, a war hero and prominent Antifederalist, Madison campaigned vigorously, assured his constituents that he would work for a bill of rights, won the election, and eventually shepherded such a bill through the first Congress. The necessary majorities of Congress proposed this bill on September 25, 1789, and the required number of states ratified it on December 15, 1791.

The Bill of Rights was adopted so closely after ratification of the Constitution and was so intimately tied to it, that it shares a place in the national archives alongside the Declaration of Independence and the seven articles of the U.S. Constitution. The First Amendment is especially important. It protects the free exercise of religion, prohibits the establishment of religion, and provides protections for freedom of speech, press, peaceable assembly, and petition. The Second Amendment protects the right to bear arms, and the Third prohibits the government from billeting soldiers in private homes without their owners' consent. The Fourth Amendment is best known for its provision against "unreasonable searches and seizures" and its provision for search warrants "particularly describing the place to be searched, and the persons or things to be seized." The Fifth Amendment provides a host of protections for individuals accused of crimes, including the right to a grand jury indictment (formal legal charges), protection against double jeopardy, a provision against compulsory self-incrimination, and a more general guarantee of "due process of law." The amendment also provides that the government must compensate individuals if it takes their property for public use. The Sixth Amendment extends rights of defendants into criminal trials. It specifies that trials must be "speedy" and "public," guarantees trial by jury in criminal cases, requires defendants to be informed of the nature of the charges against them and confronted with hostile witnesses, and provides for the all-important right to counsel. The Seventh Amendment extends the right to jury trials in civil, non-criminal, cases. The Eighth Amendment prohibits excessive bail or fines and "cruel and unusual punishments." The Ninth and Tenth Amendments respectively point to the idea that the people and states have reserved rights and powers that are not found within the Constitution to themselves.

Madison, who saw governments over larger land areas as one cure for faction, recognized that state governments often posed greater threats to civil rights and liberties than did the national government, but his proposal to use the Bill of Rights to limit both sets of governments failed and would have been especially unpopular among Antifederalists who were far more fearful of federal power than of state power. Significantly, the First Amendment specifies that "*Congress* [an institution of the national government] shall make no law," and in an important decision by the Marshall Court in *Barron v. Baltimore* (1833) that remained definitive for many years, the Supreme Court affirmed that the framers designed the Bill of Rights only to limit the national government.

As members of the first Congress debated these provisions, they had to decide how to ratify them and where to put them. One of Madison's chief concerns in pushing for the adoption of the Bill of Rights was to foreclose the possibility of a second convention that might undo the work of the first. It thus stands to reason that Congress chose to propose the bill without waiting for states to petition for another convention or that Congress chose to send the Bill of Rights to the state legislatures rather than call for another set of state ratifying conventions. Congress (rather than conventions called by Congress at the request of two-thirds or more of the states) has proposed all subsequent successful amendments, and all but the Twenty-first Amendment repealing prohibition have been ratified by state legislatures rather than by state conventions.

As to the placement of the new amendments, Madison preferred to interweave the provisions of the Bill of Rights into the document. Sherman wanted to attach them to the end of the Constitution, in part because he thought it would look absurd for delegates to be listed as having signed a document that contained subsequent provisions with which they could not have been familiar. While Madison's method would have made it easier to understand how new provisions related to others within the document, Sherman's proposal, which Congress adopted, makes it easier to trace the course of subsequent amendments, and may have magnified the impact of the Bill of Rights by putting them together. Since the Bill of Rights was ratified in 1791, Americans have added 17 other amendments.

THE POST–CIVIL WAR AMENDMENTS

The most important set of amendments was adopted at the end of the Civil War (1861–1865). No event in U.S. history stands as better testimony to the fact that constitutions can do only so much to bridge internal conflicts. The breach that eventually resulted in a national fissure was not the conflict between the large states and the small states that had threatened the convention and occupied so much of the delegates' time in 1787, but that between those states in the North that eliminated chattel slavery and those in the South that did not. As the nation expanded, the addition of new states, and the issue of the expansion of slavery into the territories (critical to the birth of the Republican Party), constantly brought the issue of North/South balance into focus and often resulted in temporary compromises, most notably in 1820 and 1850. In the meantime, abolitionists pointed to the inconsistency between slavery and the statements on human equality within the Declaration of Independence while Southern apologists took an increasingly hardline view that affirmed not simply the economic necessity, but also what they considered to be the mutual benefits for both the slaves and their owners. Implementation of the Fugitive Slave Clause was a continuing source of North/South contention, and southern states attempted to secede after the election of Abraham Lincoln in 1860.

By the war's end, it seemed clear that the nation could not continue to endure half slave and half free. The Thirteenth Amendment (1865) abolished slavery and the related provisions within the Constitution that had allowed for it. Although the notorious Dred Scott decision of 1857 had declared that blacks were not, and could not become citizens, the Fourteenth Amendment (1868) extended national citizenship to all persons born or naturalized within the United States and guaranteed that each would be entitled to national "privileges and immunities," to "due process of law" and to "equal protection" of the law. The Fifteenth Amendment (1870), which was widely evaded for almost 100 years, further prohibited discrimination in voting on the basis of race. Debates over these consequential amendments within Congress sometimes rose to the level of that of the convention of 1787.

Vigorous debates continue as to the degree to which these amendments were designed to substitute federal protection for individual rights for state protection. In time the Supreme Court has interpreted the due process clause of the Fourteenth Amendment to guarantee most rights within the first ten amendments not simply against federal, but also against state abridgements. The Court has thus arguably fulfilled Madison's own hopes on the subject.

THE IMPORTANCE OF THE
CONVENTION AND ITS AFTERMATH

Although not everyone is familiar with its details, the Constitution continues to structure institutions and shape debates within the United States, and it has inspired and influenced many other written constitutions throughout the world. It is frequently the subject of political rhetoric. While supporters describe the writing of the document as miraculous or providential, critics express disappointment over the convention's failure to free the slaves (and, thus, possibly head off the Civil War), grant equal rights to women, provide direct election of the president, apportion both houses of Congress according to population, and so on.

For those who praise the Constitution, the very longevity of the document is undoubtedly part of its appeal. This was not entirely unanticipated. In arguing against a plan for periodic reexaminations of the Constitution, James Madison argued in Federalist No. 49 that "as every appeal to the people would carry an implication of some defect in the government, frequent appeals would, in great measure, deprive the government of that veneration which time bestows on everything, and without which perhaps the wisest and freest would not possess the requisite stability" (Hamilton, Madison, and Jay 1981, 315). He further mused that while veneration would not be necessary in a nation of philosophers, "in every other nation, the most rational government will not find it a superfluous advantage to have the prejudices of the community on its side" (315).

As a people, Americans emphasize progress. This almost necessitates finding areas in which members of the current generation have excelled their forbearers. When judged by their attitudes toward slavery, toward women, toward Native Americans, and toward other minorities, the framers (at least, some of them) are often found wanting. The fact that the men at the Constitutional Convention were more articulate than most and sometimes seemed far ahead of their time, does not mean that they escaped it. Considering that it ultimately took more than 75 years and a bloody civil war to eliminate slavery in America and almost 150 years to adopt a constitutional amendment (the Nineteenth) granting women the right to vote, it is unlikely that any convention that sought to solve such issues in 1787 would have succeeded. The difficulty and ultimate failure to get delegates to accept proportional representation in both houses of Congress is but one indication of the public reception that measures for more direct democracy would have been likely to elicit.

The most important aspect of the writing and ratification of the Constitution may well be that of serving as a model for civic discourse. Every delegate who attended the Constitutional Convention or who participated in a state ratifying convention was representing not only his respective state but the American people as a whole. Most delegates took this responsibility quite seriously. Ultimately, however, they realized that they needed to compromise if they were to come to any substantial agreements that would advance national interests.

In a world where leaders have slaughtered millions of people on behalf of one or another utopian ideal—"liberty, equality, and fraternity," the establishment of a Third Reich, the dictatorship of the proletariat, or jihad, to name only a few—delegates during the American founding period recognized that it was appropriate to settle for a plan that was less than perfect but could be peacefully instituted. They demonstrated that it was possible to advocate ideas with rhetorical rather than physical force. They showed the power of both speaking and listening. They represented the diverse interests of their individual states while keeping principles and broader national interests in constant view.

One beauty of studying the Constitutional Convention and the state ratifying conventions is that they provide explanations for provisions within the Constitution that might otherwise appear inexplicable. Because of Madison's great care in taking notes, it is possible not only to find out what the founders actually ultimately proposed but also what arguments they used to justify them. Some measures within the Constitution, most notably the electoral college and equal state representation in the Senate, become much more understandable when one realizes the alternatives that were available and their possible consequences. Some proposed alternatives may look much more viable today than they did in 1787 and may warrant reconsideration, but even such reconsideration can be informed by earlier controversies.

The American people of today face crises relative to unemployment, government spending, the solvency of entitlement programs, foreign engagements, international terrorism, rising debt, declining public trust, injustice, and social disintegration, some of which are of similar magnitude to those that citizens faced in 1787. The U.S. Constitution will not last forever. Even if the nation survives for another 200 years or more, there could be a time when it will also require a substantial rewriting. Should such a time come, the nation would indeed be blessed if it could find individuals (fortunately, it could now draw from both men and women) who were as talented, as committed to peaceful discourse, and as public spirited as those who attended the convention.

In writing the introductory essay for *The Federalist*, Alexander Hamilton posed the question "whether societies of men are really capable or not establishing good government from reflection and choice, or whether they are forever destined to depend for their political constitutions on accident and force" (33). Hamilton presented a vote for ratification of the Constitution as a vote for "reflection and choice." The drafting and ratifying of the Constitution provides no guarantee that other deliberative bodies (includ-

ing possible constitutional conventions or meetings of Congress) will succeed, but it indicates that, under the right circumstances, success is possible.

SOURCES CITED IN THIS CHAPTER

Farrand, Max. 1966. *Records of the Federal Convention of 1787*. 4 vols. New Haven, CT: Yale University Press.

Hamilton, Alexander, James Madison, and John Jay. 1981. *The Federalist Papers*. Edited by Clinton Rossiter. New York: New American Library.

St. John, Jeffrey. 1990. *A Child of Fortune: A Correspondent's Report on the Ratification of the U.S. Constitution and the Battle for a Bill of Rights*. Ottawa, IL: Jameson Books., Inc.

SELECTED DOCUMENTS

THE DECLARATION OF INDEPENDENCE

In Congress, July 4, 1776
The unanimous Declaration of the thirteen united States of America,

When in the Course of human events it becomes necessary for one people to dissolve the political bands which have connected them with another and to assume among the powers of the earth, the separate and equal station to which the Laws of Nature and of Nature's God entitle them, a decent respect to the opinions of mankind requires that they should declare the causes which impel them to the separation.

We hold these truths to be self-evident, that all men are created equal, that they are endowed by their Creator with certain unalienable Rights, that among these are Life, Liberty and the pursuit of Happiness. That to secure these rights, Governments are instituted among Men, deriving their just powers from the consent of the governed, That whenever any Form of Government becomes destructive of these ends, it is the Right of the People to alter or to abolish it, and to institute new Government, laying its foundation on such principles and organizing its powers in such form, as to them shall seem most likely to effect their Safety and Happiness. Prudence, indeed, will dictate that Governments long established should not be changed for light and transient causes; and accordingly all experience hath shewn that mankind are more disposed to suffer, while evils are sufferable than to right themselves by abolishing the forms to which they are accustomed. But when a long train of abuses and usurpations, pursuing invariably the same Object evinces a design to reduce them under absolute Despotism, it is their right, it is their duty, to throw off such Government, and to provide new Guards for their future security. Such has been the patient sufferance of these Colonies; and such is now the necessity which constrains them to alter their former Systems of Government. The history of the present King of Great Britain is a history of repeated injuries and usurpations, all having in direct object the establishment of an absolute Tyranny over these States. To prove this, let Facts be submitted to a candid world.

He has refused his Assent to Laws, the most wholesome and necessary for the public good.

He has forbidden his Governors to pass Laws of immediate and pressing importance, unless suspended in their operation till his Assent should be obtained; and when so suspended, he has utterly neglected to attend to them.

He has refused to pass other Laws for the accommodation of large districts of people, unless those people would relinquish the right of Representation in the Legislature, a right inestimable to them and formidable to tyrants only.

He has called together legislative bodies at places unusual, uncomfortable, and distant from the depository of their Public Records, for the sole purpose of fatiguing them into compliance with his measures.

He has dissolved Representative Houses repeatedly, for opposing with manly firmness his invasions on the rights of the people.

He has refused for a long time, after such dissolutions, to cause others to be elected, whereby the Legislative Powers, incapable of Annihilation, have returned to the People at large for their exercise; the State remaining in the mean time exposed to all the dangers of invasion from without, and convulsions within.

He has endeavoured to prevent the population of these States; for that purpose obstructing the Laws for Naturalization of Foreigners; refusing to pass others to encourage their migrations hither, and raising the conditions of new Appropriations of Lands.

He has obstructed the Administration of Justice by refusing his Assent to Laws for establishing Judiciary Powers.

He has made Judges dependent on his Will alone for the tenure of their offices, and the amount and payment of their salaries.

He has erected a multitude of New Offices, and sent hither swarms of Officers to harass our people and eat out their substance.

He has kept among us, in times of peace, Standing Armies without the Consent of our legislatures.

He has affected to render the Military independent of and superior to the Civil Power.

He has combined with others to subject us to a jurisdiction foreign to our constitution, and unacknowledged by our laws; giving his Assent to their Acts of pretended Legislation:

For quartering large bodies of armed troops among us:

For protecting them, by a mock Trial from punishment for any Murders which they should commit on the Inhabitants of these States:

For cutting off our Trade with all parts of the world:

For imposing Taxes on us without our Consent:

For depriving us in many cases, of the benefit of Trial by Jury:

For transporting us beyond Seas to be tried for pretended offences:

For abolishing the free System of English Laws in a neighbouring Province, establishing therein an Arbitrary government, and enlarging its Boundaries so as to render it at once an example and fit instrument for introducing the same absolute rule into these Colonies

For taking away our Charters, abolishing our most valuable Laws and altering fundamentally the Forms of our Governments:

For suspending our own Legislatures, and declaring themselves invested with power to legislate for us in all cases whatsoever.

He has abdicated Government here, by declaring us out of his Protection and waging War against us.

He has plundered our seas, ravaged our coasts, burnt our towns, and destroyed the lives of our people.

He is at this time transporting large Armies of foreign Mercenaries to compleat the works of death, desolation, and tyranny, already begun with circumstances of Cruelty & Perfidy scarcely paralleled in the most barbarous ages, and totally unworthy the Head of a civilized nation.

He has constrained our fellow Citizens taken Captive on the high Seas to bear Arms against their Country, to become the executioners of their friends and Brethren, or to fall themselves by their Hands.

He has excited domestic insurrections amongst us, and has endeavoured to bring on the inhabitants of our frontiers, the merciless Indian Savages whose known rule of warfare, is an undistinguished destruction of all ages, sexes and conditions.

In every stage of these Oppressions We have Petitioned for Redress in the most humble terms: Our repeated Petitions have been answered only by repeated injury. A Prince, whose character is thus marked by every act which may define a Tyrant, is unfit to be the ruler of a free people.

Nor have We been wanting in attentions to our British brethren. We have warned them from time to time of attempts by their legislature to extend an unwarrantable jurisdiction over us. We have reminded them of the circumstances of our emigration and settlement here. We have appealed to their native justice and magnanimity, and we have conjured them by the ties of our common kindred to disavow these usurpations, which would inevitably interrupt our connections and correspondence. They too have been deaf to the voice of justice and of consanguinity. We must, therefore, acquiesce in the necessity, which denounces our Separation, and hold them, as we hold the rest of mankind, Enemies in War, in Peace Friends.

We, therefore, the Representatives of the united States of America, in General Congress, Assembled, appealing to the Supreme Judge of the world for the rectitude of our intentions, do, in the Name, and by Authority of the good People of these Colonies, solemnly publish and declare, That these united Colonies are, and of Right ought to be Free and Independent States, that they are Absolved from all Allegiance to the British Crown, and that all political connection between them and the State of Great Britain, is and ought to be totally dissolved; and that as Free and Independent States, they have full Power to levy War, conclude Peace, contract Alliances, establish Commerce, and to do all other Acts and Things which Independent States may of right do. And for the support of this Declaration, with a firm reliance on the protection of Divine Providence, we mutually pledge to each other our Lives, our Fortunes, and our sacred Honor.

John Hancock

New Hampshire:
Josiah Bartlett, William Whipple, Matthew Thornton

Massachusetts:
John Hancock, Samuel Adams, John Adams, Robert Treat Paine, Elbridge Gerry

Rhode Island:
Stephen Hopkins, William Ellery

Connecticut:
Roger Sherman, Samuel Huntington, William Williams, Oliver Wolcott

New York:
William Floyd, Philip Livingston, Francis Lewis, Lewis Morris

New Jersey:
Richard Stockton, John Witherspoon, Francis Hopkinson, John Hart, Abraham Clark

Pennsylvania:
Robert Morris, Benjamin Rush, Benjamin Franklin, John Morton, George Clymer, James Smith, George Taylor, James Wilson, George Ross

Delaware:
Caesar Rodney, George Read, Thomas McKean

Maryland:
Samuel Chase, William Paca, Thomas Stone, Charles Carroll of Carrollton

Virginia:
George Wythe, Richard Henry Lee, Thomas Jefferson, Benjamin Harrison, Thomas Nelson, Jr., Francis Lightfoot Lee, Carter Braxton

North Carolina:
William Hooper, Joseph Hewes, John Penn

South Carolina:
Edward Rutledge, Thomas Heyward, Jr., Thomas Lynch, Jr., Arthur Middleton

Georgia:
Button Gwinnett, Lyman Hall, George Walton

THE ARTICLES OF CONFEDERATION

Agreed to by Congress November 15, 1777; ratified and in force, March 1, 1781.

To all to whom these Presents shall come, we the undersigned Delegates of the States affixed to our Names send greeting.

Whereas the Delegates of the United States of America in Congress assembled did on the fifteenth day of November in the Year of our Lord One Thousand Seven Hundred and Seventy seven, and in the Second Year of the Independence of America, agree to certain articles of Confederation and perpetual Union between the States of New Hampshire, Massachusetts-bay, Rhode Island and Providence Plantations, Connecticut, New York, New Jersey, Pennsylvania, Delaware, Maryland, Virginia, North Carolina, South Carolina and Georgia, in the words following, viz:

Articles of Confederation and perpetual Union between the States of New Hampshire, Massachusetts-bay, Rhode Island and Providence Plantations, Connecticut, New York, New Jersey, Pennsylvania, Delaware, Maryland, Virginia, North Carolina, South Carolina and Georgia.

Article I. The Stile of this Confederacy shall be "The United States of America."

Article II. Each state retains its sovereignty, freedom, and independence, and every Power, Jurisdiction, and right, which is not by this confederation expressly delegated to the United States, in Congress assembled.

Article III. The said States hereby severally enter into a firm league of friendship with each other, for their common defense, the security of their liberties, and their mutual and general welfare, binding themselves to assist each other, against all force offered to, or attacks made upon them, or any of them, on account of religion, sovereignty, trade, or any other pretense whatever.

Article IV. The better to secure and perpetuate mutual friendship and intercourse among the people of the different States in this union, the free inhabitants of each of these States, paupers, vagabonds, and fugitives from justice excepted, shall be entitled to all privileges and immunities of free citizens in the several States; and the people of each State shall have free ingress and regress to and from any other State, and shall enjoy therein all the privileges of trade and commerce, subject to the same duties, impositions, and restrictions as the inhabitants thereof respectively, provided that such restrictions shall not extend so far as to prevent the removal of property imported into any State, to any other State, of which the owner is an inhabitant; provided also that no imposition, duties or restriction shall be laid by any State, on the property of the united States, or either of them.

If any person guilty of, or charged with, treason, felony, or other high misdemeanor in any State, shall flee from justice, and be found in any of the united States, he shall, upon demand of the Governor or executive power of the State from which he fled, be delivered up and removed to the State having jurisdiction of his offense.

Full faith and credit shall be given in each of these States to the records, acts, and judicial proceedings of the courts and magistrates of every other State.

Article V. For the most convenient management of the general interests of the united States, delegates shall be annually appointed in such manner as the legislatures of each State shall direct, to meet in Congress on the first Monday in November, in every year, with a power reserved to each State to recall its delegates, or any of them, at any time within the year, and to send others in their stead for the remainder of the year.

No State shall be represented in Congress by less than two, nor more than seven members; and no person shall be capable of being a delegate for more than three years in any term of six years; nor shall any person, being a delegate, be capable of holding any office under the united States, for which he, or another for his benefit, receives any salary, fees or emolument of any kind.

Each State shall maintain its own delegates in a meeting of the States, and while they act as members of the committee of the States.

In determining questions in the United States, in Congress assembled, each State shall have one vote.

Freedom of speech and debate in Congress shall not be impeached or questioned in any court or place out of Congress, and the members of Congress shall be protected in their persons from arrests or imprisonments, during the time of their going to and from, and attendance on Congress, except for treason, felony, or breach of the peace.

Article VI. No State, without the consent of the united States in Congress assembled, shall send any embassy to, or receive any embassy from, or enter into any conference, agreement, alliance or treaty with any King, Prince or State; nor shall any person holding any office of profit or trust under the united States, or any of them, accept any present, emolument, office or title of any kind whatever from any King, Prince or foreign State; nor shall the United States in congress assembled, or any of them, grant any title of nobility.

No two or more States shall enter into any treaty, confederation or alliance whatever between them, without the consent of the united States in congress assembled, specifying accurately the purposes for which the same is to be entered into, and how long it shall continue.

No State shall lay any imposts or duties, which may interfere with any stipulations in treaties, entered into by the united States in congress assembled, with any King, Prince or State, in pursuance of any treaties already proposed by congress, to the courts of France and Spain.

No vessel of war shall be kept up in time of peace by any State, except such number only, as shall be deemed necessary by the united States in congress assembled, for the defense of such State, or its trade; nor shall any body of forces be kept up by any State in time of peace, except such number only, as in the judgement of the united States, in congress assembled, shall be deemed requisite to garrison the forts necessary for the defense of such State; but every State shall always keep up a well-regulated and disciplined militia, sufficiently armed and accoutered, and shall provide and constantly have ready for use, in public stores, a due number of field pieces and tents, and a proper quantity of arms, ammunition and camp equipage.

No State shall engage in any war without the consent of the united States in congress assembled, unless such State be actually invaded by enemies, or shall have received certain advice of a resolution being formed by some nation of Indians to invade such State, and the danger is so imminent as not to admit of a delay till the united States in congress assembled can be consulted; nor shall any State grant commissions to any ships or vessels of war, nor letters of marque or reprisal, except it be after a declaration of war by the united States in congress assembled, and then only against the kingdom or State and the subjects thereof, against which war has been so declared, and under such regulations as shall be established by the united States in congress assembled, unless such State be infested by pirates, in which case vessels of war may be fitted out for that occasion, and kept so long as the danger shall continue, or until the united States in congress assembled shall determine otherwise.

Article VII. When land forces are raised by any State for the common defense, all officers of or under the rank of colonel, shall be appointed by the legislature of each State respectively, by whom such forces shall be raised, or in such manner as such State shall direct, and all vacancies shall be filled up by the State which first made the appointment.

Article VIII. All charges of war, and all other expenses that shall be incurred for the common defense or general welfare, and allowed by the united States in congress assembled, shall be defrayed out of a common treasury, which shall be supplied by the several States in proportion to the value of all land within each State, granted or surveyed for any person, as such land and the buildings and improvements thereon shall be estimated according to such mode as the united States in congress assembled, shall from time to time direct and appoint.

The taxes for paying that proportion shall be laid and levied by the authority and direction of the legislatures of the several States within the time agreed upon by the united States in congress assembled.

Article IX. The united States in congress assembled, shall have the sole and exclusive right and power of determining on peace and war, except in the cases mentioned in the sixth article—of sending and receiving ambassadors—entering into treaties and alliances, provided that no treaty of commerce shall be made whereby the legislative power of the respective States shall be restrained from imposing such imposts and duties on foreigners, as their own people are subjected to, or from prohibiting the exportation or importation of any species of goods or commodities whatsoever—of establishing rules for deciding in all cases, what captures on land or water shall be legal, and in what manner prizes taken by land or naval forces in the service of the United States shall be divided or appropriated—of granting letters of marque and reprisal in times of peace—appointing courts for the trial of piracies and felonies committed on the high seas and establishing courts for receiving and determining finally appeals in all cases of captures, provided that no member of Congress shall be appointed a judge of any of the said courts.

The United States in Congress assembled shall also be the last resort on appeal in all disputes and differences now subsisting or that hereafter may arise between two or more States concerning boundary, jurisdiction or any other causes whatever; which authority shall always be exercised in the manner following. Whenever the legislative or executive authority or lawful agent of any State in controversy with another shall present a petition to Congress stating the matter in question and praying for a hearing, notice thereof shall be given by order of Congress to the legislative or executive authority of the other State in controversy, and a day assigned for the appearance of the parties by their lawful agents, who shall then be directed to appoint by joint consent, commissioners or judges to constitute a court for hearing and determining the matter in question: but if they cannot agree, Congress shall name three persons out of each of the United States, and from the list of such persons each party shall alternately strike out one, the petitioners beginning, until the number shall be reduced to thirteen; and from that number not less than seven, nor more than nine names as Congress shall direct, shall in the presence of Congress be drawn out by lot, and the persons whose names shall be so drawn or any five of them, shall be commissioners or judges, to hear and finally determine the controversy, so always as a major part of the judges who shall hear the cause shall agree in the determination: and if either party shall neglect to attend at the day appointed, without showing reasons, which Congress shall judge sufficient, or being present shall refuse to strike, the Congress shall proceed to nominate three persons out of each State, and the secretary of Congress shall strike in behalf of such party absent or refusing; and the judgement and sentence of the court to be appointed, in the manner before prescribed, shall be final and conclusive; and if any of the parties shall refuse to submit to the authority of such court, or to appear or defend their claim or cause, the court shall nevertheless proceed to pronounce sentence, or judgement, which shall in like manner be final and decisive, the judgement or sentence and other proceedings being in either case transmitted to Congress, and lodged among the acts of Congress for the security of the parties concerned: provided that every commissioner, before he sits in judgement, shall take an oath to be administered by one of the judges of the supreme or superior court of the State, where the cause shall be tried, 'well and truly to hear and determine the matter in question, according to the best of his judgement, without favor, affection or hope of reward': provided also, that no State shall be deprived of territory for the benefit of the United States.

All controversies concerning the private right of soil claimed under different grants of two or more States, whose jurisdictions as they may respect such lands, and the States which passed such grants are adjusted, the said grants or either of them being at the same time claimed to have originated antecedent to such settlement of jurisdiction, shall on the petition of either party to the Congress of the United States, be finally determined as near as may be in the same manner as is before prescribed for deciding disputes respecting territorial jurisdiction between different States.

The United States in Congress assembled shall also have the sole and exclusive right and power of regulating the alloy and value of coin struck by their own authority, or by that of the respective States—fixing the standards of weights and measures throughout the United States—regulating the trade and managing all affairs with the Indians, not members of any of the States, provided that the legislative right of any State within its own limits be not infringed or violated—establishing or regulating post offices from one State to another, throughout all the United States, and exacting such postage on the papers passing through the same as may be requisite to defray the expenses of the said office—appointing all officers of the land forces, in the service of the United States, excepting regimental officers—appointing all the officers of the naval forces, and commissioning all officers whatever in the service of the United States—making rules for the government and regulation of the said land and naval forces, and directing their operations.

The United States in Congress assembled shall have authority to appoint a committee, to sit in the recess of Congress, to be denominated 'A Committee of the States,' and to consist of one delegate from each State; and to appoint such other committees and civil officers as may be necessary for managing the general affairs of the United States under their direction—to appoint one of their members to preside, provided that no person be allowed to serve in the office of president more than one year in any term of three years; to ascertain the necessary sums of money to be raised for the service of the United States, and to appropriate and apply the same for defraying the public expenses—to borrow money, or emit bills on the credit of the United States, transmitting every half-year to the respective States an account of the sums of money so borrowed or emitted—to build and equip a navy—to agree upon the number of land forces, and to make requisitions from each State for its quota, in proportion to the number of white inhabitants in such State; which requisition shall be binding, and thereupon the legislature of each State shall appoint the regimental officers, raise the men and cloath, arm and equip them in a solid-like manner, at the expense of the United States; and the officers and men so cloathed, armed and equipped shall march to the place appointed, and within the time agreed on by the United States in Congress assembled. But if the United States in Congress assembled shall, on consideration of circumstances judge proper that any State should not raise men, or should raise a smaller number of men than the quota thereof, such extra number shall be raised, officered, cloathed, armed and equipped in the same manner as the quota of each State, unless the legislature of such State shall judge that such extra number cannot be safely spread out in the same, in which case they shall raise, officer, cloath, arm and equip as many of such extra number as they judge can be safely spared. And the officers and men so cloathed, armed, and equipped, shall march to the place appointed, and within the time agreed on by the united States in congress assembled.

The united States in congress assembled shall never engage in a war, nor grant letters of marque or reprisal in time of peace, nor enter into any treaties or alliances, nor coin money, nor regulate the value thereof, nor ascertain the sums and expenses necessary for the defense and welfare of the United States, or any of them, nor emit bills, nor borrow money on the credit of the united States, nor appropriate money, nor agree upon the number of vessels of war, to be built or purchased, or the number of land or sea forces to be raised, nor appoint a commander in chief of the army or navy, unless nine States assent to the same: nor shall a question on any other point, except for adjourning from day to day be determined, unless by the votes of the majority of the united States in congress assembled.

The congress of the united States shall have power to adjourn to any time within the year, and to any place within the united States, so that no period of adjournment be for a longer duration than the space of six months, and shall publish the journal of their proceedings monthly, except such parts thereof relating to treaties, alliances or military operations, as in their judgement require secrecy; and the yeas and nays of the delegates of each State on any question shall be entered on the journal, when it is desired by any delegates of a State, or any of them, at his or their request shall be furnished with a transcript of the said journal, except such parts as are above excepted, to lay before the legislatures of the several States.

Article X. The committee of the States, or any nine of them, shall be authorized to execute, in the recess of congress, such of the powers of congress as the united States in congress assembled, by the consent of the nine States, shall from time to time think expedient to vest them with; provided that no power be delegated to the said Committee, for the exercise of which, by the articles of confederation, the voice of nine States in the Congress of the United States assembled be requisite.

Article XI. Canada acceding to this confederation, and adjoining in the measures of the united States, shall be admitted into, and entitled to all the advantages of this union; but no other colony shall be admitted into the same, unless such admission be agreed to by nine States.

Article XII. All bills of credit emitted, monies borrowed, and debts contracted by, or under the authority of congress, before the assembling of the united States, in pursuance of the present confederation, shall be deemed and considered as a charge against the United States, for payment and satisfaction whereof the said united States, and the public faith are hereby solemnly pledged.

Article XIII. Every State shall abide by the determination of the united States in congress assembled, on all questions which by this confederation are submitted to them. And the Articles of this confederation shall be inviolably observed by every State, and the union shall be perpetual; nor shall any alteration at any time hereafter be made in any of them; unless such alteration be agreed to in a congress of the united States, and be afterwards confirmed by the legislatures of every State.

And Whereas it hath pleased the Great Governor of the World to incline the hearts of the legislatures we respectively represent in Congress, to approve of, and to authorize us to ratify the said articles of confederation and perpetual union. Know Ye that we the undersigned delegates, by virtue of the power and authority to us given for that purpose, do by these presents, in the name and in behalf of our respective constituents, fully and entirely ratify and confirm each and every of the said articles of confederation and perpetual union, and all and singular the matters and things therein contained: And we do further solemnly plight and engage the faith of our respective constituents, that they shall abide by the determinations of the united States in congress assembled, on all questions, which by the said confederation are submitted to them. And that the articles thereof shall be inviolably observed by the States we respectively represent, and that the union shall be perpetual.

In Witness whereof we have hereunto set our hands in Congress. Done at Philadelphia in the State of Pennsylvania the ninth Day of July in the Year of our Lord one thousand seven Hundred and Seventy-eight, and in the Third Year of the independence of America.

On the part and behalf of the State of New Hampshire:
Josiah Bartlett
John Wentworth Junr. August 8th 1778

On the part and behalf of The State of Massachusetts Bay:
John Hancock
Samuel Adams
Elbridge Gerry
Francis Dana
James Lovell
Samuel Holten

On the part and behalf of the State of Rhode Island and Providence Plantations:
William Ellery
Henry Marchant
John Collins

On the part and behalf of the State of Connecticut:
Roger Sherman
Samuel Huntington
Oliver Wolcott
Titus Hosmer
Andrew Adams

On the Part and Behalf of the State of New York:
James Duane
Francis Lewis
Wm Duer
Gouv Morris

On the Part and in Behalf of the State of New Jersey, November 26, 1778.
Jno Witherspoon
Nath. Scudder

On the part and behalf of the State of Pennsylvania:
Robt Morris
Daniel Roberdeau
John Bayard Smith
William Clingan
Joseph Reed 22nd July 1778

On the part and behalf of the State of Delaware:
Tho Mckean February 12, 1779

John Dickinson May 5th 1779
Nicholas Van Dyke

On the part and behalf of the State of Maryland:
John Hanson March 1 1781
Daniel Carroll

On the Part and Behalf of the State of Virginia:
Richard Henry Lee
John Banister
Thomas Adams
Jno Harvie
Francis Lightfoot Lee

On the part and Behalf of the State of No Carolina:
John Penn July 21st 1778
Corns Harnett
Jno Williams

On the part and behalf of the State of South Carolina:
Henry Laurens
William Henry Drayton
Jno Mathews
Richd Hutson
Thos Heyward Junr

On the part and behalf of the State of Georgia:
Jno Walton 24th July 1778
Edwd Telfair
Edwd Langworthy

THE CONSTITUTION OF THE UNITED STATES

Signed September 17, 1787
Effective March 4, 1789
We the people of the United States, in order to form a more perfect union, establish justice, insure domestic tranquility, provide for the common defense, promote the general welfare, and secure the blessings of lib-

erty to ourselves and our posterity, do ordain and establish this Constitution for the United States of America.

ARTICLE I

Section 1. All legislative powers herein granted shall be vested in a Congress of the United States, which shall consist of a Senate and House of Representatives.

Section 2. 1. The House of Representatives shall be composed of members chosen every second year by the people of the several states, and the electors in each state shall have the qualifications requisite for electors of the most numerous branch of the state legislature.

2. No person shall be a representative who shall not have attained to the age of twenty-five years, and been seven years a citizen of the United States, and who shall not, when elected, be an inhabitant of that state in which he shall be chosen.

3. [*Representatives and direct taxes shall be apportioned among the several states which may be included within this union, according to their respective numbers, which shall be determined by adding to the whole number of free persons, including those bound to service for a term of years, and excluding Indians not taxed, three-fifths of all other persons.*]* The actual enumeration shall be made within three years after the first meeting of the Congress of the United States, and within every subsequent term of ten years, in such manner as they shall by law direct. The number of representatives shall not exceed one for every thirty thousand, but each state shall have at least one representative; and until such enumeration shall be made, the state of New Hampshire shall be entitled to choose three, Massachusetts eight, Rhode Island and Providence plantations one, Connecticut five, New York six, New Jersey four, Pennsylvania eight, Delaware one, Maryland six, Virginia ten; North Carolina five, South Carolina five, and Georgia three.

4. When vacancies happen in the representation from any state, the executive authority thereof shall issue writs of election to fill such vacancies.

5. The House of Representatives shall choose their speaker and other officers; and shall have the sole power of impeachment.

Section 3. 1. The Senate of the United States shall be composed of two senators from each state, [*chosen by the legislature thereof*]† for six years; and each senator shall have one vote.

---

* Changed by Section 2 of the Fourteenth Amendment.
† Changed by the Seventeenth Amendment.

2. Immediately after they shall be assembled in consequence of the first election, they shall be divided as equally as may be into three classes. The seats of the senators of the first class shall be vacated at the expiration of the second year, of the second class at the expiration of the fourth year, and of the third class at the expiration of the sixth year, so that one third may be chosen every second year; [*and if vacancies happen by resignation, or otherwise, during the recess of the legislature of any state, the executive thereof may make temporary appointments until the next meeting of the legislature, which shall then fill such vacancies.*]*

3. No person shall be a senator who shall not have attained to the age of thirty years, and been nine years a citizen of the United States, and who shall not, when elected, be an inhabitant of that state for which he shall be chosen.

4. The vice-president of the United States shall be president of the Senate, but shall have no vote, unless they be equally divided.

5. The Senate shall choose their other officers, and also a president pro tempore, in the absence of the vice-president, or when he shall exercise the office of the president of the United States.

6. The Senate shall have the sole power to try all impeachments. When sitting for that purpose, they shall be on oath or affirmation. When the president of the United States is tried, the chief justice shall preside: and no person shall be convicted without the concurrence of two thirds of the members present.

7. Judgment in cases of impeachment shall not extend further than to removal from office, and disqualifications to hold and enjoy any office of honor, trust or profit under the United States: but the party convicted shall nevertheless be liable and subject to indictment, trial, judgment and punishment, according to law.

Section 4. 1. The times, places, and manner of holding elections for senators and representatives, shall be prescribed in each state by the legislature thereof; but the Congress may at any time by law make or alter such regulations, except as to the places of choosing senators.

2. The Congress shall assemble at least once in every year, and such meeting shall be [*on the first Monday in December*],† unless they shall by law appoint a different day.

Section 5. 1. Each House shall be the judge of the elections, returns and qualifications of its own members, and a majority of each shall constitute a quorum to do business; but a smaller number may adjourn from day to

---

* Changed by the Seventeenth Amendment.
† Changed by Section 2 of the Twentieth Amendment.

day, and may be authorized to compel the attendance of absent members, in such manner, and under such penalties as each House may provide.

2. Each House may determine the rules of its proceedings, punish its members for disorderly behavior, and, with the concurrence of two thirds, expel a member.

3. Each House shall keep a journal of its proceedings, and from time to time publish the same, excepting such parts as may in their judgment require secrecy; and the yeas and nays of the members of either House on any question shall, at the desire of one fifth of those present, be entered on the journal.

4. Neither House, during the session of Congress, shall, without the consent of the other, adjourn for more than three days, nor to any other place than that in which the two Houses shall be sitting.

Section 6. 1. The senators and representatives shall receive a compensation for their services, to be ascertained by law, and paid out of the treasury of the United States. They shall in all cases, except treason, felony, and breach of the peace, be privileged from arrest during their attendance at the session of their respective Houses, and in going to and returning from the same; and for any speech or debate in either House, they shall not be questioned in any other place.

2. No senator or representative shall, during the time for which he was elected, be appointed to any civil office under the authority of the United States, which shall have been created, or the emoluments whereof shall have been increased during such time; and no person holding any office under the United States shall be a member of either House during his continuance in office.

Section 7. 1. All bills for raising revenue shall originate in the House of Representatives; but the Senate may propose or concur with amendments as on other bills.

2. Every bill which shall have passed the House of Representatives and the Senate, shall, before it becomes a law, be presented to the president of the United States; if he approves he shall sign it, but if not he shall return it, with his objections to that House in which it shall have originated, who shall enter the objections at large on their journal, and proceed to reconsider it. If after such reconsideration two thirds of that House shall agree to pass the bill, it shall be sent, together with the objections, to the other House, by which it shall likewise be reconsidered, and if approved by two thirds of that House, it shall become a law. But in all such cases the votes of both Houses shall be determined by yeas and nays, and the names of the persons voting for and against the bill shall be entered on the journal of

each House respectively. If any bill shall not be returned by the president within ten days (Sundays excepted) after it shall have been presented to him, the same shall be a law, in like manner as if he had signed it, unless the Congress by their adjournment prevent its return, in which case it shall not be a law.

3. Every order, resolution, or vote to which the concurrence of the Senate and the House of Representatives may be necessary (except on a question of adjournment) shall be presented to the president of the United States; and before the same shall take effect, shall be approved by him, or being disapproved by him, shall be repassed by two thirds of the Senate and House of Representatives, according to the rules and limitations prescribed in the case of a bill.

Section 8. The Congress shall have the power:

1. To lay and collect taxes, duties, imposts, and excises, to pay the debts and provide for the common defense and general welfare of the United States; but all duties, imposts, and excises shall be uniform throughout the United States;

2. To borrow money on the credit of the United States;

3. To regulate commerce with foreign nations, and among the several States, and with the Indian tribes;

4. To establish a uniform rule of naturalization, and uniform laws on the subject of bankruptcies throughout the United States;

5. To coin money, regulate the value thereof, and of foreign coin, and fix the standard of weights and measures;

6. To provide for the punishment of counterfeiting the securities and current coin of the United States;

7. To establish post offices and post roads;

8. To promote the progress of science and useful arts, by securing for limited times to authors and inventors the exclusive right to their respective writings and discoveries;

9. To constitute tribunals inferior to the Supreme Court;

10. To define and punish piracies and felonies committed on the high seas, and offenses against the law of nations;

11. To declare war, grant letters of marque and reprisal, and make rules concerning captures on land and water;

12. To raise and support armies, but no appropriation of money to that use shall be for a longer term than two years;

13. To provide and maintain a navy;

14. To make rules for the government and regulation of the land and naval forces;

15. To provide for calling forth the militia to execute the laws of the Union, suppress insurrections and repel invasions;

16. To provide for organizing, arming, and disciplining the militia, and for governing such part of them as may be employed in the service of the United States, reserving to the States respectively, the appointment of the officers, and the authority of training the militia according to the discipline prescribed by Congress.

17. To exercise exclusive legislation in all cases whatsoever, over such district (not exceeding ten miles square) as may, by cession of particular states, and the acceptance of Congress, become the seat of the government of the United States, and to exercise like authority over all places purchased by the consent of the legislature of the state in which the same shall be, for the erection of forts, magazines, arsenals, dockyards, and other needful buildings; and

18. To make all laws which shall be necessary and proper for carrying into execution the foregoing powers, and all other powers vested by this Constitution in the government of the United States, or in any department or officer thereof.

Section 9. 1. The migration or importation of such persons as any of the states now existing shall think proper to admit, shall not be prohibited by the Congress prior to the year one thousand eight hundred and eight, but a tax or duty may be imposed on such importation, not exceeding ten dollars for each person.

2. The privilege of the writ of habeas corpus shall not be suspended, unless when in cases of rebellion or invasion the public safety may require it.

3. No bill of attainder or ex post facto law shall be passed.

4. [*No capitation, or other direct, tax shall be laid, unless in proportion to the census or enumeration hereinbefore directed to be taken.*]*

5. No tax or duty shall be laid on articles exported from any State.

6. No preference shall be given by any regulation of commerce or revenue to the ports of one state over those of another: nor shall vessels bound to, or from, one state be obliged to enter, clear, or pay duties in another.

7. No money shall be drawn from the treasury, but in consequence of appropriations made by law; and a regular statement and account of the receipts and expenditures of all public money shall be published from time to time.

8. No title of nobility shall be granted by the United States: and no person holding any office of profit or trust under them, shall, without the consent

---

* Changed by the Sixteenth Amendment.

of the Congress, accept of any present, emolument, office, or title, of any kind whatever, from any king, prince, or foreign state.

Section 10. 1. No state shall enter into any treaty, alliance, or confederation; grant letters of marque and reprisal; coin money; emit bills of credit; make anything but gold and silver coin a tender in payment of debts; pass any bill of attainder, ex post facto law, or law impairing the obligation of contracts, or grant any title of nobility.

2. No state shall, without the consent of the Congress, lay any imposts or duties on imports or exports, except what may be absolutely necessary for executing its inspection laws: and the net produce of all duties and imposts laid by any state on imports or exports, shall be for the use of the treasury of the United States; and all such laws shall be subject to the revision and control of the Congress.

3. No state shall, without the consent of the Congress, lay any duty of tonnage, keep troops, or ships of war in time of peace, enter into any agreement or compact with another state, or with a foreign power, or engage in war, unless actually invaded, or in such imminent danger as will not admit of delay.

ARTICLE II

Section 1. 1. The executive power shall be vested in a president of the United States of America. He shall hold his office during the term of four years, and, together with the vice-president, chosen for the same term, be elected as follows:

2. Each state shall appoint, in such manner as the legislature thereof may direct, a number of electors, equal to the whole number of senators and representatives to which the state may be entitled in the Congress: but no senator or representative, or person holding an office of trust or profit under the United States, shall be appointed an elector.

3. [*The electors shall meet in their respective states, and vote by ballot for two persons, of whom one at least shall not be an inhabitant of the same state with themselves. And they shall make a list of all the persons voted for, and of the number of votes for each; which list they shall sign and certify, and transmit sealed to the seat of the government of the United States, directed to the president of the Senate. The president of the Senate shall, in the presence of the Senate and House of Representatives, open all the certificates, and the votes shall then be counted. The person having the greatest number of votes shall be the president, if such number be a majority of the whole number of electors appointed; and if there be more than one who have such majority, and have an equal number of votes, then the House of Representatives shall immediately choose by ballot one of them for president; and if*]

*no person have a majority, then from the five highest on the list the said House shall in like manner choose the president. But in choosing the president, the votes shall be taken by states, the representation from each state having one vote; a quorum for this purpose shall consist of a member or members from two thirds of the states, and a majority of all the states shall be necessary to a choice. In every case, after the choice of the president, the person having the greatest number of votes of the electors shall be the vice-president. But if there should remain two or more who have equal votes, the Senate shall choose from them by ballot the vice president.]**

3. The Congress may determine the time of choosing the electors, and the day on which they shall give their votes; which day shall be the same throughout the United States.

4. No person except a natural born citizen, or a citizen of the United States, at the time of the adoption of this Constitution, shall be eligible to the office of president; neither shall any person be eligible to that office who shall not have attained to the age of thirty-five years, and been fourteen years a resident within the United States.

5. *[In case of the removal of the president from office, or of his death, resignation, or inability to discharge the powers and duties of the said office, the same shall devolve on the vice president, and the Congress may by law provide for the case of removal, death, resignation, or inability, both of the president and vice-president, declaring what officer shall then act as president, and such officer shall act accordingly, until the disability be removed, or a president shall be elected.]†*

6. The president shall, at stated times, receive for his services a compensation, which shall neither be increased nor diminished during the period for which he shall have been elected, and he shall not receive within that period any other emolument from the United States, or any of them.

7. Before he enter on the execution of his office, he shall take the following oath or affirmation:—"I do solemnly swear (or affirm) that I will faithfully execute the office of president of the United States, and will to the best of my ability, preserve, protect and defend the Constitution of the United States."

Section 2. 1. The president shall be commander in chief of the army and navy of the United States, and of the militia of the several states, when called into the actual service of the United States; he may require the opinion, in writing, of the principal officer in each of the executive departments, upon any subject relating to the duties of their respective offices,

---

* Changed by the Twelfth Amendment.
† Changed by the Twenty-fifth Amendment.

and he shall have power to grant reprieves and pardons for offenses against the United States, except in cases of impeachment.

2. He shall have power, by and with the advice and consent of the Senate, to make treaties, provided two thirds of the senators present concur; and he shall nominate, and by and with the advice and consent of the Senate, shall appoint ambassadors, other public ministers and consuls, judges of the Supreme Court, and all other officers of the United States, whose appointments are not herein otherwise provided for, and which shall be established by law: but the Congress may by law vest the appointment of such inferior officers, as they think proper, in the president alone, in the courts of law, or in the heads of departments.

3. The president shall have power to fill up all vacancies that may happen during the recess of the Senate, by granting commissions which shall expire at the end of their next session.

Section 3. He shall from time to time give to the Congress information of the state of the Union, and recommend to their consideration such measures as he shall judge necessary and expedient; he may, on extraordinary occasions, convene both Houses, or either of them, and in case of disagreement between them with respect to the time of adjournment, he may adjourn them to such time as he shall think proper; he shall receive ambassadors and other public ministers; he shall take care that the laws be faithfully executed, and shall commission all the officers of the United States.

Section 4. The president, vice-president, and all civil officers of the United States, shall be removed from office on impeachment for, and conviction of, treason, bribery, or other high crimes and misdemeanors.

ARTICLE III

Section 1. The judicial power of the United States shall be vested in one Supreme Court, and in such inferior courts as the Congress may from time to time ordain and establish. The judges, both of the Supreme and inferior courts, shall hold their offices during good behavior, and shall, at stated times, receive for their services, a compensation, which, shall not be diminished during their continuance in office.

Section 2. 1. The judicial power shall extend to all cases, in law and equity, arising under this Constitution, the laws of the United States, and treaties made, or which shall be made, under their authority;—to all cases affecting ambassadors, other public ministers and consuls;—to all cases of admiralty and maritime jurisdiction;—to controversies to which the United States shall be a party;—to controversies between two or more states; [*between a state* *and citizens of another state;—]** between citizens of different states;—between citizens of the same state claiming lands under grants of different states, [*and between a state, or the citizens thereof, and foreign states citizens or subjects.*]†

2. In all cases affecting ambassadors, other public ministers and consuls, and those in which a state shall be party, the Supreme Court shall have original jurisdiction. In all the other cases before mentioned, the Supreme Court shall have appellate jurisdiction, both as to law and to fact, with such exceptions, and under such regulations as the Congress shall make.

3. The trial of all crimes, except in cases of impeachment, shall be by jury; and such trial shall be held in the state where the said crimes shall have been committed; but when not committed within any state, the trial shall be at such place or places as the Congress may by law have directed.

Section 3. 1. Treason against the United States shall consist only in levying war against them, or in adhering to their enemies, giving them aid and comfort. No person shall be convicted of treason unless on the testimony of two witnesses to the same overt act, or on confession in open court.

2. The Congress shall have power to declare the punishment of treason, but no attainder of treason shall work corruption of blood, or forfeiture except during the life of the person attainted.

ARTICLE IV

Section 1. Full faith and credit shall be given in each state to the public acts, records, and judicial proceedings of every other state. And the Congress may by general laws prescribe the manner in which such acts, records and proceedings shall be proved, and the effect thereof.

Section 2. 1. The citizens of each state shall be entitled to all privileges and immunities of citizens in the several states.

2. A person charged in any state with treason, felony, or other crime, who shall flee from justice, and be found in another state, shall on demand of the executive authority of the state having jurisdiction of the crime.

3. [*No person held to service or labor in one state under the laws thereof, escaping into another, shall in consequence of any law or regulation therein, be discharged from such service or labor, but shall be delivered up on claim of the party to whom such service or labor may be due.*]‡

Section 3. 1. New states may be admitted by the Congress into this Union; but no new state shall be formed or erected within the jurisdiction of any

---

* Changed by the Eleventh Amendment.
† Changed by the Eleventh Amendment.
‡ Changed by the Thirteenth Amendment.

other state, nor any state be formed by the junction of two or more states, or parts of states, without the consent of the legislatures of the states concerned as well as of the Congress.

2. The Congress shall have power to dispose of and make all needful rules and regulations respecting the territory or other property belonging to the United States; and nothing in this Constitution shall be so construed as to prejudice any claims of the United States, or of any particular state.

Section 4. The United States shall guarantee to every state in this Union a republican form of government, and shall protect each of them against invasion; and on application of the legislature, or of the executive (when the legislature cannot be convened) against domestic violence.

ARTICLE V

The Congress, whenever two thirds of both Houses shall deem it necessary, shall propose amendments to this Constitution, or, on the application of the legislature of two thirds of the several states, shall call a convention for proposing amendments, which in either case, shall be valid to all intents and purposes, as part of this Constitution when ratified by the legislatures of three fourths of the several states, or by conventions in three fourths thereof, as the one or the other mode of ratification may be proposed by the Congress; Provided that no amendment which may be made prior to the year one thousand eight hundred and eight shall in any manner affect the first and fourth clauses in the ninth section of the first article; and that no state, without its consent, shall be deprived of its equal suffrage in the Senate.

ARTICLE VI

1. All debts contracted and engagements entered into, before the adoption of this Constitution, shall be as valid against the United States under this Constitution, as under the Confederation.

2. This Constitution, and the laws of the United States which shall be made in pursuance thereof; and all treaties made, or which shall be made, under the authority of the United States, shall be the supreme law of the land; and the Judges in every state shall be bound thereby, anything in the Constitution or laws of any state to the contrary notwithstanding.

3. The senators and representatives before mentioned, and the members of the several state legislatures, and all executive and judicial officers, both of the United States and of the several states, shall be bound by oath or affirmation to support this Constitution; but no religious test shall ever be required as a qualification to any office or public trust under the United States.

ARTICLE VII

The ratification of the conventions of nine states shall be sufficient for the establishment of this Constitution between the states so ratifying the same. Done in Convention by the unanimous consent of the States present the seventeenth day of September in the year of our Lord one thousand seven hundred and eighty-seven, and of the independence of the United States of America the twelfth. In witness whereof we have hereunto subscribed our names.

G. *Washington*—Presid: and deputy from Virgina
New Hampshire
John Langdon
Nicholas Gilman
Massachusetts
Nathaniel Gorham
Rufus King
Connecticut
Wm. Saml. Johnson
Roger Sherman
New York
Alexander Hamilton
New Jersey
Wil: Livingston
David Brearley
Wm. Paterson
Jona Dayton
Pennsylvania
B. Franklin
Thomas Mifflin
Robt. Morris
Geo. Clymer
Thos. FitzSimons
Jared Ingersoll
James Wilson
Gouv. Morris
Delaware
Geo: Read
Gunning Bedford jun
John Dickinson
Richard Bassett

Jaco: Broom
Maryland
James McHenry
Dan of St Thos. Jenifer
Danl Carroll
Virginia
John Blair—
James Madison Jr.
North Carolina
Wm. Blount
Richd. Dobbs Spaight
HU Williamson
South Carolina
J. Rutledge
Charles Cotesworth Pickney
Charles Pickney
Pierce Butler
Georgia William Few
Abr Baldwin
Attest *William Jackson* Secretary

In Convention Monday September 17th 1787.

Articles in addition to, and amendment of, the Constitution of the United States of America, proposed by Congress, and ratified by the legislatures of the several states pursuant to the fifth article of the original Constitution.

AMENDMENTS

First Ten Amendments proposed by Congress Sept. 25, 1789.
Ratified by three-fourths of the States December 15, 1791.

AMENDMENT I

Congress shall make no law respecting an establishment of religion, or prohibiting the free exercise thereof; or abridging the freedom of speech, or of the press; or the right of the people peaceably to assemble, and to petition the government for a redress of grievances.

AMENDMENT II

A well regulated militia, being necessary to the security of a free state, the right of the people to keep and bear arms, shall not be infringed.

AMENDMENT III

No soldier shall, in time of peace be quartered in any house, without the consent of the owner, nor in time of war, but in a manner to be prescribed by law.

AMENDMENT IV

The right of the people to be secure in their persons, houses, papers, and effects, against unreasonable searches and seizures, shall not be violated, and no warrants shall issue, but upon probable cause, supported by oath or affirmation, and particularly describing the place to be searched, and the persons or things to be seized.

AMENDMENT V

No person shall be held to answer for a capital, or otherwise infamous crime, unless on a presentment or indictment of a grand jury, except in cases arising in the land or naval forces, or in the militia, when in actual service in time of war or public danger; nor shall any person be subject for the same offense to be twice put in jeopardy of life or limb; nor shall be compelled in any criminal case to be a witness against himself, nor be deprived of life, liberty, or property, without due process of law: nor shall private property be taken for public use without just compensation.

AMENDMENT VI

In all criminal prosecutions, the accused shall enjoy the right to a speedy and public trial, by an impartial jury of the state and district wherein the crime shall have been committed, which district shall have been previously ascertained by law, and to be informed of the nature and cause of the accusation; to be confronted with the witnesses against him; to have compulsory process for obtaining witnesses in his favor, and to have the assistance of counsel for his defense.

AMENDMENT VII

In suits at common law, where the value in controversy shall exceed twenty dollars, the right of trial by jury shall be preserved, and no fact tried by a jury shall be otherwise reexamined in any court of the United States, than according to the rules of the common law.

AMENDMENT VIII

Excessive bail shall not be required, nor excessive fines imposed, nor cruel and unusual punishments inflicted.

AMENDMENT IX

The enumeration in the Constitution of certain rights shall not be construed to deny or disparage others retained by the people.

AMENDMENT X

The powers not delegated to the United States by the Constitution, nor prohibited by it to the states, are reserved to the states respectively, or to the people.

AMENDMENT XI

Proposed by Congress March 5, 1794. Ratified January 8, 1798.

The judicial power of the United States shall not be construed to extend to any suit in law or equity, commenced or prosecuted against one of the United States by citizens of another state, or by citizens or subjects of any foreign state.

AMENDMENT XII

Proposed by Congress December 12, 1803. Ratified September 25, 1804.

The electors shall meet in their respective states, and vote by ballot for president and vice-president, one of whom, at least, shall not be an inhabitant of the same state with themselves; they shall name in their ballots the person voted for as president, and in distinct ballots, the person voted for as vice-president, and they shall make distinct lists of all persons voted for as president and of all persons voted for as vice-president, and of the number of votes for each, which lists they shall sign and certify, and transmit sealed to the seat of the government of the United States, directed to the president of the Senate;—The president of the Senate shall, in the presence of the Senate and House of Representatives, open all the certificates and the votes shall then be counted;—The person having the greatest number of votes for president, shall be the president, if such number be a majority of the whole number of electors appointed; and if no person have such majority, then from the persons having the highest numbers not exceeding three on the list of those voted for as president, the House of Representatives shall choose immediately, by ballot, the president. But in choosing the president, the votes shall be taken by states, the representation from each state having one vote; a quorum for this purpose shall consist of a member or members from two thirds of the states, and a majority of all the states shall be necessary to a choice. [*And if the House of Representatives shall not choose a president whenever the right of choice shall devolve upon them, before the fourth day of March next following, then the vice-president shall act as president, as in the case of the* *death or other constitutional disability of the president.*]* The person having the greatest number of votes as vice-president shall be the vice-president, if such number be a majority of the whole number of electors appointed, and if no person have a majority, then from the two highest numbers on the list, the Senate shall choose the vice-president; a quorum for the purpose shall consist of two thirds of the whole number of Senators, and a majority of the whole number shall be necessary to a choice. But no person constitutionally ineligible to the office of president shall be eligible to that of vice-president of the United States.

AMENDMENT XIII
Proposed by Congress February 1, 1865. Ratified December 18, 1865.
Section 1. Neither slavery nor involuntary servitude, except as punishment for crime whereof the party shall have been duly convicted, shall exist within the United States, or any place subject to their jurisdiction.
Section 2. Congress shall have power to enforce this article by appropriate legislation.

AMENDMENT XIV
Proposed by Congress June 16, 1866. Ratified July 23, 1868.
Section 1. All persons born or naturalized in the United States, and subject to the jurisdiction thereof, are citizens of the United States and of the state wherein they reside. No state shall make or enforce any law which shall abridge the privileges or immunities of citizens of the United States; nor shall any state deprive any person of life, liberty, or property, without due process of law; nor deny to any person within its jurisdiction the equal protection of the laws.
Section 2. Representatives shall be apportioned among the several states according to their respective numbers, counting the whole number of persons in each state, excluding Indians not taxed. But when the right to vote at any election for the choice of electors for president and vice-president of the United States, representatives in Congress, the executive and judicial officers of a state, or the members of the legislature thereof, is denied to any of the male inhabitants of such state, being twenty-one years of age, and citizens of the United States, or in any way abridged, except for participation in rebellion, or other crime, the basis of representation therein shall be reduced in the proportion which the number of such male citizens shall bear to the whole number of male citizens twenty-one years of age in such state.

---

* Superseded by Section 3 of the Twentieth Amendment.

Section 3. No person shall be a senator or representative in Congress, or elector of president and vice president, or hold any office, civil or military, under the United States, or under any state, who having previously taken an oath, as a member of Congress, or as an officer of the United States, or as a member of any state legislature, or as an executive or judicial officer of any state, to support the Constitution of the United States, shall have engaged in insurrection or rebellion against the same, or given aid or comfort to the enemies thereof. But Congress may by a vote of two thirds of each House, remove such disability.

Section 4. The validity of the public debt of the United States, authorized by law, including debts incurred for payment of pensions and bounties for services in suppressing insurrection or rebellion, shall not be questioned. But neither the United States nor any state shall assume or pay any debt or obligation incurred in aid of insurrection or rebellion against the United States, or any claim for the loss or emancipation of any slave; but all such debts, obligations, and claims shall be held illegal and void.

Section 5. The Congress shall have power to enforce, by appropriate legislation, the provisions of this article.

AMENDMENT XV

Proposed by Congress February 27, 1869. Ratified March 30, 1870.

Section 1. The right of citizens of the United States to vote shall not be denied or abridged by the United States or by any state on account of race, color, or previous condition of servitude.

Section 2. The Congress shall have power to enforce this article by appropriate legislation.

AMENDMENT XVI

Proposed by Congress July 12, 1909. Ratified February 25, 1913.

The Congress shall have power to lay and collect taxes on incomes, from whatever source derived, without apportionment among the several states, and without regard to any census or enumeration.

AMENDMENT XVII

Proposed by Congress May 16, 1912. Ratified May 31, 1913.

The Senate of the United States shall be composed of two senators from each state, elected by the people thereof, for six years; and each senator shall have one vote. The electors in each state shall have the qualifications requisite for electors of the most numerous branch of the state legislature.

When vacancies happen in the representation of any state in the Senate, the executive authority of such state shall issue writs of election to fill such vacancies: Provided, That the legislature of any state may empower the executive thereof to make temporary appointments until the people fill the vacancies by election as the legislature may direct.

This amendment shall not be so construed as to affect the election or term of any senator chosen before it becomes valid as part of the Constitution.

AMENDMENT XVIII

Proposed by Congress December 17, 1917. Ratified January 16, 1919.

Section 1. [*After one year from the ratification of this article, the manufacture, sale, or transportation of intoxicating liquors within, the importation thereof into, or the exportation thereof from the United States and all territory subject to the jurisdiction thereof for beverage purposes is hereby prohibited.*]

Section 2. [*The Congress and the several states shall have concurrent power to enforce this article by appropriate legislation.*]

Section 3. [*This article shall be inoperative unless it shall have been ratified as an amendment to the Constitution by the legislatures of the several states, as provided in the Constitution, within seven years from the date of the submission hereof to the states by Congress.*]*

AMENDMENT XIX

Proposed by Congress June 5, 1919. Ratified August 26, 1920.

The right of citizens of the United States to vote shall not be denied or abridged by the United States or by any state on account of sex.

The Congress shall have power by appropriate legislation to enforce the provisions of this article.

AMENDMENT XX

Proposed by Congress March 3, 1932. Ratified January 23, 1933.

Section 1. The terms of the president and vice-president shall end at noon on the 20th day of January, and the terms of Senators and Representatives at noon on the 3d day of January, of the years in which such terms would have ended if this article had not been ratified; and the terms of their successors shall then begin.

Section 2. The Congress shall assemble at least once in every year, and such meeting shall begin at noon on the 3d day of January, unless they shall by law appoint a different day.

---

* The Eighteenth Amendment was repealed by the Twenty-first Amendment, December 5, 1933.

Section 3. If, at the time fixed for the beginning of the term of the president, the president-elect shall have died, the vice-president-elect shall become president. If a president shall not have been chosen before the time fixed for the beginning of his term, or if the president-elect shall have failed to qualify, then the vice-president-elect shall act as president until a president shall have qualified; and the Congress may by law provide for the case wherein neither a president-elect nor a vice-president-elect shall have qualified, declaring who shall then act as president, or the manner in which one who is to act shall be selected, and such person shall act accordingly until a president or vice-president shall have qualified.

Section 4. The Congress may by law provide for the case of the death of any of the persons from whom the House of Representatives may choose a president whenever the right of choice shall have devolved upon them, and for the case of the death of any of the persons from whom the Senate may choose a vice-president whenever the right of choice shall have devolved upon them.

Section 5. Sections 1 and 2 shall take effect on the 15th day of October following the ratification of this article.

Section 6. This article shall be inoperative unless it shall have been ratified as an amendment to the Constitution by the legislatures of three-fourths of the several states within seven years from the date of its submission.

AMENDMENT XXI

Proposed by Congress February 20, 1933. Ratified December 5, 1933.

Section 1. The Eighteenth Article of amendment to the Constitution of the United States is hereby repealed.

Section 2. The transportation or importation into any state, territory, or possession of the United States for delivery or use therein of intoxicating liquors in violation of the laws thereof, is hereby prohibited.

Section 3. This article shall be inoperative unless it shall have been ratified as an amendment to the Constitution by conventions in the several states, as provided in the Constitution, within seven years from the date of the submission thereof to the states by the Congress.

AMENDMENT XXII

Proposed by Congress March 24, 1947. Ratified February 26, 1951.

Section 1. No person shall be elected to the office of the president more than twice, and no person who has held the office of president, or acted as president, for more than two years of a term to which some other person was elected president shall be elected to the office of the president more than once. But this article shall not apply to any person holding the office of president when this article was proposed by the Congress, and shall not prevent any person who may be holding the office of president, or acting as president, during the term within which this article becomes operative from holding the office of president or acting as president during the remainder of such term.

Section 2. This article shall be inoperative unless it shall have been ratified as an amendment to the Constitution by the legislatures of three-fourths of the several states within seven years from the date of its submission to the states by the Congress.

AMENDMENT XXIII

Proposed by Congress June 16, 1960. Ratified March 29, 1961.

Section 1. The district constituting the seat of government of the United States shall appoint such manner as the Congress may direct:

A number of electors of president and vice-president equal to the whole number of Senators and Representatives in Congress to which the district would be entitled if it were a state, but in no event more than the least populous state; they shall be in addition to those appointed by the states, but they shall be considered, for the purposes of election of president and vice-president, to be electors appointed by a state; and they shall meet in the district and perform such duties as provided by the twelfth article of amendment.

Section 2. The Congress shall have the power to enforce this article by appropriate legislation.

AMENDMENT XXIV

Proposed by Congress August 27, 1962. Ratified January 23, 1964.

Section 1. The right of citizens of the United States to vote in any primary or other election for president or vice-president, for electors for president or vice-president, or for Senator or Representative in Congress, shall not be denied or abridged by the United States or any state by failure to pay any poll tax or other tax.

Section 2. The Congress shall have the power to enforce this article by appropriate legislation.

AMENDMENT XXV

Proposed by Congress July 6, 1965. Ratified February 10, 1967.

Section 1. In case of the removal of the president from office or of his death or resignation, the vice-president shall become president.

Section 2. Whenever there is a vacancy in the office of the vice-president, the president shall nominate a vice-president who shall take office upon confirmation by a majority vote of both Houses of Congress.

Section 3. Whenever the president transmits to the president pro tempore of the Senate and the Speaker of the House of Representatives his written declaration that he is unable to discharge the powers and duties of his office, and until he transmits to them a written declaration to the contrary, such powers and duties shall be discharged by the vice-president as acting president.

Section 4. Whenever the vice-president and a majority of either the principal officers of the executive departments or of such other body as Congress may by law provide, transmit to the president pro tempore of the Senate and the Speaker of the House of Representatives their written declaration that the president is unable to discharge the powers and duties of his office, the vice-president shall immediately assume the powers and duties of the office as acting president.

Thereafter, when the president transmits to the president pro tempore of the Senate and the Speaker of the House of Representatives his written declaration that no inability exists, he shall resume the powers and duties of his office unless the vice-president and a majority of either the principal officers of the executive department or of such other body as Congress may by law provide, transmit within four days to the president pro tempore of the Senate and the Speaker of the House of Representatives their written declaration that the president is unable to discharge the powers and duties of his office. Thereupon Congress shall decide the issue, assembling within forty-eight hours for that purpose if not in session. If the Congress, within twenty-one days after receipt of the latter written declaration, or, if Congress is not in session, within twenty-one days after Congress is required to assemble, determines by two-thirds vote of both Houses that the president is unable to discharge the powers and duties of his office, the vice-president shall continue to discharge the same as acting president; otherwise, the president shall resume the powers and duties of his office.

AMENDMENT XXVI

Proposed by Congress March 23, 1971. Ratified June 30, 1971.

Section 1. The right of citizens of the United States, who are eighteen years of age or older, to vote shall not be denied or abridged by the United States or by any State on account of age.

Section 2. The Congress shall have power to enforce this article by appropriate legislation.

AMENDMENT XXVII

Proposed by Congress September 25, 1789. Ratified May 8, 1992.

No law, varying the compensation for the services of the Senators and Representatives, shall take effect, until an election of Representatives shall have intervened.

THE VIRGINIA PLAN

State of the resolutions submitted to the consideration of the House by the honorable Mr. Randolph, as altered, amended, and agreed to, in a Committee of the whole House.

1. Resolved that it is the opinion of this Committee that a national government ought to be established consisting of a Supreme Legislative, Judiciary, and Executive.

2. Resolved. that the national Legislature ought to consist of Two Branches.

3. Resolved that the members of the first branch of the national Legislature ought to be elected by the People of the several States for the term of Three years. to receive fixed stipends, by which they may be compensated for the devotion of their time to public service to be paid out of the National Treasury. to be ineligible to any Office established by a particular State or under the authority of the United-States (except those peculiarly belonging to the functions of the first branch) during the term of service, and under the national government for the space of one year after it's expiration.

4. Resolved. that the members of the second Branch of the national Legislature ought to be chosen by the individual Legislatures. to be of the age of thirty years at least. to hold their offices for a term sufficient to ensure their independency, namely seven years. to receive fixed stipends, by which they may be compensated for the devotion of their time to public service—to be paid out of the National Treasury to be ineligible to any office established by a particular State, or under the authority of the United States (except those peculiarly belonging to the functions of the second branch) during the term of service, and under the national government, for the space of one year after it's expiration.

5. Resolved that each branch ought to possess the right of originating acts.

6. Resolved. that the national Legislature ought to be empowered to enjoy the legislative rights vested in Congress by the confederation—and moreover to legislate in all cases to which the separate States are incompetent: or in which the harmony of the United States may be interrupted by the exercise of individual legislation. to negative all laws passed by the several States contravening, in the opinion of the national Legislature, the articles of union, or any treaties subsisting under the authority of the union.

7. Resolved. that the right of suffrage in the first branch of the national Legislature ought not to be according to the rule established in the articles of confederation: but according to some equitable ratio of representation— namely, in proportion to the whole number of white and other free citizens and inhabitants of every age, sex, and condition including those bound to servitude for a term of years, and three fifths of all other persons not comprehended in the foregoing description, except Indians, not paying taxes in each State.

8. Resolved. that the right of suffrage in the second branch of the national Legislature ought to be according to the rule established for the first.

9. Resolved. that a national Executive be instituted to consist of a single person. to be chosen by the National Legislature. for the term of seven years. with power to carry into execution the national Laws, to appoint to Offices in cases not otherwise provided for to be ineligible a second time, and to be removable on impeachment and conviction of mal practice or neglect of duty. to receive a fixed stipend, by which he may be compensated for the devotion of his time to public service to be paid out of the national Treasury.

10. Resolved. that the national executive shall have a right to negative any legislative act: which shall not be afterwards passed unless by two third parts of each branch of the national Legislature.

11. Resolved. that a national Judiciary be established to consist of One Supreme Tribunal. The Judges of which to be appointed by the second Branch of the National Legislature. to hold their offices during good behaviour to receive, punctually, at stated times, a fixed compensation for their services: in which no encrease or diminution shall be made so as to affect the persons actually in office at the time of such encrease or diminution.

12. Resolved. That the national Legislature be empowered to appoint inferior Tribunals.

13. Resolved. that the jurisdiction of the national Judiciary shall extend to cases which respect the collection of the national revenue: impeachments of any national officers: and questions which involve the national peace and harmony.

14. Resolved. that provision ought to be made for the admission of States, lawfully arising within the limits of the United States, whether from a voluntary junction of government and territory, or otherwise, with the consent of a number of voices in the national Legislature less than the whole.

15. Resolved. that provision ought to be made for the continuance of Congress and their authorities until a given day after the reform of the articles of Union shall be adopted; and for the completion of all their engagements.

16. Resolved that a republican constitution, and its existing laws, ought to be guaranteed to each State by the United States.

17. Resolved. that provision ought to be made for the amendment of the articles of Union, whensoever it shall seem necessary.

18. Resolved. that the Legislative, Executive, and Judiciary powers within the several States ought to be bound by oath to support the articles of Union.

19. Resolved. that the amendments which shall be offered to the confederation by the Convention, ought at a proper time or times, after the approbation of Congress to be submitted to an assembly or assemblies of representatives, recommended by the several Legislatures, to be expressly chosen by the People to consider and decide thereon.

Received this sheet from the President of the United States, with the journals of the general Convention, March 19th, 1796.

Timothy Pickering
Secy of State

THE NEW JERSEY PLAN

1. Resolved that the articles of Confederation ought to be so revised, corrected and enlarged, as to render the federal Constitution adequate to the exigencies of Government, and the preservation of the Union.

2. Resolved that in addition to the powers vested in the United States in Congress, by the present existing articles of Confederation, they be authorized to pass acts for raising a revenue, by levying a duty or duties on all goods or merchandises of foreign growth or manufacture, imported into any part of the United States, by Stamps on paper, vellum or parchment, and by a postage on all letters or packages passing through the general post-office, to be applied to such federal purposes as they shall deem proper and expedient; to make rules and regulations for the collection thereof; and the same from time to time, to alter and amend in such manner as they shall

think proper: to pass Acts for the regulation of trade and commerce as well with foreign nations as with each other: provided that all punishments, fines, forfeitures and penalties to be incurred for contravening such acts rules and regulations shall be adjudged by the Common law Judiciaries of the State in which any offense contrary to the true intent and meaning of such Acts rules and regulations shall have been committed or perpetrated, with liberty of commencing in the first instance all suits and prosecutions for that purpose in the superior common law Judiciary in such State, subject nevertheless, for the correction of all errors, both in law and fact in rendering Judgment, to an appeal to the Judiciary of the United States.

3. Resolved that whenever requisitions shall be necessary, instead of the rule for making requisitions mentioned in the articles of Confederation, the United States in Congress assembled be authorized to make such requisitions in proportion to the whole number of white and other free citizens and inhabitants of every age, sex, and condition including those bound to servitude for a term of years and three fifths of all other persons not comprehended in the foregoing description, except Indians not paying taxes; that if such requisitions be not complied with, in the time specified therein, to direct the collection thereof in the non complying States and for that purpose to devise and pass acts directing and authorizing the same; provided that none of the powers hereby vested in the United States in Congress assembled shall be exercised without the consent of at least—States, and in that proportion if the number of Confederated States should hereafter be increased or diminished.

4. Resolved that the United States in Congress assembled be authorized to elect a federal Executive to consist of—persons, to continue in office for the term of—years, to receive punctually at stated times a fixed compensation for their services, in which no increase or diminution shall be made so as to affect the persons composing the Executive at the time of such increase or diminution, to be paid out of the federal treasury; to be incapable of holding any other office or appointment during their time of service and for—years thereafter; to be ineligible a second time, and removable by Congress on application by a majority of the Executives of the several States; that the Executives, besides their general authority to execute the federal acts, ought to appoint all federal officers not otherwise provided for, and to direct all military operations; provided that none of the persons composing the federal Executive shall on any occasion take command of any troops, so as personally to conduct any enterprise as General or in other capacity.

5. Resolved that a federal Judiciary be established to consist of a supreme Tribunal the Judges of which to be appointed by the Executive, and to hold

their offices during good behavior, to receive punctually at stated times a fixed compensation for their services in which no increase or diminution shall be made, so as to affect the persons actually in office at the time of such increase or diminution; that the Judiciary so established shall have authority to hear and determine in the first instance on all impeachments of federal officers, and by way of appeal in the dernier resort in all cases touching the rights of Ambassadors, in all cases of captures from an enemy, in all cases of piracies and felonies on the high Seas, in all cases in which foreigners may be interested, in the construction of any treaty or treaties, or which may arise on any of the Acts for regulation of trade, or the collection of the federal Revenue: that none of the Judiciary shall during the time they remain in office be capable of receiving or holding any other office or appointment during their time of service, or for—thereafter.

6. Resolved that all Acts of the United States in Congress assembled made by virtue and in pursuance of the powers hereby and by the articles of Confederation vested in them, and all Treaties made and ratified under the authority of the United States shall be the supreme law of the respective States so far forth as those Acts or Treaties shall relate to the said States or their Citizens, and that the Judiciary of the several States shall be bound thereby in their decisions, any thing in the respective laws of the Individual States to the contrary notwithstanding; and that if any State, or any body of men in any State shall oppose or prevent the carrying into execution such acts or treaties, the federal Executive shall be authorized to call forth the power of the Confederated States, or so much thereof as may be necessary to enforce and compel an obedience to such Acts, or an observance of such Treaties.

7. Resolved that provision be made for the admission of new States into the Union.

8. Resolved the rule for naturalization ought to be the same in every State.

9. Resolved that a Citizen of one State committing an offense in another State of the Union, shall be deemed guilty of the same offense as if it had been committed by a Citizen of the State in which the offense was committed.

FEDERALIST NO. 10

The Utility of the Union as a Safeguard Against Domestic Faction and Insurrection (continued)

Daily Advertiser
Thursday, November 22, 1787
(James Madison)
To the People of the State of New York:

Among the numerous advantages promised by a well constructed Union, none deserves to be more accurately developed than its tendency to break and control the violence of faction. The friend of popular governments never finds himself so much alarmed for their character and fate, as when he contemplates their propensity to this dangerous vice. He will not fail, therefore, to set a due value on any plan which, without violating the principles to which he is attached, provides a proper cure for it. The instability, injustice, and confusion introduced into the public councils, have, in truth, been the mortal diseases under which popular governments have everywhere perished; as they continue to be the favorite and fruitful topics from which the adversaries to liberty derive their most specious declamations. The valuable improvements made by the American constitutions on the popular models, both ancient and modern, cannot certainly be too much admired; but it would be an unwarrantable partiality, to contend that they have as effectually obviated the danger on this side, as was wished and expected. Complaints are everywhere heard from our most considerate and virtuous citizens, equally the friends of public and private faith, and of public and personal liberty, that our governments are too unstable, that the public good is disregarded in the conflicts of rival parties, and that measures are too often decided, not according to the rules of justice and the rights of the minor party, but by the superior force of an interested and overbearing majority. However anxiously we may wish that these complaints had no foundation, the evidence, of known facts will not permit us to deny that they are in some degree true. It will be found, indeed, on a candid review of our situation, that some of the distresses under which we labor have been erroneously charged on the operation of our governments; but it will be found, at the same time, that other causes will not alone account for many of our heaviest misfortunes; and, particularly, for that prevailing and increasing distrust of public engagements, and alarm for private rights, which are echoed from one end of the continent to the other. These must be chiefly, if not wholly, effects of the unsteadiness and injustice with which a factious spirit has tainted our public administrations.

By a faction, I understand a number of citizens, whether amounting to a majority or a minority of the whole, who are united and actuated by some common impulse of passion, or of interest, adversed to the rights of other citizens, or to the permanent and aggregate interests of the community.

There are two methods of curing the mischiefs of faction: the one, by removing its *causes*; the other, by controlling its *effects*.

There are again two methods of removing the causes of faction: the one, by destroying the liberty which is essential to its existence; the other, by giving to every citizen the same opinions, the same passions, and the same interests.

It could never be more truly said than of the first remedy, that it was worse than the disease. Liberty is to faction what air is to fire, an aliment without which it instantly expires. But it could not be less folly to abolish liberty, which is essential to political life, because it nourishes faction, than it would be to wish the annihilation of air, which is essential to animal life, because it imparts to fire its destructive agency.

The second expedient is as impracticable as the first would be unwise. As long as the reason of man continues fallible, and he is at liberty to exercise it, different opinions will be formed. As long as the connection subsists between his reason and his self-love, his opinions and his passions will have a reciprocal influence on each other; and the former will be objects to which the latter will attach themselves. The diversity in the faculties of men, from which the rights of property originate, is not less an insuperable obstacle to a uniformity of interests. The protection of these faculties is the first object of government. From the protection of different and unequal faculties of acquiring property, the possession of different degrees and kinds of property immediately results; and from the influence of these on the sentiments and views of the respective proprietors, ensues a division of the society into different interests and parties.

The latent causes of faction are thus sown in the nature of man; and we see them everywhere brought into different degrees of activity, according to the different circumstances of civil society. A zeal for different opinions concerning religion, concerning government, and many other points, as well of speculation as of practice; an attachment to different leaders ambitiously contending for pre-eminence and power; or to persons of other descriptions whose fortunes have been interesting to the human passions, have, in turn, divided mankind into parties, inflamed them with mutual animosity, and rendered them much more disposed to vex and oppress each other than to co-operate for their common good. So strong is this propensity of mankind to fall into mutual animosities, that where no substantial occasion presents itself, the most frivolous and fanciful distinctions have been sufficient to kindle their unfriendly passions and excite their most violent conflicts. But the most common and durable source of factions has been the various and unequal distribution of property. Those who hold and those who are without property have ever formed distinct interests in society. Those who are creditors, and those who are debtors, fall under a like discrimination. A landed interest, a manufacturing interest, a mercantile interest, a moneyed interest, with many lesser interests, grow up of necessity in civilized nations, and divide them into different classes, actuated by different sentiments and views. The regulation of these various and interfering interests forms the principal task of modern legislation, and involves the spirit of party and faction in the necessary and ordinary operations of the government.

No man is allowed to be a judge in his own cause, because his interest would certainly bias his judgment, and, not improbably, corrupt his integrity. With equal, nay with greater reason, a body of men are unfit to be both judges and parties at the same time; yet what are many of the most important acts of legislation, but so many judicial determinations, not indeed concerning the rights of single persons, but concerning the rights of large bodies of citizens? And what are the different classes of legislators but advocates and parties to the causes which they determine? Is a law proposed concerning private debts? It is a question to which the creditors are parties on one side and the debtors on the other. Justice ought to hold the balance between them. Yet the parties are, and must be, themselves the judges; and the most numerous party, or, in other words, the most powerful faction must be expected to prevail. Shall domestic manufactures be encouraged, and in what degree, by restrictions on foreign manufactures? are questions which would be differently decided by the landed and the manufacturing classes, and probably by neither with a sole regard to justice and the public good. The apportionment of taxes on the various descriptions of property is an act which seems to require the most exact impartiality; yet there is, perhaps, no legislative act in which greater opportunity and temptation are given to a predominant party to trample on the rules of justice. Every shilling with which they overburden the inferior number, is a shilling saved to their own pockets.

It is in vain to say that enlightened statesmen will be able to adjust these clashing interests, and render them all subservient to the public good. Enlightened statesmen will not always be at the helm. Nor, in many cases, can such an adjustment be made at all without taking into view indirect and remote considerations, which will rarely prevail over the immediate interest which one party may find in disregarding the rights of another or the good of the whole.

The inference to which we are brought is, that the causes of faction cannot be removed, and that relief is only to be sought in the means of controlling its effects.

If a faction consists of less than a majority, relief is supplied by the republican principle, which enables the majority to defeat its sinister views by regular vote. It may clog the administration, it may convulse the society; but it will be unable to execute and mask its violence under the forms of the Constitution. When a majority is included in a faction, the form of popular government, on the other hand, enables it to sacrifice to its ruling passion or interest both the public good and the rights of other citizens. To secure the public good and private rights against the danger of such a faction, and at the same time to preserve the spirit and the form of popular government, is then the great object to which our inquiries are directed. Let me add that it is the great desideratum by which this form of government can be rescued from the opprobrium under which it has so long labored, and be recommended to the esteem and adoption of mankind.

By what means is this object attainable? Evidently by one of two only. Either the existence of the same passion or interest in a majority at the same time must be prevented, or the majority, having such coexistent passion or interest, must be rendered, by their number and local situation, unable to concert and carry into effect schemes of oppression. If the impulse and the opportunity be suffered to coincide, we well know that neither moral nor religious motives can be relied on as an adequate control. They are not found to be such on the injustice and violence of individuals, and lose their efficacy in proportion to the number combined together, that is, in proportion as their efficacy becomes needful.

From this view of the subject it may be concluded that a pure democracy, by which I mean a society consisting of a small number of citizens, who assemble and administer the government in person, can admit of no cure for the mischiefs of faction. A common passion or interest will, in almost every case, be felt by a majority of the whole; a communication and concert result from the form of government itself; and there is nothing to check the inducements to sacrifice the weaker party or an obnoxious individual. Hence it is that such democracies have ever been spectacles of turbulence and contention; have ever been found incompatible with personal security or the rights of property; and have in general been as short in their lives as they have been violent in their deaths. Theoretic politicians, who have patronized this species of government, have erroneously supposed that by reducing mankind to a perfect equality in their political rights, they would, at the same time, be perfectly equalized and assimilated in their possessions, their opinions, and their passions.

A republic, by which I mean a government in which the scheme of representation takes place, opens a different prospect, and promises the cure for which we are seeking. Let us examine the points in which it varies from pure democracy, and we shall comprehend both the nature of the cure and the efficacy which it must derive from the Union.

The two great points of difference between a democracy and a republic are: first, the delegation of the government, in the latter, to a small number of citizens elected by the rest; secondly, the greater number of citizens, and greater sphere of country, over which the latter may be extended.

The effect of the first difference is, on the one hand, to refine and enlarge the public views, by passing them through the medium of a chosen body of citizens, whose wisdom may best discern the true interest of their country, and whose patriotism and love of justice will be least likely to sacrifice it to temporary or partial considerations. Under such a regulation, it may well happen that the public voice, pronounced by the representatives of the people, will be more consonant to the public good than if pronounced by the people themselves, convened for the purpose. On the other hand, the effect may be inverted. Men of factious tempers, of local prejudices, or of sinister designs, may, by intrigue, by corruption, or by other means, first obtain the suffrages, and then betray the interests, of the people. The question resulting is, whether small or extensive republics are more favorable to the election of proper guardians of the public weal; and it is clearly decided in favor of the latter by two obvious considerations:

In the first place, it is to be remarked that, however small the republic may be, the representatives must be raised to a certain number, in order to guard against the cabals of a few; and that, however large it may be, they must be limited to a certain number, in order to guard against the confusion of a multitude. Hence, the number of representatives in the two cases not being in proportion to that of the two constituents, and being proportionally greater in the small republic, it follows that, if the proportion of fit characters be not less in the large than in the small republic, the former will present a greater option, and consequently a greater probability of a fit choice.

In the next place, as each representative will be chosen by a greater number of citizens in the large than in the small republic, it will be more difficult for unworthy candidates to practice with success the vicious arts by which elections are too often carried; and the suffrages of the people being more free, will be more likely to centre in men who possess the most attractive merit and the most diffusive and established characters.

It must be confessed that in this, as in most other cases, there is a mean, on both sides of which inconveniences will be found to lie. By enlarging too much the number of electors, you render the representatives too little acquainted with all their local circumstances and lesser interests; as by reducing it too much, you render him unduly attached to these, and too little fit to comprehend and pursue great and national objects. The federal Constitution forms a happy combination in this respect; the great and aggregate interests being referred to the national, the local and particular to the State legislatures.

The other point of difference is, the greater number of citizens and extent of territory which may be brought within the compass of republican than of democratic government; and it is this circumstance principally which renders factious combinations less to be dreaded in the former than in the latter. The smaller the society, the fewer probably will be the distinct parties and interests composing it; the fewer the distinct parties and interests, the more frequently will a majority be found of the same party; and the smaller the number of individuals composing a majority, and the smaller the compass within which they are placed, the more easily will they concert and execute their plans of oppression. Extend the sphere, and you take in a greater variety of parties and interests; you make it less probable that a majority of the whole will have a common motive to invade the rights of other citizens; or if such a common motive exists, it will be more difficult for all who feel it to discover their own strength, and to act in unison with each other. Besides other impediments, it may be remarked that, where there is a consciousness of unjust or dishonorable purposes, communication is always checked by distrust in proportion to the number whose concurrence is necessary.

Hence, it clearly appears, that the same advantage which a republic has over a democracy, in controlling the effects of faction, is enjoyed by a large over a small republic,—is enjoyed by the Union over the States composing it. Does the advantage consist in the substitution of representatives whose enlightened views and virtuous sentiments render them superior to local prejudices and schemes of injustice? It will not be denied that the representation of the Union will be most likely to possess these requisite endowments. Does it consist in the greater security afforded by a greater variety of parties, against the event of any one party being able to outnumber and oppress the rest? In an equal degree does the increased variety of parties comprised within the Union, increase this security. Does it, in fine, consist in the greater obstacles opposed to the concert and accomplishment of the secret wishes of an unjust and interested majority? Here, again, the extent of the Union gives it the most palpable advantage.

The influence of factious leaders may kindle a flame within their particular States, but will be unable to spread a general conflagration through the other States. A religious sect may degenerate into a political faction in a part of the Confederacy; but the variety of sects dispersed over the entire face of it must secure the national councils against any danger from that source. A rage for paper money, for an abolition of debts, for an equal division of property, or for any other improper or wicked project, will be less apt to pervade the whole body of the Union than a particular member of it; in the same proportion as such a malady is more likely to taint a particular county or district, than an entire State.

In the extent and proper structure of the Union, therefore, we behold a republican remedy for the diseases most incident to republican government. And according to the degree of pleasure and pride we feel in being republicans, ought to be our zeal in cherishing the spirit and supporting the character of Federalists.

PUBLIUS

SELECTED BIBLIOGRAPHY

Adair, Douglass. 1974. "Fame and the Founding Fathers." In *Fame and the Founding Fathers: Essays*, edited by Trevor Colburn, 3–26. New York: W.W. Norton.

Adair, Douglass and Marvin Harvey. 1955. "Was Alexander Hamilton a Christian Statesman?" *William and Mary Quarterly*, 3rd ser., 12 (April): 308–29.

Adams, Willi Paul. 2001. *The First American Constitutions: Republican Ideology and the Making of State Constitutions in the Revolutionary Era*. Lanham, MD: Rowman & Littlefield.

Aldrich, John H., and Ruth W. Grant. 1993, "The Antifederalists, the First Congress, and the First Parties." *Journal of Politics* 55 (May): 295–326.

Alexander, John K. 1990. *The Selling of the Constitutional Convention: A History of News Coverage*. Madison, WI: Madison House.

American Political Science Association and American Historical Association. 1986. *This Constitution: Our Enduring Legacy*. Washington, DC: Congressional Quarterly.

Anderson, Thornton. 1993. *Creating the Constitution: The Convention of 1787 and the First Congress*. University Park: Pennsylvania State University Press.

Bailyn, Bernard. 1967. *The Ideological Origins of the American Revolution*. Cambridge, MA: Belknap Press of Harvard University Press.

———, ed. 1993. *The Debate on the Constitution: Federalists and Antifederalist Speeches, Articles, and Letters During the Struggle Over Ratification*. 2 vols. New York: Library of America.

Banning, Lance. 1995. *The Sacred Fire of Liberty: James Madison and the Founding of the American Republic*. Ithaca, NY: Cornell University Press.

Baum, Marsha L, and Christian G. Fritz. 2000. "American Constitution-Making: The Neglected State Constitutional Sources." *Hastings Constitutional Law Quarterly* 27 (Winter): 199–242.

Beard, Charles A. 1949. *An Economic Interpretation of the Constitution of the United States*. New York: Macmillan.

Becker, Carl L. 1970. *The Declaration of Independence: A Study in the History of Political Ideas.* New York: Vintage Books.

Beeman, Richard. 2009. *Plain, Honest Men: The Making of the American Constitution.* New York: Random House.

Belz, Herman, Ronald Hoffman, and Peter J. Albert, eds. 1992. *To Form a More Perfect Union: The Critical Ideas of the Constitution.* Charlottesville: University Press of Virginia.

Bennett, William J., ed. 1997. *Our Sacred Honor: Words of Advice from the Founders in Stories, Letters, Poems, and Speeches.* New York: Simon and Schuster.

Benton, Wilbourne E., ed. 1986. *1787: Drafting the U.S. Constitution.* 2 vols. College Station: Texas A & M University Press.

Berkin, Carol. 2002. *A Brilliant Solution: Inventing the American Constitution.* New York: Harcourt.

Bernstein, David. 1987. "The Constitutional Convention: Facts and Figures." *The History Teacher* 21 (November): 11–19.

Bernstein, Richard B., with Kym S. Rice. 1987. *Are We to be a Nation? The Making of the Constitution.* Cambridge, MA: Harvard University Press.

Bigler, Philip and Annie Lorsbach. 2009. *Liberty and Learning: The Essential James Madison.* Harrisonburg, VA: The James Madison Center.

Billias, George Athan. 1976. *Elbridge Gerry: Founding Father and Republican Statesman.* New York: McGraw Hill.

Bishop, Hillman Metcalf. 1950. *Why Rhode Island Opposed the Federal Constitution.* Providence, RI: Roger Williams Press.

Bloom, Sol. 1935. *The Story of the Constitution.* Washington, DC: United States Constitutional Sesquicentennial Commission.

Bodenhamer, David J. *The Revolutionary Constitution.* New York: Oxford University Press, 2012.

Borgeaud, Charles. 1982. "The Origins and Development of Written Constitutions." *Political Science Quarterly* 7 (December): 613–32.

Bowen, Catherine Drinker. 1966. *Miracle at Philadelphia: The Story of the Constitutional Convention, May to September 1787.* Boston: Little, Brown.

Boyd, Steven R. 1979. *The Politics of Opposition: Antifederalists and the Acceptance of the Constitution.* Millwood, NY: KTO Press.

Bradford, M. M. 1981. *Founding Fathers: Brief Lives of the Framers of the United States Constitution,* 2nd ed. Lawrence: University Press of Kansas.

———. 1993. *Original Intentions: On the Making and Ratification of the United States Constitution.* Athens: University of Georgia Press.

———. 2007. *What Would the Founders Do? Our Questions, Their Answers.* New York: Basic Books.

Broadwater, Jeff. 2006. *George Mason: Forgotten Founder.* Chapel Hill: The University of North Carolina Press.

Brookhiser, Richard. 2003. *Gentleman Revolutionary: Gouverneur Morris—The Rake Who Wrote the Constitution.* New York: The Free Press.

———. 2011. *James Madison*. New York: Basic Books.

Brown, Richard D. 1976. "The Founding Fathers of 1776 and 1787: A Collective View." *William and Mary Quarterly*, 3rd. ser., 33 (July): 465–80.

Burstein, Andrew and Nancy Isenberg. 2010. *Madison and Jefferson*. New York: Random House.

Butzner, Jane, compiler. 1941. *Constitutional Chaff—Rejected Suggestions of the Constitutional Convention of 1787 with Explanatory Argument*. New York: Columbia University Press.

Calvert, Jane E. 2009. *Quaker Constitutionalism and the Political Thought of John Dickinson*. New York: Cambridge University Press.

Carey, George W. 1989. *The Federalist: Design for a Constitutional Republic*. Urbana: University of Illinois Press.

Carr, William G. 1990. *The Oldest Delegate: Franklin in the Constitutional Convention*. Newark: University of Delaware Press.

Cerami, Charles. 2005. *Young Patriots: The Remarkable Story of Two Men, Their Impossible Plan and the Revolution That Created the Constitution*. Napierville, IL: Sourcebooks, Inc.

Chadwick, Bruce. 2010. *Triumvirate: The Story of the Unlikely Alliance That Saved the Constitution and United the Nation*. Naperville, IL: Sourcebooks, Inc.

Chernow, Ron. 2004. *Alexander Hamilton*. New York: Penguin Press.

Chidsey, Donald B. 1964. *The Birth of the Constitution: An Informal History*. New York: Crown Publishers.

Clarkson, Paul S., and R. Samuel Jett. 1970. *Luther Martin of Maryland*. Baltimore, MD: Johns Hopkins Press.

Clinton, Robert L. 1997. *God and Man in the Law: The Foundations of Anglo-American Constitutionalism*. Lawrence: University Press of Kansas.

Cogan, Neil H., ed. 1997. *The Complete Bill of Rights: The Drafts, Debates, Sources, and Origins*. New York: Oxford University Press.

Coleman, Nannie McCormick. 1910. *The Constitution and Its Framers*. Chicago: The Progress Company.

Collier, Christopher. 2003. *All Politics is Local: Family, Friends, and Provincial Interests in the Creation of the Constitution*. Hanover, NH: University Press of New England.

Collier, Christopher, and James Lincoln Colier. 1986. *Decision in Philadelphia: The Constitutional Convention of 1787*. New York: Random House.

Conley, Patrick T., and John P. Kaminski, eds. 1988. *The Constitution and the States: The Role of the Original Thirteen in the Framing and Adoption of the Federal Constitution*. Madison, WI: Madison House.

Connelly, William F., Jr. 2010. *James Madison Rules America: The Constitutional Origins of Congressional Partisanship*. Lanham, MD: Rowman & Littlefield.

Cooke, Donald E. 1970. *America's Great Document—The Constitution*. Maplewood, NJ: Hammond.

Corwin, Edward S. 1964. "The Progress of Constitutional Theory between the Declaration of Independence and the Meeting of the Philadelphia Convention."

American Constitutional History: Essays by Edward S. Corwin. Edited by Alpheus T. Mason and Gerald Garvey. New York: Harper and Row.

Cousins, Norman, ed. 1958. *"In God We Trust": The Religious Beliefs and Ideas of the American Founding Fathers.* New York: Harper and Brothers.

Craige, Burton. 1987. *The Federal Convention of 1787: North Carolina in the Great Crisis.* Richmond, VA: Expert Graphics.

Curtis, George Ticknor. 1961. *History of the Origin, Formation, and Adoption of the Constitution of the United States with Notices of Its Principal Framers.* 2 vols. New York: Harper and Brothers.

Dahl, Robert. 2001. *How Democratic Is the American Constitution?* New Haven, CT: Yale University Press.

DeRose, Chris. 2011. *Founding Rivals: Madison vs. Monroe: The Bill of Rights and the Election That Saved a Nation.* New York: Regnery.

Diamond, Martin. 1981. *The Founding of the Democratic Republic.* Itasca, IL: F. F. Peacock Publishers.

Dill, Alonzo. 1979. *George Wythe: Teacher of Liberty.* Williamsburg, VA: Independence Bicentennial Commission.

Dinan, John J. *The American State Constitutional Tradition.* Lawrence, KS: University Press of Kansas, 2006.

Dos Passos, John. 1957. *The Men Who Made the Nation.* Garden City, NY: Doubleday.

Dougherty, Keith L. 2001. *Collective Action under the Articles of Confederation.* Cambridge, UK: Cambridge University Press.

Dreisbach, Daniel L., Mark D. Hall, and Jeffry Morrison, eds. 2004. *The Founders on God and Government.* Lanham, MD: Rowman & Littlefield.

Dudley, William, ed. 1995. *The Creation of the Constitution: Opposing Viewpoints.* San Diego, CA: Greenhaven Press.

Edling, Max M. 2003. *A Revolution in Favor of Government: Origins of the U.S. Constitution and the Making of the American State.* New York: Oxford University Press.

Eidelberg, Paul. 1968. *The Philosophy of the American Constitution: A Reinterpretation of the Intentions of the Founding Fathers.* New York: The Free Press.

Eisinger, Chester E. 1947. "The Freehold Concept in Eighteenth-Century American Letters." *William and Mary Quarterly,* 3rd ser., 4 (1947): 42–59.

Elkins, Stanley, and Eric McKitrick. 1961. "The Founding Fathers: Young Men of the Revolution." *Political Science Quarterly* 76 (June): 181–216.

Elliott, Jonathan, ed. 1888. *The Debates in the Several State Conventions on the Adoption of the Federal Constitution.* 5 vols. New York: Burt Franklin.

Ellis, Joseph J. 2000. *Founding Brothers: The Revolutionary Generation.* New York: Vintage Books.

———. 2004. *His Excellency: George Washington.* New York: Alfred A. Knopf.

———. 2007. *American Creation: Triumphs and Tragedies at the Founding of the Republic.* New York: Alfred A. Knopf.

Engeman, Thomas S., and Michael P. Zuchert, eds. 2004. *Protestantism and the American Founding*. Notre Dame, IN: University of Notre Dame Press.

Epstein, David F. 1984. *The Political Theory of* The Federalist. Chicago: University of Chicago Press.

Ernst, Robert. 1968. *Rufus King: American Federalist*. Chapel Hill: University of North Carolina Press.

Farber, Daniel A., and Suzanna Sherry. 1990. *A History of the American Constitution*. Saint Paul, MN: West Publishing.

Farrand, Max. 1913. *The Framing of the Constitution of the United States*. New Haven, CT: Yale University Press

———. 1921. *The Fathers of the Constitution: A Chronicle of the Establishment of the Union*. New Haven, CT: Yale University Press.

Farrand, Max., ed. 1966 (1937). *The Records of the Federal Convention*. 4 vols. New Haven, CT: Yale University Press.

Ferris, Robert G., ed. 1976. *Signers of the Constitution*. Washington, DC: United States Department of the Interior, National Park Service.

Finkelman, Paul. 1996. *Slavery and the Founders: Race and Liberty in the Age of Jefferson*. Armonk, NY: M. E. Sharpe.

Fiske, John. 1888. *The Critical Period of American History, 1783–1789*. Boston: Houghton Mifflin.

Flower, Milton E. 1983. *John Dickinson: Conservative Revolutionary*. Charlottesville: University Press of Virginia.

Ford, Paul Leicester, ed. 1970. *Essays on the Constitution of the United States Published during Its Discussion by the People, 1787–1788*. New York: Burt Franklin.

Fox, Frank W. 2003. *The American Founding*, 2nd ed. Boston: Pearson Custom Publishing.

Freehling, William W. 1972. "The Founding Fathers and Slavery." *American Historical Review* 77 (February): 81–93.

Gibson, Alan. 2006. *Interpreting the Founding: Guide to the Enduring Debates over the Origin and Foundations of the American Republic*. Lawrence: University Press of Kansas.

———. 2007. *Understanding the Founding: The Crucial Questions*. Lawrence: University Press of Kansas.

Gillespie, Michael Allen, and Michael Lienesch, eds. 1989. *Ratifying the Constitution*. Lawrence: University Press of Kansas.

Goldstone, Lawrence. 2005. *Dark Bargain: Slavery, Profits and the Struggle for the Constitution*. New York: Walker & Company.

Goldwin, Robert A. 1990. *Why Blacks, Women, and Jews Are Not Mentioned in the Constitution and Other Unorthodox Views*. Washington, DC: AEI Press.

———. 1997. *From Parchment to Power: How James Madison Used the Bill of Rights to Save the Constitution*. Washington, DC: AEI Press.

Greene, Jack P. 1986. *Peripheries and Center: Constitutional Development in the Extended Politics of the British Empire and the United States, 1607–1788.* Athens: University of Georgia Press.

Greene, Thurston. 1991. *The Language of the Constitution: A Sourcebook and Guide to the Ideas, Terms, and Vocabulary Used by the Framers of the United States Constitution.* Westport, CT: Greenwood Press.

Gregg, Gary L., II. 1999. *Vital Remnants: America's Founding and the Western Tradition.* Wilmington, DE: ISI Books.

Grundfest, Jerry. 1982. *George Clymer: Philadelphia Revolutionary, 1739–1813.* New York: Arno Press.

Gutzman, Kevin R. *James Madison and the Making of America.* New York: St. Martin's Press, 2012.

Hall, David W. 2003. *The Geneva Reformation and the American Founding.* Lanham, MD: Lexington Books.

Hall, Kermit L., ed. 1984. *A Comprehensive Bibliography of American Constitutional and Legal History, 1896–1979.* 5 vols. and 2-vol. supplement of 1991 that covers the years 1980–1987. Millwood, NY: Kraus International Publications.

Hamilton, Alexander, James Madison, and John Jay. 1961. *The Federalist Papers.* Edited by Clinton Rossiter. New York: New American Library.

Hartz, Louis. 1955. *The Liberal Tradition in America: An Interpretation of American Political Thought since the Revolution.* New York: Harcourt, Brace and World.

Haskett, Richard D. 1950. "William Paterson, Attorney General of New Jersey: Public Office and Private Profit in the American Revolution," *William and Mary Quarterly,* 3rd ser., 7 (January): 26–38.

Hauptly, Denis J. 1987. *"A Convention of Delegates": The Creation of the Constitution.* New York: Athenaeum.

Heideking, Jürgen. *The Constitution Before the Judgment Seat: The Prehistory and Ratification of the American Constituton, 1787–1791,* ed. By John P. Kaminski and Richard Leffler. Charlottesville: University of Virginia Press, 2012.

Hendrick, Burton J. 1937. *Bulwark of the Republic: A Biography of the Constitution.* Boston: Little, Brown.

Hendrickson, David D. 2003. *Peace Pact: The Lost World of the American Founding.* Lawrence: University Press of Kansas.

Historians of the Independence National Historical Park, National Park Service, compilers. 1987. *1787: The Day-to-Day Story of the Constitutional Convention.* New York: Exeter Books.

Hobson, Charles F. 1979. "The Negative on State Laws: James Madison, the Constitution, and the Crisis of Republican Government." *William and Mary Quarterly,* 3rd ser., 36 (April): 213–35.

Hoffert, Robert W. 1992. *A Politics of Tensions: The Articles of Confederation and American Political Ideals.* Niwot: University Press of Colorado.

Holmes, David L. 2006. *The Faiths of the Founding Fathers.* New York: Oxford University Press.

Holton, Woody. 2007. *Unruly Americans and the Origins of the Constitution*. New York: Hill and Wang.

Hueston, John C. 1990. "Note: Altering the Course of the Constitutional Convention: The Role of the Committee of Detail in Establishing the Balance of State and Federal Powers." *Yale Law Journal* 200 (December): 765–83.

Hutson, James H., ed. 1987. *Supplement to Max Farrand's* The Records of the Federal Convention of 1787. New Haven, CT: Yale University Press.

Hutson, James H. 2003. *Forgotten Features of the Founding: The Recovery of Religious Themes in the Early American Republic*. Lanham, MD: Lexington Books.

Ireland, Owen S. 1995. *Religion, Ethnicity, and Politics: Ratifying the Constitution in Pennsylvania*. University Park: Pennsylvania State University Press.

Isaacson, Walter, 2003. *Benjamin Franklin: An American Life*. New York: Simon and Schuster.

Jefferson, Thomas. 1904. *The Works of Thomas Jefferson*. Edited by Paul Leicester Ford. New York: G. G. Putnam's Sons, Knickerbocker Press.

———. 1964. *Notes on the State of Virginia*. New York: Harper and Row, Publishers.

Jensen, Merrill. 1966. *The Articles of Confederation*. Madison: University of Wisconsin Press.

———. 1976. *Constitutional Documents and Records, 1776–1787*. Vol. 1 of *The Documentary History of the Ratification of the Constitution*. Madison: State Historical Society of Wisconsin.

Jillson, Calvin C. 1981. "Constitution-Making: Alignment and Realignment in the Federal Convention of 1787." *American Political Science Review* 75 (September): 598–612.

Johnson, Calvin H. 2003–2004. "Homage to Clio: The Historical Continuity from the Articles of Confederation into the Constitution," *Constitutional Commentary* 20 (Winter): 463–513.

———. 2005. *Righteous Anger at the Wicked States: The Meaning of the Founders' Constitution*. New York: Cambridge University Press.

Kaminski, John P. 1995. *A Necessary Evil? Slavery and the Debates Over the Constitution*. Madison, WI: Madison House.

Kammen, Michael. 1987. *A Machine That Would Go of Itself: The Constitution in American Culture*. New York: Alfred A. Knopf.

Kann, Mark E. 1999. *A Republic of Men: The American Founders, Gendered Language, and Patriarchal Politics*. New York: New York University Press.

Kasper, Eric T. 2010. *To Secure the Liberty of the People: James Madison's Bill of Rights and the Supreme Court's Interpretation*. DeKalb: Northern Illinois Press.

Kauffman, Bill. 2008. *Forgotten Founder, Drunken Prophet: The Life of Luther Martin*. Wilmington, DE: ISI Books.

Kay, Richard S. 1987. "The Illegality of the Constitution." *Constitutional Commentary* 4 (Winter): 57–80.

Kenyon, Cecilia, ed. 1984. *The Antifederalists*. Boston: Northeastern University Press.

Kesavan, Vasan. 2002. "When Did the Articles of Confederation Cease to Be Law?" *Notre Dame Law Review* 78 (December): 35–82.

Ketcham, Ralph. 1993. *Framed for Posterity: The Enduring Philosophy of the Constitution.* Lawrence: University Press of Kansas.

Kmiec, Douglas M., and Stephen B. Presser. 1998. *The History, Philosophy and Structure of the American Constitution.* Cincinnati, OH: Anderson Publishing Co.

Koch, Adrienne. 1950. *Jefferson and Madison: The Great Collaboration.* New York: Oxford University Press.

Kromkowski, Charles A. 2002. *Recreating the American Republic: Rules of Apportionment, Constitutional Change, and American Political Development, 1700–1870.* Cambridge: Cambridge University Press.

Kruman, Marc W. 1997. *Between Authority and Liberty: State Constitution Making in Revolutionary America.* Chapel Hill: University of North Carolina Press.

Kurland, Philip B., and Ralph Lerner. 1987. *The Founders' Constitution.* 5 vols. Chicago: University of Chicago Press.

Loewen, James W. 2007. *Lies My Teacher Told Me: Everything Your American History Book Got Wrong.* New York: Simon & Schuster.

Levinson, Sanford. 2006. *Our Undemocratic Constitution: Where the Constitution Goes Wrong (And How the People Can Correct It).* New York: Oxford University Press.

Levy, Leonard W. 1998. *Original Intent and the Framers' Constitution.* New York: Macmillan.

Liebiger, Stuart. 1999. *Founding Friendship: George Washington, James Madison, and the Creation of the American Republic.* Charlottesville: University Press of Virginia.

Lindop, Edmund. 1987. *Birth of the Constitution.* Hillsdale, NJ: Enslow Publishers.

Locke, John. 1955. *Of Civil Government: Second Treatise.* Chicago: Henry Regnery.

Lutz, Donald S. 1988. *The Origins of American Constitutionalism.* Baton Rouge: Louisiana State University Press.

———. 1998. *Colonial Origins of the American Constitution: A Documentary History.* Indianapolis, IN: Liberty Fund.

Maier, Pauline. 1970. "Popular Uprisings and Civil Authority in Eighteenth-Century America," *William and Mary Quarterly,* 3rd ser., 27 (January): 3–35.

———. 1997. *American Scripture: Making the Declaration of Independence.* New York: Alfred A. Knopf.

———. 2010. *Ratification: The People Debate the Constitution, 1787–1788.* New York: Simon & Schuster.

Main, Jackson T. 1961. *The Antifederalists: Critics of the Constitution, 1781–1788.* Chicago: Quadrangle books.

Matthews, Marty D. 2004. *Forgotten Founder: The Life and Times of Charles Pinckney.* Columbia: University of South Carolina Press.

Mayo, Lawrence Shaw. 1970. *John Langdon of New Hampshire.* Port Washington, NY: Kennicat Press.

McDonald, Forrest. 1958. *We the People: The Economic Origins of the Constitution.* Chicago: University of Chicago Press.

———. 1985. *Novus Ordo Seclorum: The Intellectual Origins of the Constitution.* Lawrence: University Press of Kansas.

McDonald, Forrest, and Allen Shapiro McDonald. 1968. *Confederation and Constitution, 1781–1789.* New York: Harper and Row Publishers.

McGee, Dorothy H. 1968. *Framers of the Constitution.* New York: Dodd, Mead.

McGuire Robert A. 2003. *To Form a More Perfect Union: A New Economic Interpretation of the United States Constitution.* New York: Oxford University Press.

McLaughlin, Andrew C. 1897. "James Wilson in the Philadelphia Convention." *Political Science Quarterly* 12 (March): 1–20.

———. 1905. *The Confederation and the Constitution, 1782–1789.* New York: Harper and Brothers.

Meacham, Jon. 2006. *American Gospel: God, the Founding Fathers, and the Making of a Nation.* New York: Random House.

Meyers, Marvin, ed. *The Mind of the Founder: Sources of the Political Thought of James Madison.* Indianapolis, IN: Bobbs-Merrill.

Meyerson, Michael I. 2008. *Liberty's Blueprint: How Madison and Hamilton Wrote the Federalist Papers, Defined the Constitution, and Made Democracy Safe for the World.* New York: Basic Books.

Miller, William L. 1992. *The Business of May Next: James Madison and the Founding.* Charlottesville: University Press of Virginia.

Morgan, Edmund S. 1977. *The Birth of the Republic, 1763–1789*, rev. ed. Chicago: University of Chicago Press.

———.1988. *Inventing the People: The Rise of Popular Sovereignty in England and America.* New York: W. W. Norton.

Morison, S. E. 1929. "Elbridge Gerry, Gentleman-Democrat." *The New England Quarterly* 2 (January): 6033.

Morris, Richard B. 1985. *Witnesses at the Creation: Hamilton, Madison, Jay, and the Constitution.* New York: New American Library.

———. 1986. *The Framing of the Federal Constitution.* Washington, DC: U.S. Department of the Interior.

———. 1987. *The Forging of the Union: 1781–1789.* New York: Harper & Row.

Morris, Thomas D. 1996. *Southern Slavery and the Law, 1619–1860.* Chapel Hill: University of North Carolina Press.

Natelson, Robert G. 2003. "The Constitutional Contributions of John Dickinson." *Pennsylvania State Law Review* 108 (Fall): 415–77.

Nelson, William E. 1987. "Reason and Compromise in the Establishment of the Federal Constitution, 1787–1801." *William and Mary Quarterly*, 3rd ser., 44 (July): 458–84.

Nordham, George Washington. 1987. *George Washington: President of the Constitutional Convention.* Chicago: Adams Press.

O'Connor, J. S. 1979. *William Paterson: Lawyer and Statesman, 1745–1806.* New Brunswick, NJ: Rutgers University Press.

Onuf, Peter S. 1983. *The Origins of the Federal Republic: Jurisdictional Controversies in the United States, 1775–1787.* Philadelphia: University of Pennsylvania Press.

Padover, Saul K. 1962. *To Secure These Blessings: The Great Debate of the Constitutional Convention of 1787, Arranged According to Topics.* New York: Washington Square Press/Ridge Press Book.

Paine, Thomas. 1986 (1776). *Common Sense.* New York: Penguin Books.

Pangle, Thomas L. 1988. *The Spirit of Modern Republicanism: The Moral Vision of the American Founders and the Philosophy of Locke.* Chicago: University of Chicago Press.

Penegar, Kenneth Lawing. 2011. *The Political Trial of Benjamin Franklin: A Prelude to the American Revolution.* New York: Algora Publishing.

Peters, William. 1987. *A More Perfect Union.* New York: Crown Publishers.

Phelps, Glenn A. 1993. *George Washington and American Constitutionalism.* Lawrence: University Press of Kansas.

Rakove, Jack N. 1987. "The Great Compromise: Ideas, Interests, and the Politics of Constitution Making." *William and Mary Quarterly,* 3rd ser., 44 (July): 424–57.

———. 1990. *James Madison and the Creation of the American Republic.* Glenview, IL: Scott, Foresman.

———. 1996. *Original Meanings: Politics and Ideas in the Making of the Constitution.* New York: Alfred A. Knopf.

Rappleye, Charles. 2010. *Robert Morris: Financier of the American Revolution.* New York: Simon & Schuster.

Read, James H. 2000. *Power Versus Liberty: Madison, Hamilton, Wilson, and Jefferson.* Charlottesville: University Press of Virginia.

Reardon, John J. 1974. *Edmund Randolph: A Biography.* New York: Macmillan.

Revelery, W. Taylor, III. 1974. "Constitutional Allocation of the War Powers between the President and the Congress: 1787–1788." *Virginia Journal of International Law* 15 (Fall): 73–147.

Rhodehamel, John H. 1987. *Letters of Liberty: A Documentary History of the U.S. Constitution.* Los Angeles: Constitutional Rights Foundation.

———. 1998. *The Great Experiment: George Washington and the American Republic.* New Haven, CT: Yale University Press.

Richards, Leonard L. 2002. *Shays' Rebellion: The American Revolution's Final Battle.* Philadelphia: University of Pennsylvania Press.

Roberts, Cokie. 2004. *Founding Mothers: The Women Who Raised Our Nation.* New York: William Morrow.

Roche, John P. 1961. "The Founding Fathers: A Reform Caucus in Action," *American Political Science Review* 55 (December): 799–816.

Rohr, John A. 1986. *To Run a Constitution: The Legitimacy of the Administrative State.* Lawrence: University Press of Kansas.

Rosen, Gary. 1999. *American Compact: James Madison and the Problem of Founding*. Lawrence: University Press of Kansas.

Rossiter, Clinton. 1964. *Alexander Hamilton and the Constitution*. New York: Harcourt, Brace and World.

———. 1966. *1787: The Grand Convention*. New York: W. W. Norton.

Ruane, Michael E., and Michael D. Schaffer. 1987. *1787: Inventing America: A Day-by-Day Account of the Constitutional Convention*. Philadelphia: Philadelphia Inquirer.

Rutland, Robert A. 1962. *The Birth of the Bill of Rights, 1776–1791*. New York: Collier Books.

———. 1966. *The Ordeal of the Constitution: The Antifederalists and the Ratification Struggle of 1787–1788*. Norman: University of Oklahoma Press.

———. 1987. *James Madison: The Founding Father*. New York: Macmillan.

Sabato, Larry J. 2007. *A More Perfect Constitution*. New York: Walker & Company.

Sandoz, Ellis, ed. 1991. *Political Sermons of the American Founding Era, 1730–1805*. Indianapolis, IN: Liberty Fund. Index published in 1997.

Schwarzenbach, Sibyl A., and Patricia Smith, eds. 2003. *Women and the United States Constitution: History, Interpretation, and Practice*. New York: Columbia University Press.

Seed, Geoffrey. 1978. *James Wilson*. Millwood, NY: KTO Press.

Shalhope, Robert E. 1972. "Toward a Republican Synthesis: The Emergence of an Understanding of Republicanism in American Historiography." *William and Mary Quarterly*, 3rd ser., 29 (January): 49–80.

Sheldon, Garrett Ward. 2001. *The Political Philosophy of James Madison*. Baltimore, MD: Johns Hopkins University Press.

Siemers, David J. 2003. *Antifederalists: Men of Great Faith and Forbearance*. Lanham, MD: Rowman & Littlefield.

Sikes, Lewright B. 1979. *The Public Life of Pierce Butler, South Carolina Statesman*. Washington, DC: University Press of America.

Simon, Sheila S. 2005. *Odd Couple of the Constitution: James Madison and Alexander Hamilton*. Baltimore: PublishAmerica.

Slonin, Shlomo. 1986. "The Electoral College at Philadelphia: The Evolution of an ad hoc Congress for the Selection of a President." *Journal of American History* 73 (June): 35–58.

Smith, Charles Page. 1956. *James Wilson: Founding Father, 1742–1798*. Chapel Hill: University of North Carolina Press.

Smith, Craig R. 1993. *To Form a More Perfect Union: The Ratification of the Constitution and the Bill of Rights, 1787–1791*. Lanham, MD: University Press of America.

Smith, David G. 1965. *The Convention and the Constitution: The Political Ideas of the Founding Fathers*. New York: St. Martin's Press.

Solberg, Winton, ed. 1958. *The Federal Convention and the Formation of the Union of the American States*. Indianapolis, IN: Bobbs-Merrill.

St. John, Jeffrey. 1987. *Constitutional Journal: A Correspondent's Report from the Convention of 1787*. Ottawa, IL: Jameson Books.

———. 1990. *A Child of Fortune: A Correspondent's Report on the Ratification of the U.S. Constitution and Battle for a Bill of Rights*. Ottawa, IL: Jameson Books.

Staloff, Darren. 2005. *Hamilton, Adams, Jefferson: The Politics of Enlightenment and the American Founding*. New York: Hill and Wang.

Stewart, David O. 2007. *The Summer of 1787: The Men Who Invented the Constitution*. New York: Simon & Schuster.

Storing, Herbert J. 1981. *The Complete Anti-Federalist*. 7 vols. Chicago: University of Chicago Press.

———. 1981. *What the Anti-Federalists Were For*. Chicago: University of Chicago Press.

Thach, Charles C. 1922. *The Creation of the Presidency, 1775–1789: A Study in Constitutional History*. Baltimore, MD: Johns Hopkins University Press.

Thorpe, Francis N., ed. 1907. *The Federal and State Constitutions, Colonial Charters, and Other Organic Laws of the United States*. 7 vols. Washington, DC: U.S. Government Printing Office.

Toth, Michale C. 2011. *Founding Federalist: The Life of Oliver Ellsworth*. Wilmington, DE: ISI Books.

Trenchard John, and Thomas Gordon. 1995 (first published in four volumes in 1755). *Cato's Letters or Essays on Liberty, Civil and Religious, and Other Important Subjects*. Edited by Ronald Hamowy. 2 vols. Indianapolis, IN: Liberty Fund.

Tushnet, Mark. 2010. *Why the Constitution Matters*. New Haven, CT: Yale University Press.

Ulmer, S. Sidney. 1966 "Sub-group Formation in the Constitutional Convention." *Midwest Journal of Political Science* 10 (August): 288–303.

Utley, Robert L., Jr., ed. 1989. *Principles of the Constitutional Order: The Ratification Debates*. Lanham, MD: University Press of America.

Van Doren, Charles. 1948. *The Great Rehearsal: The Story of the Making and Ratifying of the Constitution of the United States*. New York: Viking Press.

Vile, John R. 1992. "Three Kinds of Constitutional Founding and Change: The Convention Method and Its Alternatives." *Political Research Quarterly* 56 (December): 881–95.

———. 2005. *The Constitutional Convention of 1787: A Comprehensive Encyclopedia of America's Founding*. 2 vols. Santa Barbara, CA: ABC-CLIO.

———. 2010. *Encyclopedia of Constitutional Amendments, Proposed Amendments, and Amending Issues, 1789–2010*, 3rd ed. Santa Barbara, CA: ABC-CLIO

———. 2011. *A Companion to the United States Constitution and Its Amendments*. Lanham, MD: Rowman & Littlefield.

Vile, John R., William D. Pederson, and Frank J. Williams, eds. 2008. *James Madison: Philosopher, Founder, and Statesman*. Athens: Ohio University Press.

Wakelyn, John L. 2004. *Birth of the Bill of Rights: Encyclopedia of the Antifederalists*. 2 vols. Westport, CT: Greenwood Press.

Waldman, Steven. 2008. *Founding Faith: How Our Founding Fathers Forged a Radical New Approach to Religious Liberty*. New York: Random House.

Waldstreicher, David. 2009. *Slavery's Constitution: From Revolution to Ratification*. New York: Hill and Wang.

Webking, Robert H. 1988. *The American Revolution and the Politics of Liberty*. Baton Rouge: Louisiana State University Press.

Weiner, Gregg. *Madison's Metronome: The Constitution, Majority Rule, and the Tempo of American Politics*. Lawrence: University Press of Kansas, 2012.

West, Thomas G. 1997. *Vindicating the Founders: Race, Sex, Class, and Justice in the Origins of America*. Lanham, MD: Rowman & Littlefield.

Wexler, Jay. 2011. *The Odd Clauses: Understanding the Constitution through Ten of Its Most Curious Provisions*. Boston: Beacon Press.

Whitney, David C. 1974. *Founders of Freedom in America: Lives of the Men Who Signed the Constitution of the United States and So Helped to Establish the United States of America*. Chicago: J. J. Ferguson Publishing.

Wills, Garry. 1978. *Inventing America: Jefferson's Declaration of Independence*. Garden City, NY: Doubleday.

———. 2001. *Explaining America: The Federalist*. New York: Penguin.

———. 2003. *"Negro President": Jefferson and the Slave Power*. Boston: Houghton Mifflin.

Winik, Jay. 2007. *The Great Upheaval: America and the Birth of the Modern World*. New York: HarperCollins Publishers.

Wirls, Daniel, and Stephen Wirls. 2004. *The Invention of the United States Senate*. Baltimore, MD: Johns Hopkins University Press.

Wood, Gordon S. 1969. *The Creation of the American Republic, 1776–1787*. Chapel Hill: University of North Carolina Press.

———. 1987. *The Making of the Constitution*. Waco, TX: Markham Press Fund.

Wright, Robert K., Jr., and Morris J. MacGregor, Jr. 1987. *Soldier Statesmen of the Constitution*. Washington, DC: Center for Military History, United States Army.

Zagarri, Rosemarie. 1987. *The Politics of Size: Representation in the United States, 1776–1850*. Ithaca, NY: Cornell University Press.

Zahniser, Marvin R. 1967. *Charles Cotesworth Pinckney: Founding Father*. Chapel Hill: University of North Carolina Press.

INDEX

ABOUT THE AUTHOR

Dr. John R. Vile is a professor of political science and dean of the University Honors College at Middle Tennessee State University. A graduate of the College of William and Mary and the University of Virginia, he is the author and editor of numerous books about the U.S. Constitution and related subjects. These include *The Constitutional Convention of 1787* (2 vols.), *A Companion to the United States Constitution and Its Amendments* (5th ed.), *Essential Supreme Court Decisions: Summaries of Leading Cases in U.S. Constitutional Law* (15th ed.), *Encyclopedia of the First Amendment* (coeditor, 2 vols.), *Encyclopedia of Constitutional Amendments, Proposed Amendments, and Amending Issues, 1789–2010* (2 vols., 3rd ed.), and others.

CPSIA information can be obtained at www.ICGtesting.com
Printed in the USA
BVOW031223050712

294338BV00001B/13/P